The
Equal
Parent

PAUL MORGAN-BENTLEY

The Equal Parent

How sharing the load helps
the whole family thrive

THREAD

Published by Thread in 2023

An imprint of Storyfire Ltd.
Carmelite House
50 Victoria Embankment
London EC4Y 0DZ

www.thread-books.com

ISBN: 978-1-80419-120-0
eBook ISBN: 9-781-80314-397-2

Printed and bound in Great Britain

The FSC® label means that materials used for the product
have been responsibly sourced.

For Robin and Solly

CONTENTS

INTRODUCTION

YOU KNOW WHAT YOU'RE
LETTING YOURSELF IN FOR, DON'T YOU?

It is close to 3 a.m., and I can feel my son's weight on my chest after a milk feed. His ears are glowing with the light from my phone. I should take him to his cot, but he is sleeping and I do not dare. I am also transfixed by what I have just read. It is a hospital website's page for new fathers, and expectations could not be lower. In a bizarre opening, it warns men that having a baby might make them cry. 'Watching your baby coming into the world can be the most incredible experience,' it states. 'Many new parents experience very strong emotions; some cry, do not worry this is natural.'

The website goes on to tell fathers that after the birth they will be able to 'go home to get some much needed rest' but cautions that they might be expected to pitch in and help to keep their new baby alive and well in the future, but only occasionally and if no other family members are around. 'You may find that relatives and friends are able to help in the early days so that the baby's mother can rest and feed the baby,' it states. 'However, you may live far from relatives and your partner may have only you to help, so it's a good idea to have a week or so off work if you can.' Under some further suggestions, it offers: 'You could look after the baby so that the baby's mum can get a good rest each day.'[1]

I think of my relationship with my son: these moments after his night feeds; holding his hand as he moans in his cot, trying to help him learn to settle himself to sleep; desperately fanning his forehead and dousing it with wet wipes during a high fever; kissing his cheeks, bouncy like bao buns, until his giggles go from screeches to hiccups; and panicking when hives spread across his stomach in the bath. I am far from a perfect father, but it is impossible to relate to the caricature 1950s dad that the health service website speaks to. I am sure that many of the men in my life who have children, and their partners, would feel the same.

Following the birth of my son, I took six months of parental leave from work. What I did was unusual but should not be remarkable. Millions of women every year take maternity leave, and it is legal in many countries for men to take equal-length parental leave. But I soon learned that while people speak carefully in front of women who take time off work to look after their babies, this was not always the case with me. 'You'll still go to the office a bit, right?' an acquaintance asked when I told him the news. A male friend with children phoned me. 'You know what you're letting yourself in for, don't you? You're doing it when he's a newborn? That is a nightmare. The night feeds and screaming. I couldn't do it. I had to get back to work.'

While the vast majority of my family, friends and colleagues were supportive of my decision to take extended parental leave from my son's birth, I soon learned to recognise a look. It was generally from older men. The types who had three or four kids but never changed a nappy. It was a combination of bewilderment and suspicion. They looked me up and down, reassessing, perhaps checking to see if I had grown breasts.

But I have always been like this: a man who did not just want to have children but wanted to be a fully present, bonded, loving, exhausted, despairing, nurturing, primary parent. I love having children around and the way their presence affects an environment.

The chaos of them. The way children relax a stuffy occasion such as a dinner party or wedding reception by banging into table legs, spilling their drinks and saying mad things. The way they yank us out of the performance of adulthood.

I find it hard to relate to dads who have not been around enough to know what their babies can eat, what they should wear or what time they have their naps. I have always been good with babies and have grown up helping to look after my big Jewish family of nieces and nephews, eating meals to a soundtrack of them playing, laughing and fighting. The idea of a future without children in my life felt impossible. Growing up, I always imagined in some vague, unconscious way that I would have a child and would be there for him or her fully, like we are told mothers are meant to.

There is no word to define how I feel. The closest is 'maternal', which is obviously not quite right. The *Chambers Concise Dictionary* on my bookcase at home defines 'maternal' as 'belonging to, typical of or like a mother' and 'maternity' as 'the qualities typical of a mother'. What are these qualities? The entry for 'mother' includes 'the protective, nurturing, or loving qualities associated with a mother'. Under 'father', there is no mention of loving or nurturing. Being a father is defined as 'to beget (offspring); to procreate'. Being 'fatherly' is defined as being 'benevolent, protective and encouraging, as a father ideally is to a child'. Paternity is about 'the authorship, source or origin of something'.[2] To me, the words paternal and paternalism suggest creation, strength and quiet authority.

I do not feel paternal, as the word is defined, and I do not relate to the attributes that society tells us a paternal man should have: being strong, dependable, unemotional and good for an occasional fun trip. I do not feel parental, which sounds cold and stale, or fatherly, like a priest. I am a man, and I also feel protective, nurturing and loving towards my son. I do not feel any shame about this. Why would anyone?

Equally, some of my female friends, who are in their thirties like I am, feel immense pressure to be mothers but just do not want children. They do not feel maternal. Thousands of miles of glossy magazine columns have been filled with accounts from women who felt utter despair that they could not bond with their babies in the way they believed they should have just because of their sex. They describe how they wanted children but were made to feel unworthy because they did not instantly feel what we are told all women – and only women – should feel.

While it may seem that, generally, more women feel maternal than men, so many men and women veer from what is expected of the sexes. Scientists have found that when a baby has a mother and a father, the mother usually feels more urgency and panic in responding to their baby crying. Something changes in her brain to cause this. However, when a baby has two fathers, the men can respond in the same way mothers do to their babies. Their brains also change.[3] This has nothing to do with their sexuality or genetics (in the case of gay fathers, at least one will not be genetically related to the child). It is because without the expectation that a woman will take care of their child, the men have to step up (and get up). It is about our bodies responding to the terror that comes with having proper responsibility.

In so many other areas of life there has rightly been a destruction of traditional gender stereotypes. It is outrageous to believe anything other than that women are equal to men at work, that they – shock-horror – have libidos, that men can be creative, sew and bake. Children's books celebrate girls climbing trees, becoming doctors and playing football. Yet while women work as hard as men professionally, they are also presumed, almost always, to be the parent with primary responsibility. No matter how involved a father is in his child's care, he is, at best, expected to be the other parent. This is something that is ingrained in us as children and then reinforced if you are expecting a baby, from as early as the first medical appointment.

Of course the woman is the focus during pregnancy, but do health service leaflets, websites and posters on the walls of maternity units have to reduce fathers' roles to just helping to build furniture and sometimes offering to change a nappy? Why are so many fathers banished from hospitals within a few hours of their child's first breath, treated like visitors, when they could be encouraged to spend those formative moments caring for their new child together with the mother, as a team, finally able to share the responsibility now the baby is no longer in her body? Why are nurses so shocked when a father brings his child to a vaccination appointment? Why do schools almost always seem to call the mother when a child is unwell, even when her child has two parents and both of them work? Often it seems as if the institutions that we lean on as parents – the healthcare services, schools and workplaces – are failing to keep up with how society is already evolving. When it comes to children, the default expectation remains that a woman will be there for them at all times, whether or not they have a partner and want to share the duties as well as the love.

When I am not looking after my son and getting angry about hospital websites, I am an investigative journalist at *The Times* newspaper in London and specialise in in-depth reporting and undercover work. I am also a gay man and live with my husband, Robin, and our son, Solly, on the outskirts of London. Robin took extended parental leave after Solly was born through surrogacy, so we were both off work with him together for the first six weeks of his life and then Robin took over for most of the second half of the year. With Solly having two fathers, we have had the relatively unusual experience of coming to parenthood without any expectations as to who should perform which roles. While we have not always succeeded – and have often spectacularly failed – we have tried to split the responsibility for our son as equally as possible.

Although my experience as a gay dad has, I think, offered me a particular perspective on how unequal parenting can often be for men and women, this is not a book about same-sex parenting. It is also not a 'Men's Lives Matter' or 'Fathers for Justice' rant. It is absolutely not a call to erase motherhood or women's experiences. I would never claim to be able to speak for women – or mothers. In writing this book, I interviewed a range of women, from those who agreed that dads could be equal parents to those who challenged my views. I am not a parenting expert, and this is not a book that will tell you how to get your baby to nap, what to feed your baby, how to treat nappy rash or which bottles are best for colic. This is though, I hope, a book for anyone as mystified as my husband and I are as to why it is still so rare for parents to split responsibility for their children equally and why it is seen as unusual for men to care for their children in a nurturing way. It is about my first-hand experiences of being a man on extended leave from work with a baby, and about what that has meant, from the funny to the exhausting. It is about the chemist who called me 'MummyDaddy', the breastfeeding mothers at baby classes who could not have been less bothered that I was there with them and the woman in the café who offered to be our son's mother because she could not believe he would be properly cared for by male parents.

I have described the utter joy and terror my husband and I felt caring for our son at hospital on the first night of his life and our bewilderment that other dads often are not allowed to experience this, and that mothers have to do this alone, after giving birth, sometimes when they cannot walk following an epidural or cannot carry anything after a caesarean section. I have investigated why men do not usually take proper time off work in the first year of their children's lives when this is legally allowed in many countries.

Surely gender equality does not just mean women working as hard as men professionally. It means men also working as hard as women in other aspects of life. It means men telling their bosses that they are taking leave from work to care for their children, and workplaces and governments seeing the benefits of encouraging this. It means men feeling the insecurity that comes with returning to work, putting in requests for more flexible working and wondering if everyone has forgotten them or holds a grudge about them having been away. It means experiencing colleagues and acquaintances saying things like 'how was your time off?' or 'you must feel rested' after the most exhausting months of their lives keeping a baby alive and happy. It means hiring managers not being able to discriminate against women in their twenties and thirties on the grounds that they might take maternity leave soon because the same would be true of men.

I wrote this book as a celebration of men caring for their children and to explore the truths behind the lazy assumptions we can all sometimes find ourselves making about parental roles. Whenever I refer to parents, I mean any adult who has responsibility for a child. This can include non-genetic parents, adoptive parents, parents with or without a romantic life partner and other legal guardians. As far as I am concerned, parenting is about the actual role of looking after a child, not genetics.

I spoke to leading researchers about the science of mothers' and fathers' instincts and the outcomes for children whose parents, regardless of their sex or genetics, are fully engaged. I wanted to understand the impact parenting gender stereotypes have on our sons and daughters and what this means they grow up expecting they should be as men and women. There is no doubt that there has already been progress towards parenting equality. I cannot think of a single father of my age who has not changed nappies. The same could not be said of my father's generation of men. However, we need to acknowledge how far there still is to go.

Men who go to baby classes, children's doctor appointments and do the nursery or school run are often now praised for being 'hands-on' dads. 'He is wonderfully hands-on,' someone will say, because a father does a bottle feed at 11 p.m. every day. Imagine saying that a mother is 'hands-on' because she bothers to pick up her child from school. That this sounds ridiculous when applied to a mother, but not to a father, demonstrates how far away we are still from achieving proper equality of the sexes.

My experience of parenting has led me to believe passionately that fathers should be doing everything they can to be fully present during substantial periods of their babies' lives. It should not be unusual for dads to be as immersed as mothers in the endless maths that is tweaking feeding and sleeping schedules, or to be as involved as mothers in decisions about whether to do any sleep training and how to wean babies onto solid food. Fathers should be around enough to see their share of those first gassy smiles, the first rolls, for the mind-numbing monotony of *Cocomelon*, *Little Baby Bum* and *Paw Patrol* – and, indeed, for the comments from other parents who 'absolutely never' let their children watch TV. Men should feel such responsibility for their babies that they wake as easily as mothers do at the sound of a cry from the monitor.

While over the past few years I have read as much research as I have Julia Donaldson books, and I have interviewed lots of mothers, fathers, scientists and parenting experts, I do not have all of the answers as to how we can change the world and achieve parenting equality. But I hope that by sharing what I have found, and my family's experiences, with honesty, that future might be a little less distant.

If a woman wants to go back to work after taking some of her maternity leave entitlement and have her male partner take over, she should be supported in doing so by a society that does not view this decision with suspicion. If a man wants to take extended parental leave to care for his baby, he should not feel masculine shame. This is a book about what we can all do – from individuals to medical staff, schools, businesses, community groups and governments – to encourage men to take their fair share of responsibility as parents, and why experts are convinced this will benefit all of us: mothers, fathers and, most importantly, our children.

CHAPTER ONE

GO HOME AND GET SOME REST

Panic and Bonding in the Days after Birth

Our newborn son, Solly, is a few hours old and I am crouching over him with my hands out, trying to touch his chest lightly enough to confirm he is breathing without waking him. My husband, Robin, and I have swaddled him terribly, and waves of beige blanket fill his see-through hospital cot like loose toilet roll. We have been up through the night watching our boy with the lights low. Doing what millions of new parents must do. Listening, feeling and looking and then listening, feeling and looking, again and again, just to make 100 per cent sure he is still alive, that we have not screwed it all up already.

Solly rolls his perfect little head to the side, away from us – relief, he is still breathing – and then brown sick shoots from his mouth, staining the side of the cot. We panic, my husband reaching for Solly while I run to find a midwife. She walks over calmly – why isn't she rushing? – and then cleans him up and puts him back down. She says this is normal, probably just some blood and gunk he swallowed during his birth. My veins are wild with more love and terror than I have ever felt in my life. Here he is, our son, the child we wanted so desperately and have spent years trying to have. He seems calm.

He is sucking his thumb. Robin and I keep watching him. How can anything else ever matter?

Other questions come to mind in the hours that follow. Why are so many fathers told that they cannot be here for these first hours of their child's life? How can so many hospitals expect them to go home, sleep alone, leave their partner and baby and come back to get them in the morning? How do they sleep without being able to check manically that their baby is still alive? How do mothers do this alone? What do they do when their baby vomits brown blood and they are exhausted, wincing through afterpains, unable to move fully following an epidural or surgery, surrounded by strangers on a ward? Do they have a button to press? Do they just scream?

As a gay male couple, Robin and I could not have a baby naturally. We like to make family members wince by joking that we tried repeatedly but our attempts were unsuccessful. We had our son by creating embryos with an anonymous egg donor at a fertility clinic and then one of these embryos, who would become Solly, was carried altruistically by Rachel, now one of our closest friends, whom we met through a not-for-profit British surrogacy organisation. Later in the book, I will describe in detail how we became fathers and met Rachel, her husband James, and their sons Charlie and Jack. For now, I mention it because our situation was unusual.

After we cut the cord, gave Solly his first bottle feed and all cried and hugged – even the men cried! – Rachel chose to have her own room to eat toast, drink tea and sleep, while we were given another room with a double bed and a cot, so we could spend the night with Solly. Rachel could see us and Solly whenever she wanted and joined us when she woke up. The arrangement meant that Robin and I got to experience what so many fathers in Britain and many other countries miss: being there throughout our newborn baby's time in hospital following his birth. Why should this be unusual?

What message do we send to mothers and fathers by excluding men physically from being with their children after they are born?

Within moments of birth, society's expectations seem pretty clear. While the baby is no longer in the mother's body, the weight of responsibility remains with her, whether she wants to share this with a partner or not. Her partner, if she has one, continues a supporting role, rather than one of equal responsibility. But if parents want to care for their children as a unit, is it not counter-intuitive to separate them so quickly? And, most importantly, is this really in the child's best interests?

It is well established that skin-to-skin contact between a mother and her baby in the hours after birth is important, if possible, both for the baby's health and because holding your child's body to your naked chest can be such a powerful bonding experience. The World Health Organization and the United Nations Children's Fund, also known as UNICEF, recommend that all healthy mothers and babies have skin-to-skin contact for at least an hour.[1] Many hospitals encourage mothers to do this almost constantly, throughout the days after birth. Decades of research show that the direct contact helps to stabilise the baby's heartbeat, breathing and temperature, as well as lowering the baby's stress and encouraging breastfeeding if the mother wants this, with the newborn's primitive reflexes making it almost climb up her body in search of her nipple.[2] What is less known is that there are benefits for the baby whether this experience is with a mother exclusively or shared with a partner. Experts also believe that enabling fathers to have this time with their newborn babies can prime them for longer-term committed caregiving.

Robin and I both had skin-to-skin contact with Solly in the hours after his birth. We took it in turns to sit in an armchair and hold him. I can still see Solly's newborn face, his tiny bright eyes and little left arm below me and feel his skin warming against my chest. He was wearing a beige woollen hat that was too small for his head and kept creeping up and popping off. There was a white blanket around his back. His breathing slowed with mine. Robin took over and Solly nestled into the cove between his left arm and chest and started sucking his thumb. He must have been particularly comfortable in Robin's arms as we realised later that he had pooed black meconium in tar-like splodges onto Robin's arm and jeans. The benefits to us of this time were obvious – those first moments together were magical – but studies suggest that they also would have been important for Solly.

In 2007, researchers in Sweden published a study involving 29 men whose babies were born by caesarean section and could not have skin-to-skin contact with their mothers. Fourteen of the fathers were randomly chosen to sit by the baby's cot after the birth, and the others held their babies to their naked chests. The babies that were cuddled by their fathers cried 'significantly less', for an average of 13 seconds every five-minute period, compared to 33 seconds for the other babies. The babies that had skin-to-skin contact with their fathers fell asleep after about 60 minutes, while the others took 110 minutes on average.[3]

A similar Chinese study observed 108 babies born via caesarean sections, half of whom were randomly assigned to have skin-to-skin contact with their fathers immediately. The babies in this group had more stable heart rates and forehead temperatures and cried less, while the fathers had lower scores for anxiety.[4] More recently, in January 2021, a study of 95 babies born via caesarean sections in Chile was published showing that those who experienced skin-to-skin contact with their fathers had significantly higher and more stable heart rates than those who had no skin-to-skin contact.[5]

Individual studies like these ones are based on small samples. In 2016, researchers at the University of Singapore and Linköping University, Sweden, worked together to review 12 relevant studies published between 1995 and 2015. The review found that skin-to-skin contact between fathers and babies 'had positive impacts on infants' outcomes, including temperature and pain' as well as improving fathers' levels of stress and anxiety and promoting greater interaction between the dads and their children.[6]

While more research is needed and on a wider scale, the findings suggest fathers can play an important part in soothing their babies when a mother is unable to do this. Given that about one in five pregnant women worldwide gives birth by caesarean section[7] (in the UK the rate is around one in four,[8] and in the US it is closer to one in three[9]), with some unable to hold their babies afterwards, this is relevant to a large number of babies, very possibly millions every year. Whenever a mother cannot have skin-to-skin contact with her baby, it is in the child's best interests that they have this with a partner, if possible, instead. Mothers can also be made aware that if they want to share this experience with a partner, their baby will continue to benefit.

Evalotte Mörelius, one of the Swedish researchers who reviewed 12 of the studies in this area, is professor of nursing at Edith Cowan University in Perth, Western Australia, and specialises in the care of newborn babies, particularly those born prematurely. She described an array of benefits when fathers share responsibility for caring for their babies in the first hours and days after birth, including increased reported feelings of closeness to their babies, better relationships with their children long term, improved mental health for mothers and the babies having a stronger support system.

In one of her studies, published in 2015, the parents of 37 babies agreed to have continuous skin-to-skin contact with their newborns for a week, alternating while the other slept or had time off.[10] 'When they compared with their peers and friends, the fathers said they felt much closer to their babies,' she said. 'We also found that partners in the randomised group chosen to have skin-to-skin contact with their babies reported having better spouse relationships when the baby was four months compared to the other group.'

Mörelius said the study pushed fathers to share responsibility for their newborn babies with the mothers, and the experience meant they both felt they had a shared goal and could empathise with each other, rather than mothers feeling the weight of primary responsibility with fathers simply helping when they could. It also meant the mothers were able to relax more and to let go of control. 'If you trust your partner, you can go to sleep and sleep deeply,' she said.

Nils Bergman, a Swedish public health physician who is a research affiliate at the Karolinska Institute, Sweden, dedicates his full working time to researching and promoting skin-to-skin contact between parents and babies. He is a strong advocate of the benefits of fathers, as well as mothers, doing this in the first hours of their children's lives.

Bergman and his team's work has included taking blood samples from men as they support their partners in labour and then in the hours after the birth of their children.[11] By Bergman's own admission, asking them to give blood repeatedly during this time, for no urgent medical reason, was a 'really unreasonable request'. About one in every 50 men they approached agreed to take part. These men included 15 whose partners had caesarean sections and other small groups whose partners had births led by midwives in hospitals and at home. All the fathers had skin-to-skin contact with their newborn babies within two hours of birth, whenever the mother was happy for them to do this.

Bergman found that levels of prolactin, a hormone that rises in stressful situations, fell dramatically in all of the new fathers once they started skin-to-skin contact with their babies. The prolactin levels had been the highest in the men whose partners had caesarean sections and lowest in those whose partners had home births. He said that, crucially, the levels of prolactin did not fall immediately after the births but only after they began skin-to-skin contact. Bergman believes this hormonal response – with the new fathers' bodies calming while holding their babies for the first time – will have been central to them learning to cope with the stress of having a new child and remaining committed parents when times are hard throughout their upbringing.

While there are benefits of involving fathers in the earliest stages of bonding, the practicalities of allowing for this to happen can be tricky. In Britain, there is no overarching policy governing whether men should be allowed to stay on maternity wards with mothers following the birth of their children. Each hospital trust decides for itself. Some treat fathers as visitors who can only be there for one brief period during the day. It is a divisive issue.

In January 2020, staff at Edinburgh's Royal Infirmary complained that while they were meant to encourage fathers to go home because of lack of space, lots of male partners were ignoring them and, in their words, 'using the ward like a hotel'. They said men were sleeping in chairs, on the floors and squeezed into hospital beds with their partners. Some of the dads were asking for food and others ordered takeaway to the hospital.[12] In heated exchanges in the comment sections below the articles, on social media and on TV, some agreed with the concerns, most convincingly raising the issue of privacy for women who are in a vulnerable state following childbirth. Others objected, citing the importance of partners being encouraged and supported to become fully immersed in caring for their newborns.

The concerns about women's privacy and dignity should, surely, be paramount. If mothers have to share open post-birth wards and there is genuinely no space for fathers, or if any of the mothers are alarmed by the presence of other people's partners, their voices must be the ones heard. But why is there no space? There are just over half a million babies born per year at National Health Service (NHS) hospitals in England.[13] Only about one in four hospitals usually allow partners to stay with mothers on postnatal wards throughout the time after their child is born.[14] If many hospitals are able to accommodate partners, why can't they all?

Northumbria Healthcare NHS Foundation Trust, in the north east of England, is one that encourages partners to stay with mothers and babies no matter how long they have to be in hospital after the birth.[15] At the Northumbria Specialist Emergency Care Hospital (NSECH), which the Trust runs, mothers typically have private rooms with en-suite bathrooms, reclining armchairs and fold-out camp beds for partners. The hospital simply asks that partners stay in their family's room at all times and bring their own provisions for their stay, such as food. The hospital can offer this free service partly because it was built so recently, opening in 2015.[16] Unlike many old NHS hospitals, which were designed by a previous generation of men whose idea of postnatal care was a pint at the pub nursing a cigar, this hospital was built to encourage fathers to be directly involved in supporting mothers and sharing care for their children.

Jenna Wall, head of midwifery for the Trust, said that because childbirth could be traumatic, it was crucial that anyone giving birth and their partners were given the best chance of a positive experience:

> Both parents can suffer trauma if they don't have the birth experience that they were expecting. That was the foundation of the lack of restrictions around visiting in Northumbria. Rather than childbirth being a physical experience, in terms of you going for treatment of a condition, it is viewed more around the maternity experience and that adaptation to parenthood and supporting the family. We appreciated that becoming a parent is a huge adaptation, regardless of your parental role. People are reshaping their entire life. Ensuring everyone is together supports the wellbeing of the family unit.

Allowing for partners to stay can be of huge help in the hours after birth. 'In terms of physical recovery, if someone can pass you a couple of snacks and a clean sanitary towel at two in the morning when you're shuffling off the toilet, that's hugely advantageous,' Wall said. 'If somebody, after you've fed and changed your baby, can rock him for an hour and take over the parenting while you have half an hour's sleep and recover from your caesarean section, of course it's advantageous.'

She also described psychological benefits for mothers when they have a private room to recover in with a partner, including being able to reflect on what has happened and have someone with them who can fill in bits of the story, because often they have gone through sedation or intense pain and cannot clearly remember. Midwives at the Trust encourage fathers, or even grandparents, to have skin-to-skin contact with their babies, particularly if a mother has had a caesarean section or a complex birth. She said:

> This is partly why those facilities in the rooms are so important, so they have a comfortable space to do that as well, in either a reclining chair or a bed. We just ask that dads keep their underpants on because midwives aren't used to seeing boy bits.

During the pandemic, Northumbria Healthcare did not have to impose restrictions on mothers and partners because there are so many private rooms in the maternity unit. At some other hospitals, mothers were banned from having a partner with them during labour, as well as in the hours and days afterwards. When lockdowns were in place, word got around in the north east of England about rules not changing at the Northumbria Trust and the numbers of births at the hospital soared, with people travelling further than they otherwise would have to have children there.

As a mother of two with a high-pressure job, Wall said she felt personally connected to the idea of changing attitudes around gender stereotypes in parenting and encouraging fathers to see direct caregiving as a shared responsibility. Like many working mothers, she has continually experienced presumptions about women having primary responsibility for their children's day-to-day care, even if they have another parent. 'I have a relatively challenging job, but the expectation is that it will always be me who goes to parents evening, and if the kids are poorly the expectation is that it will be me who looks after them,' she said.

At other NHS hospital trusts in the UK, maternity wards can be very different. Leah Hazard is a practising NHS midwife and the author of the bestselling memoir *Hard Pushed: A Midwife's Story*.[17] We spoke on video about partners being on maternity wards while I was upstairs at my parents' house during a day off work and my mum, Esther, was looking after Solly before she had to run out for an appointment. The interview overran, and towards the end of my recording, you can hear my mum shouting my name every few minutes with increasing panic as a very energetic Solly tears up her house. Hazard said that while, in general, it can be helpful to have partners with mothers and their babies after birth, and most fathers are compassionate and considerate of other people on the wards, hospitals often cannot accommodate them:

> Most maternity hospitals in the UK and probably throughout the industrialised world have not been built with this rela-tionship [between a fully involved father and baby] in mind. The mother or birthing parent will usually be in a three- or four-bedded bay, with the beds divided by curtains. Within each bed space there is probably other furniture such as a chair, a bedside locker, maybe an extendable table for eating.

It is crowded. Design-wise there is very little space for another person to be there all the time.

Many maternity units are very busy and care for women who are extremely vulnerable following the birth of their children and can be from a range of different ethnicities and cultures. Hazard said:

They've been through a huge physical and emotional ordeal even if it has gone well. They may be post-operative if they have had forceps or a caesarean section. Absolutely they will be bleeding, facing challenges with infant feeding, whether by breast or bottle. You've got predominantly women who are generally in a partial state of undress, particularly if they are trying to establish breastfeeding. They're sitting around with their pyjama tops open, going back and forth to the toilet to change pads or go to the shower. So, in general, yes partners are respectful, but it is certainly not uncommon at all to have women who feel uncomfortable in the presence of generally male partners in their immediate vicinity. Although we'd love to facilitate everybody being there all the time, hospitals are just not designed with that in mind.

Hazard has two teenage daughters. Her first child was born in hospital during an emergency caesarean section and her husband was asked to leave within a few hours of the birth. While her experience was not uncommon, she described it as traumatic and said her 'whole existence changed that day'. It was also transformative for her husband. 'I realised after what a huge undertaking it was for me to manage myself and our baby without him,' she said. In the panic before the birth, he was sent to a small room, which he described as like a cupboard, to change into scrubs while she was sent to the operating theatre. She said:

I didn't realise until he told me years later how terrified he had been. He thought the baby and I were both going to die, that he was going to be leaving the hospital by himself. He had this very detailed vision of how that would look and feel. For him to have felt that way and then have to leave us a couple of hours later, even though everything was fine, must have been incredibly difficult.

Their second daughter was born at home. They had planned a home birth, but the baby came so quickly the midwives had not arrived yet. Hazard's husband caught the baby, and she was in such shock she could not hold her in the moments after birth. As a result, he had the first proper skin-to-skin contact. 'That was hugely powerful. It was euphoric,' Hazard said. 'He still teases her about it because she was trying to breastfeed off her dad's hairy nipple.'

While home births are an option for parents if they choose this and it is medically suitable, they are not for everybody. And it should not be the case that women have to give birth at home to ensure their partners can be around to support them afterwards.

Hazard said that Britain's health service is so desperately under-staffed, with maternity units at breaking point, particularly following the pandemic, that there are countless fundamental problems to solve before even considering the possibility of routinely providing space for partners on postnatal hospital wards by building private rooms. Staffing is so tight that midwife-led units, which do not have doctors or typical hospital furniture and can be more accommodating of partners, are often closed, with hospitals prioritised for midwives' shifts. As an example of the struggle faced by maternity services in Britain, Hazard described the 'golden hour' after birth when midwives do their checks while almost disappearing into the background so the family unit can be together to bond:

This is where the system is broken. It is wonderful that we've always had what we call the 'golden hour' after birth when everyone in the family can be together. But because most maternity units are so overworked and understaffed, that time is more and more hurried, and there is now a conveyor belt sense of 'right, she's delivered, she's fine, the baby's had the first feed, tick that box, baby's been weighed, tagged, assessed, documented, why is the mother still here? Off to the ward.'

In recent years, as more and more of our friends have become parents, Robin and I have become accustomed to hearing the horror stories. Almost every new mother seems to have experienced one of the terrifying scenarios: a midwife-led unit being shut at the last minute, staff shortages, problems during labour, the baby's heartbeat slowing, emergency caesarean sections, problems finding an anaesthetist for pain relief, and packed wards. With all the medical advances of the past century, it seems incomprehensible that childbirth is still so difficult for many mothers. Would this be the case if men went through childbirth? I very much suspect not. We would have our own family rooms, huge funding for staff and drugs on tap. In this imaginary alternative universe, there is also no way the system would not ensure female partners could be around in hospital afterwards, to help look after the new dads and change their share of the new baby's nappies.

Bergman, the scientist who specialises in parents having skin-to-skin contact with their babies, was horrified when I told him about the British system and fathers being treated as visitors on postnatal wards. Unlike some of the other experts I interviewed, he argued strongly that some parenting stereotypes are rooted in biological differences between the sexes, rather than because of societal pressures, with women naturally more primed for nurturing. However, he said this should not mean fathers do any less than their fair share of the hard work of parenting, or that they have any less value or importance as parents.

'Fathers getting kicked out of hospital is a problem. In fact, it is a social crime that they are not allowed to spend this time with mothers and babies,' he said. 'There can be a loss of a profound connection, an emotional connection which ensures resilience in fathers that will span the rest of their lifetime.'

In Sweden there have been significant changes to postnatal care since the 1990s. One academic study published in 2009 reported that family suites on hotel wards were already 'becoming increasingly popular' and that these private rooms meant midwives could routinely invite fathers to stay overnight with their partners and new babies. The study reported that 'almost all fathers are engaged in prenatal visits and are present during and after birth'.[18] As a minimum, Bergman recommended that fathers in other countries who are sent home from hospitals should have skin-to-skin contact with their child before they leave and within two hours of the birth.

It is impossible to generalise about whether fathers can or cannot always be with their babies after birth within other specific countries because policies vary depending on the health system, the choice of birth setting, and, even within individual hospitals, rules can change overnight, as they did repeatedly during the Covid-19 pandemic.

While writing this book, I made it a habit to ask people who had children in other countries about their birth experiences. As is so often the case, wealth makes a huge difference. In various countries, parents can often ensure fathers are not sent home after birth by paying for an individual room, either in a private hospital or within some public hospitals. In Britain, giving birth at a private hospital and staying for one night typically costs more than £5,000, while private rooms within public NHS hospitals can cost as much as

£450 per night.[19] A friend who has given birth twice in New York in recent years said her husband was allowed to remain with her throughout the time afterwards, both when they paid for a private room and when she was on a general ward. Another woman who gave birth in New York said:

> They gave us an hour and a half in the recovery room together and then he [the father] had to leave until the next morning, which was horrible as we didn't know yet that I had broken my tailbone [also known as the coccyx] during the delivery because I had a monster epidural. When I woke up in the middle of the night, I was basically paralysed and in horrific pain. I had to cope with that as well as the stress of having to try to breastfeed a newborn baby. My husband was still only allowed in during visiting hours the next day and the day after.

Other male friends felt they benefitted from going home after the birth of their babies, particularly with second or third children, as it meant they could be around at home for the older siblings. Surely it is best to have the choice though.

In Denmark, there is now a movement to transform the design of hospital maternity rooms to make them as calming and homely as possible. This has included ensuring there is space for partners to support mothers and other birthing parents, and to promote the best possible experience for the whole family to bond as the new child is born. Esben Bala Skouboe, a civil engineer, designed a birth room at a regional hospital in Herning, Denmark, almost two decades ago, and it has become an archetype for how this can be achieved.

In 2006, Bala Skouboe's wife gave birth to their first child, Olivia, at the hospital in Herning. He was struck by how much more positive the experience would be for mothers, partners and for the staff at the hospital with a few design changes:

It is one of the biggest moments in people's lives but at the hospital there were these slaughterhouse aesthetics, with pipes coming out of the walls, stainless-steel tables and white, glazed tiles on the walls so the blood is easy to wash down. It was all the highest quality but pure utilitarian. There had been no thought put into how this environment makes you feel. This meant that it was completely down to the midwife to make things comfortable for us.

By chance, the hospital was being rebuilt at the time. After his daughter was born, Bala Skouboe spoke to the head of midwifery and she liked his ideas, so much so that he was employed to oversee the design of one of the new maternity rooms.

About a year later, the room was ready. There is a hospital bed and a birthing bath but also a regular bed and a large sofa, with trendy hanging lights on dimmers and lamps on coffee tables. Slow and soothing footage, filmed by a videographer in local beauty spots, can be projected to span across the walls, with the sounds enhanced by a concert composer to promote calm breathing. There are 11 options for the wall scenery, with the footage taken at a beach, in a forest, among wildflowers and in winter scenes, chosen through discussions with local women about the areas they found most calming. It is all very hygge.

When parents-to-be arrive, they are shown how to use a simple tablet that controls the lighting and the footage on the walls if they want to use this. The dads are encouraged to use the tablet. It also guides them through the stages of labour, suggesting massages and exercises that they could help their partners do at different points. There is an emergency button in the room, but at the time of writing, about 4,000 births later, it has never been used. Staff can also use a small button to flood the room with bright light if this is ever needed for clinical reasons.

Bala Skouboe said that in Denmark fathers are encouraged to stay with mothers and babies throughout and following births, and that was a key focus of his designs. 'I did skin-to-skin contact after my children were born; we shared it. I also had them on my chest,' he said:

We wanted to create this sensual, meaningful experience that would support the healing process and bonding. Part of that is the man being given agency in the room, to be active and able to help, to take responsibility in supporting the mother. That carries on after the birth. The sofa and bed allow them to have skin-to-skin contact with their baby after the birth, but also between the father and the mother, a pause, for them to start finding themselves as a family. After about an hour they all move together to another private room. Dads are encouraged to stay, which lowers work for the midwives and supports the family building process. It is horrible that fathers are kicked out in other countries. This is where you create your family – and your memories.

There are now 12 of these birth rooms designed by Bala Skouboe in three hospitals in Denmark and there are plans for more of them to be built across the country. Bala Skouboe's second child, Isabella, was born in the hospital room in Herning that he designed.

There are daunting challenges facing maternity services that need to be tackled before many hospitals can consider trying to offer all families free postnatal private rooms. However, when new hospitals are built, they should look to the ones in Denmark, and in Northumbria, to see how the design of maternity units can make such a profound difference to women and all new parents in terms of recovery from potential trauma, the ability to cope with the overwhelming new responsibility of having a newborn and establishing the expectation that all parents, whatever their sex, are responsible for caring for their babies.

Slowly, change is starting to happen. In June 2022, a major hospital in Leeds, also in the north of England, revealed plans for the UK's largest single-site maternity centre, with the capacity to deliver up to 10,500 babies a year. The announcement stated that there would be a focus on 'keeping families together', with en-suite postnatal rooms so partners can stay. Kelly Cohen, clinical director for women's services at Leeds Teaching Hospitals NHS Trust, said: 'Parents will be starting or growing their family life in their own private space which is great for infection control but also means they can get to bond with their new baby in a private room with their own bathroom.'[20]

At other hospitals, at the very minimum, staff must protect the 'golden hour' after hospital births. One small and practical change that could make a difference to families would be for midwives to suggest that fathers could have skin-to-skin contact during this time if they and the mother want this. Partners should then be encouraged to continue to offer to properly share the time holding and directly caring for the baby once the family is back at home, rather than just doing the dishes and making cups of tea. Of course, you do not have to have had skin-to-skin contact with a baby in the first hours after birth in order to be a committed father. Research suggests this can help though.

Currently, men are not only often discouraged from being with their children in many hospitals in the hours following their births; the messaging throughout pregnancy and childbirth enforces this idea of men being part-time parents. When a male friend was expecting twins and attended a medical appointment, he was given a booklet on parenting that included just one page for dads, which focused on the importance of them having powerful arms to protect their baby. A male colleague went to an antenatal class and the five-minute section for fathers consisted of a video narrated by a cartoon baby with a caricature cockney accent. A book that my husband and I relied on daily for advice when our son was tiny, and was generally incredibly helpful, included a line about dads often making a fuss if they bathe with a baby and the baby does a wee.

I know lots of men are awful. I have seen the videos of dads retching when they are forced, just once, to change a nappy bulging with bright yellow, liquid poo. But is this really the assumed position, generally, about men? If an average man's child wees in the bath with him, does he really throw a tantrum, like a child himself? Does he scream, splash and jump out, willy wagging, leaving the mother alone in the bathroom with their baby in one hand and a mop in the other to soak up the mess?

Maybe it is about time men were patronised. Men have had quite a good time of it generally when it comes to equality. Should we really care if in this one area of life – maternity – men are treated like idiots – or excluded? I think we should because this nonsense benefits no one. By warning new dads that we may occasionally have to be there for our children, it reinforces the idea that general absence is normal. By warning us about being emotional when we have a baby, it reinforces the idea that emotional vulnerability in men is shameful. By describing fathers as an occasional help for the mother, it positions the baby and the volume of its every scream as almost entirely the mother's to soothe.

I reread the hospital website for new fathers – the one that warns dads they may have to chip in occasionally and help look after their new baby – when Solly was 11 months old. At the time, a tight rock of anxiety sat on my diaphragm for the third day in a row because he had come out in hives all over his body. Every time he scratched, another red-and-white weal appeared, like elongated mosquito bites. They did not seem to bother him massively, but Robin and I could not stop looking at them, willing them to fade.

We had recently moved home. Was it bed bugs? Some kind of lice in the wooden flooring? Had we changed washing powder? Was this a reaction to us moving out of London and exposing him to too much pollen? He had also recently started nursery. Was it just a virus? Could it be a symptom of something more serious?

We googled and put our phones down, traumatised, spent hours on hold failing to get a GP appointment and then, when successful, were told there was a waiting list of four to six months to see an NHS dermatologist, even for a baby. The rashes came and went – Solly just has sensitive skin – but the rock in my chest rarely moves. I have learned, since Solly was born, that the love you feel as a parent can literally make you feel breathless, because it is embedded in the fear that comes with proper responsibility.

While Robin and I both felt a very strong instant bond to Solly, I now look back and can see how our love and dedication to him deepened because we were both fully present for the intense challenges and joy that started that first night and followed throughout those first few weeks.

Solly was born on the first day of lockdown in Britain because of the pandemic. We were incredibly lucky that we could be at his birth. So many women were forced to give birth without family support, and fathers were unable to be there, in the weeks and months that followed, as hospitals became stricter about letting in anyone other than the people actually giving birth.

The pandemic meant that Solly did not meet the rest of his family in person for almost three months. We had none of our parents, siblings or friends around to watch him or hold him occasionally so we could relax our arms and our minds and get some rest. Health visitors usually check in on parents in the weeks after birth, but we had one in-person visit and were told to check his growth by weighing ourselves on our bathroom scales before doing it again while holding him. We never bothered. His chubby legs and cheeks suggested he was getting enough formula. The timing meant that Robin, Solly and I were together for every minute of every day when he was newborn. Just us.

With hindsight, I can never quite remember the full exhaustion of that time. It comes back in flashes of moments. Rocking Solly left to right for what feels like an hour when he screams in the middle of the night and then desperately calling out for Robin to take over. Lying face down on the floor afterwards, begging the carpet for him to go back to sleep. Feeding Solly with one hand while using the phone in my other hand to do crosswords and try to get holes-in-one on Golf Clash, a game I played obsessively in the first weeks of his life and then never looked at again once Solly was sleeping through the night. Dreaming through the drone of white noise while Robin does his feeds. Washing bottles and pans in the kitchen while wearing Solly in a sling, looking down at the top of his head, leaning forward and seeing his dummy bobbing. Quietly sipping soup while he lies in a Sleepyhead mattress on the kitchen table next to us. Singing nursery rhymes over and over again to keep Solly entertained while he kicks on a blanket on the floor. Obsessively checking the temperature in the room to make sure he is not too hot. Adding layers so he is not too cold.

Fathers need these moments. Rather than just supporting in the background, we also need to share substantial time holding our babies ourselves, to feel their weight in our hands every day. In Nell Frizzell's book *The Panic Years*, about the years of flux in women's late twenties and early thirties, she put forward a compelling argument as to why it is all too easy for fathers to be absent if they have not spent these formative hours with their babies. She wrote:

> So many cultural tropes centre on the absent fathers, the men who walk away, work long hours, forget their children's birthdays, but so little is said about why... The truth is that

by 'protecting' men from the grit and gristle, the sleepless-
ness and the screaming, the regret and reality, the fear and
the failure of parenting, we might, eventually, close them
off from it entirely. Which makes it infinitely easier to leave,
once things take a tricky turn… Fathers need the beast, as
well as the beauty of babies, otherwise their love will be a
flaky one – too easily crumbled by absence, rejection and
misunderstanding.[21]

I listened to the audiobook of *The Panic Years* and nodded to
those words in my car as I drove past my house, in loops, to keep
Solly asleep for just a few minutes longer because he had barely
napped that day. I would have screamed amen, but I did not want
to wake him.

I thought of Bergman and his experiment suggesting how
important it is that fathers literally feel their bodies calming through
the panic of having a new child, while holding them to their skin,
preparing them to be present throughout the madness that will
follow. I thought of those first few weeks of Solly's life. My baby on
my chest. Hearing his breaths slowing into deep sleep. Breathing
with him. The milky smell of his head, just above his ears. Feeling
my temples calm and the top of my head, just above my forehead,
just for a moment, tingling. The love for your child is not flaky,
whatever your sex, when you have fed them, and held them, and
changed them, and soothed them with cream, night after night
after night, from the very first night.

CHAPTER TWO

WHO DOES THE NIGHTS?

The Mother and Father Instinct

Solly is screaming – a relentless 'alaaaaaa, alaaaaaa, alaaaaaa' – and I am furious. Not with him but with Robin, who is lying next to me, eyes shut and mouth ajar, still in the depths of a dream.

I sit up to go to Solly in his crib at the bottom of our bed and make sure I am being as clumsy and loud as possible as my eyes feel through the darkness. I launch myself up by leaning down hard on the mattress just by Robin's face. I pull the covers, huff and then huff again, louder. As I reach for Solly and put a dummy back in his mouth, shushing to quiet him and calm myself, Robin stirs and mouths a little kiss, his eyes still shut, and then settles back down. I have no idea what time it is. Some point between Solly's last milk feed at 11 p.m. and the next one at 3 a.m.

Why does this keep happening? Solly is between three and four months old and while we both used to wake up when he cried at night, now Robin barely stirs while I jump in panic. We have friends with newborn babies and the cliché generally seems true – the mothers wake up before the fathers when their babies cry at night. If this is a biological response based on the sex of the parent, why am I responding like mothers usually do and why is Robin responding like a lot of other men?

The answer had been, almost literally, staring us in the face during night feeds. Like many parents, Robin and I had become increasingly reliant on TV for company when doing feeds at night and had our own series that we watched. We had got Solly (and ourselves) onto a pretty regular routine by that point. At about 7 p.m. he had a bottle and went to sleep in his crib before Robin and I had dinner, and I then joined Solly in our bedroom. Robin stayed awake until 11 p.m., by which point Solly would have started crying for his next bottle. Robin would then feed and burp him in the living room while watching *Lovesick*, a comedy about a man with chlamydia. I then did the next feed at about 3 a.m., usually while watching *Modern Family*. I went through seven series in the first few months.

Our living room was transformed into a night-feed nirvana. A chest-height wooden cabinet that used to be a proud fixture of the room became a makeshift feeding station, both for Solly and for us. There was a 'Perfect Prep' machine – like a home coffee machine but for formula – flanked, on one side, by clean bottles and, on the other, a large vase filled with sweets. Before every feed I would shove a handful into my mouth as a middle-of-the-night pick-me-up.

In convenient timing, a documentary series about newborn babies was one of the most watched shows on Netflix during those first months of Solly's life. Initially I assumed the documentary images were at the top of our account homepage for creepy data reasons related to us buying new baby clothes and furniture. In fact, it was there because it was in the top ten list of most-watched programmes in Britain so, while balancing a bottle into Solly's little mouth and listening to him guzzle, I switched it on.

The first episode of the series, called 'Babies', was about the love formed between a child and their parents and featured research from Ruth Feldman, director of the Centre for Developmental Social Neuroscience at Reichman University, Israel, with a joint appointment at Yale University's Child Study Centre. After decades of studying hundreds of new families, measuring their hormone levels and scanning their brains, Feldman and her team had concluded that fathers' bonds with their babies were often as strong as mothers'. They also found that non-genetic parents had bonds with their children that were equivalent to those experienced by genetic parents, and that while most men did not wake as easily as women at night when their children cried, something extraordinary happened to men's brains when they took on primary responsibility for their children. Feldman's findings made sense to me, mirroring my early experiences as a father, and yet they are at odds with how society expects men and women to behave as parents.

After Feldman gave birth aged 22 to her first child, Estie, she set out to discover what happened in parents' brains when they felt that unique connection to their child and fell in love with them. Central to this feeling of bonding in mammals is a hormone called oxytocin. Scientific research over the past two decades, including by Feldman, has found that mothers' levels of oxytocin can rise during pregnancy and childbirth and remain high in the weeks after childbirth.[1] The hormone then appears to increase the more the mother touches her baby, with the brain giving the mother a feeling of intense reward through interaction, making her want to engage with the baby more and more.[2]

Feldman and her team then recruited 80 couples and measured the fathers' levels of oxytocin following the birth of their children, as well as the mothers'. While the dads did not get the surge of oxytocin through being pregnant or giving birth, their levels of the hormone rose so high after their children were born that soon they were identical to those in the mothers.[3] Feldman described this finding as a 'huge surprise' and explained that it was all about fathers becoming actively involved in caring for their children. 'The more you do with a baby and really lift your sleeves and take care of the child, and wash it and feed it, engage in a parental role, the more your oxytocin system will activate,' she said on the programme. 'Fatherhood is biological. It's as deep as motherhood.'

This interaction between babies and their parents, or any other dedicated caregiver, is also crucial to the child's social development. Feldman's team's research, which has followed babies to adulthood, suggests that sharing these direct moments with babies – smiling and the baby smiling back, making them giggle, touching and the baby responding, singing and cooing together – teaches them subconsciously how to form secure attachments with other people. These are social skills that stay with them for life, helping them to form friendships and experience romantic love when they are older.[4]

A big question remained. If fathers really can feel attached to their babies in as deep a way as mothers do, why is it so often the mother who cannot sleep properly at night and who wakes first when their baby cries? The answer came when Feldman's team scanned parents' brains and noticed the difference in size between the amygdalae depending on the sex of the parent.

The amygdalae are the parts of the brain that cause alertness to danger and make us feel anxiety and panic. There are two: one amygdala on each side of the brain. They are what tell you to run after an explosion and wake you up in a sweat at night before an exam. The scientists found that the oxytocin surge in mothers during childbirth appeared to 'activate' their amygdalae in a primitive way, causing them to be more vigilant and worry about the baby. Once the mother's amygdalae were 'open', they appeared to remain in this state afterwards, even as the child grew older and less obviously dependant on them. Fathers' brains looked very different, with their amygdalae typically about a quarter of the size of those observed in mothers.[5] The hypothesis was that fathers can feel an equal intensity of love for their babies, but they do not feel equal alertness. With much smaller amygdalae, they appeared to lack the so-called 'mother's instinct'.

As more and more gay men have become fathers through surrogacy, Feldman returned to the subject. What happens to fathers' brains when there is no mother? She and her team recruited 48 gay couples in committed relationships who had a child through surrogacy and cared for their child from the first day of their life. They measured the fathers' levels of oxytocin and scanned their brains. They found that when fathers are primary caregivers, their amygdalae are as large as those typically seen in mothers' brains, as well as their oxytocin levels being just as high. While the physical experiences of pregnancy and childbirth activate this 'instinct' in mothers – an enhanced alertness, with their amygdalae becoming bigger – similar changes happen when men have primary responsibility for their babies.[6] 'It doesn't really matter whether you are the biological parent or a committed caregiving parent. It's a choice to be a parent to that infant,' Feldman said on the programme.

Her team's findings seemed to answer my question. I was waking up first at night when Solly was a few months old because I was on parental leave. At this point in Solly's first year, I was spending almost all my time looking after him and Robin was working during the days. I was Solly's primary carer, and my brain must have responded to the responsibility that came with that, making me hyper-alert. The same almost certainly would have happened to Robin's brain when he took over parental leave for the second half of the year and felt the full weight of primary responsibility, in turn allowing me to relax and sleep better.

Sarah Blaffer Hrdy, a biological anthropologist and professor emerita at the University of California, Davis, told me that this research on fathers' brains changing like mothers' when they had primary responsibility for their babies was 'one of the most exciting papers in science I have ever read'. Hrdy's books, including the multi-award-winning *Mother Nature* and *Mothers and Others*,[7] explored decades of research into parenting behaviours across modern societies, hunter-gatherer peoples and primate communities. She has long argued that humans could not have evolved without mothers having dedicated help from others. Parenting is too hard for anyone to do completely alone. While she believes absolutely in the importance of mothers, she also argues against the 'long, pointless, and ill-informed debate over whether or not women have "maternal instincts"'.[8] Her wide-ranging research suggests that fathers – and any other person who dedicates themselves to caring for a baby – can have similar biological responses to mothers if they look after their baby enough.

Hrdy uses the term 'allomothers' (with 'allo' from the Greek for 'other than') to describe anyone other than a genetic mother who provides committed caregiving to a child. She describes me and Robin as 'allomothers' to Solly. She would use the term for any other father who properly takes on parental responsibility. Even though I am not Solly's genetic father, with Robin's sperm used during fertility treatment that resulted in him being born, she also describes both me and Robin as his biological fathers because of the hormonal and neurological changes that will have occurred within us as a result of us spending so much time caring for our son. For the same reason, she says mothers through adoption are biological mothers.

'To say that a woman who did not give birth to a baby was not a biological mother, to me, is inaccurate because she has all these very biological responses,' she said. 'Prolactin [a hormone usually associated with breastfeeding] can go up in an adoptive mother. Oxytocin would be changed. There are the neural changes that Feldman and others have documented in Israel now.' I am biased, but I found this rethinking of the term 'biological parent' really beautiful. Referring to me, Hrdy said: 'You are very biologically a father.'

After proudly sending me photographs of her grandchildren, Hrdy shared a small personal experiment she conducted in 2014 when her first grandchild was born. As she arrived by taxi at her daughter Katrinka's home to meet Maximus, her 11-day-old grandson, Hrdy took a sterile plastic vial from her purse, spat into it and screwed the top on tight, before entering the home and putting it into her daughter's freezer. She met her grandson and, in her words, spent the time 'holding and nuzzling him'. She then spat into another vial and had the samples tested at a laboratory. After cuddling the baby, there had been a 63 per cent jump in her levels of oxytocin, the 'bonding' hormone known to spike in new mothers.

A fortnight later, her husband, Dan, met his grandson for the first time as well, and he did the same experiment. His oxytocin levels rose by 26 per cent immediately after holding the baby. After two more days of interaction, his oxytocin levels were also up by 63 per cent. Hrdy said: 'There was no difference in the end result between me and my husband; it just took him a little more exposure to his grandson to get there.'

While Hrdy has concluded from her wider studies that men can care for babies in as nurturing a way as women, she wonders why some choose to be dedicated fathers while so many others are absent. In a speech in 2014, she described the 'extraordinary potential for nurture' in men, adding:

Fathers clearly have this potential to respond to babies, and you have this species where mothers need help so very much. In that case, how is it that paternal care varies so much? You have some men who are totally dedicated to their children – the Mrs Doubtfires out there – and you have other men, men certain of paternity, who behave as if they didn't even know they had children.[9]

When we spoke, she said that more research is needed to understand what drives absent fathers to leave their children:

> Nurturing emotions in men are not hard-wired. They are more flexible than most people realise, dependent on how much time they spend with the baby and who is responsible for the baby's wellbeing. The experiences of undergoing gestation and birth and those hormone changes in the mother prime her for these responses. Men are capable of them too, it just takes them a little more time, a little more exposure.

Hrdy said the most important factor determining whether a father is committed is 'prolonged intimate contact with the infant'.

Why does this matter? While it is interesting that men and non-genetic parents or carers have the potential to bond as intensely with their babies as mothers do, and even to respond as quickly to their cries at night, why do they need to do this? Biologically, if a mother is around to wake up when her baby screams, what is the benefit of a father doing so as well?

Hrdy's books focus on the importance to children of having more than one committed caregiver. These do not only have to be genetic parents; they can include anyone focused on caring for a child, from a genetic mother to a father, step-parents, foster carers, adopted parents, grandparents and others. Historically, in the most basic living environments, having others around to help a mother look after a baby meant the child was much more likely to survive.[10] Studies also suggest that children today continue to benefit if they have a few stable, close attachment figures, with the different relationships helping them grow up with more self-confidence and better able to empathise with other perspectives.[11] I will explore these studies in more detail later in the book.

Put simply, babies seem to benefit from more than one person being committed to their care, whatever their genetic relationship. In an age when women, rightly, have careers, there are also now obvious advantages of sharing the burdens of parenting as well as the joys. This is true 'at so many levels,' Hrdy said:

> Earning one's own living, freedom to work and pursue a chosen career, these are as empowering for women as they are for men. Meanwhile, caretaking broadens men's emotional horizons and helps them escape having to live up to unattainable, and often unrewarding, definitions of masculinity. The psychological benefits of men sharing the responsibilities of caring for children are tremendous, all around, including for society at large.

It is apt that the marker of parental instinct and primary responsibility is which parent wakes up first when their baby cries at night. Sleep is so central to the experience of being a new parent. While everyone struggles with less sleep after having a child, the research suggests that mothers lose more of it. This is clearly unfair. It has somehow become an unquestionable truth among some that fathers of newborns must not be woken up at night because they need to go to work in the morning. Whoever came up with this unwritten rule never looked after a six-week-old baby with colic all day after an all-nighter of screaming (or maybe they did and thought, never again).

Every time I hear a dad of a newborn saying he is sleeping in the spare room because he is back at work, I feel my heart rate quickening and my lips start to twitch, begging to speak. I have to make a quick decision as to whether or not to ignore it or to ruin his life by telling his partner the truth. Why should being fresh-faced for a day of accountancy work in an office be more important than being rested enough to care for your baby safely while on maternity leave?

By splitting parental leave, Robin and I have done both and came to the same conclusion. Paid work is not more exhausting or important than keeping a tiny new child alive and happy. The science indicates that it is a choice for men to be a primary parent. Fathers can hone that instinct to respond to their children by showing up and getting involved. Committed caregiving makes fathers feel the responsibility that makes them wake at night. Of course, that does not happen if you bugger off to the spare room.

As anyone who has had a baby will know, sleep, and the amount of it that you are having, or not having, is the obsession that follows you everywhere you go. In the months before the birth, friends with young children stare at you with wild eyes and instruct you to stock up on as much of the stuff as you can while you can still get it, like it is something you can hold. When the baby arrives, the conversation continues relentlessly. How is he sleeping? Is he going through the night? How much are you sleeping? You offer a 'yeah, quite good, four hours at a time', remembering the one time that the baby went the longest between 7 p.m. and 11 p.m., and they say, 'Oh dear, you must be going mad.' Some unthinkably stupid people even decide this is the time to tell you that their children were sleeping through the night by his age. Everyone lies about how much babies sleep. You know it, they know it, but it carries on. It is infuriating. There is nothing worse than getting through a night of continual waking with a newborn to then read a message on the antenatal group WhatsApp chat about how someone else's baby just slept eight hours straight.

People would ask us, 'Who does the nights?' as if one of us exclusively would have taken on a traditional mother's role, while the other slept in the spare room. Robin and I just did what felt fairest. We split the feeds at night so we could both sometimes get semi-decent stretches of unbroken sleep, me at some point between 8 p.m. and 3 a.m. and Robin somewhere between midnight and 7 a.m. The days were tiring on less sleep than normal, and waking up during the night was a challenge, but we knew many new parents, typically mothers, have had it much worse.

I am going to try to be honest here. From memory (it is still hazy) Solly was a pretty average sleeper as a newborn. He was not doing nights by two months like French babies apparently do, but we were also relatively lucky. He did not have colic, with screaming for more than a few minutes at a time very rare. He immediately took to a dummy so lured us into a false sense of security in the first few weeks, quickly doing two- to three-hour stints. We would pop a dummy in after a feed and he would be off for a little while, either in a sling, buggy or in his crib. While our breasts were growing from all the middle-of-the-night sweets, Solly remained on formula milk, so feeds were much easier for us to share than for breastfeeding mothers who may or may not choose to express milk so a partner or other family member can help them. I have huge admiration for mothers who do all the feeds through the night, either by choice or not. I would have found that unimaginably hard.

At around three or four months, just as we were becoming smug about Solly's sleep getting better, he started waking once an hour crying for his dummy. At that age he was too young to know how to put them back into his mouth by himself, so one of us had to get out of bed and put it back in, repeatedly, through the night. While I would often wake before Robin – presumably my amygdalae had annexed most of the rest of my brain by this point – he would usually also be disturbed and did his share of dummy runs. The sound of Solly crying ripped through my mind and tightened my chest, but the anticipation was worse. Robin and I would lie there in the seconds after he settled again with knots in our ribs, not daring to move.

During the morning, I would pace with Solly in a sling, forcing my eyes open and daydreaming about inventing a machine that could safely replace dummies for babies, a sort of arcade toy-catcher claw connected to his crib. I read forums online and once-an-hour waking seemed to be normal for babies of Solly's age during a sleep regression. Some warned we would be replacing the dummy like this for the next four months unless we got rid of it. Robin was working from home in a daze. We did not want to get rid of the dummy as it was so useful for calming Solly, and we had read research suggesting they may help to prevent sudden infant death syndrome (SIDS), also known as cot death. The advice was that if babies had dummies they should be used regularly and only be removed from six months.[12] Instead, we came up with a plan. We called it 'dummy training'.

During the day, while Robin worked, I lay Solly down on a mat in our living room with two small piles of dummies either side of his head. Like a deranged baby gym instructor, I repeatedly showed him where the dummies were and guided his hands towards them. Who knows how many times I did this? Maybe 400. It took two days, but he got the knack of it. After a week, he was a little dummy ninja, instinctively reaching up to get them and then twiddling them in his little hands. We bought more dummies and surrounded his head with a crown of them when he went to sleep. Our nights were saved. We also moved him to a bigger cot in his own room and that seemed to help; we had probably been disturbing him by snoring.

Soon after, we drove to Derbyshire to visit Rachel, Solly's surrogate, and because this is where his birth had to be registered after months of this being impossible during the earliest days of the pandemic. We could only see each other outdoors because of restrictions on social contact. The trip got us out of our normal routine, and we only put Solly back to sleep for the night when we were home at 9 p.m. Instead of waking him at 11 p.m. for his usual night feed, we decided to see how long he would go. He woke up at around 5 a.m. So from then on we ditched the 11 p.m. feed.

For a while after that, he would almost sleep through the night but wake very early. He did not do full-night sleeps from 7 p.m. until 7 a.m. until he was about seven months old and was weaned and eating proteins such as chicken and fish. The books we had read stated that weaning would not help with sleep as there are more calories in baby formula. Apparently Solly had not read them.

The other tricks that worked for us were blackout blinds in his room and a white-noise machine (although we forgot this on a trip at about five months, and he did not seem to care so we then got rid of it). We have also had a consistent routine before bedtime involving playtime upstairs, a bath, books and, until he was just over one year old, a bottle.

At about 18 months, Solly went through a stage of refusing to go to sleep at night and one of us would have to sit by his cot, singing, shushing and rubbing his back. After about half an hour, when he had drifted off, there was then the awful dance of trying to get out of the room and shut the door without setting him off by creaking a floorboard or banging your toe. Robin was much better at putting him down than I was. He would come out of the room after a success and I would be waiting outside, raising my arms up in the air and silently cheering. It was unsustainable. We decided to do some sleep training, and it was much easier than we thought it would be.

The first night Robin put Solly in his cot, Solly cried for between five and ten minutes before settling down by himself. I found this much harder to cope with than Robin, who had to force me not to go in. The second night it took about 30 seconds. After that, for a while, Solly almost always went to sleep happily, whichever one of us put him down, and rarely woke at night. When he did, we would hear him moan and shuffle – probably to find a dummy – and then settle himself back to sleep.

Soon after turning two, Solly had another phase of night waking – which we think may have been down to nightmares, or separation anxiety, or who bloody knows? – but thankfully it did not last very long. He moved to a toddler bed at two and a half, and after a couple of tough nights, he got used to it and slept through the night again. We have got no idea what is going to happen when we get rid of the dummies at night. Wish us luck.

While we had some difficult moments due to lack of sleep, we know we had a relatively easy ride. Many parents face the agonising reality of a newborn baby who will not sleep and cries relentlessly, no matter what they do to try to soothe them. More than one in every ten new mothers experiences postnatal depression, and many fathers also experience this.[13]

In her 2020 *New York Times*-bestselling book *Cribsheet*,[14] Emily Oster, a professor of economics at Brown University, used data to consider the most reliable scientific evidence on many parenting questions usually loaded with judgment such as breastfeeding, sleep training, TV and potty training. On sleep, she highlighted an Australian study involving 328 children, half of whom were randomised to be included in a sleep-training regime and the other randomly picked as a control group.[15] Oster wrote: 'Two and four months later, the authors found that the mothers of babies in the sleep-training arm were less likely to be depressed and more likely to have better physical health… The finding is consistent across studies.'[16]

The book I have written is not about whether or not you should sleep train your baby. Robin and I were convinced after doing our own research, but many parents worry about the impact of allowing babies to cry even for short periods and prefer always to comfort them immediately. It is a personal choice that is not for everyone. We are all just trying to get by and make sure our children are as happy as they can be. The point I am making is that sleep matters, and it is deeply unfair for one parent's sleep to be prioritised over another's.

Having considered the evidence, Oster wrote about how improved sleep alleviated depression in parents, stating that if parents had not sleep trained their baby, there were other ways they could improve their sleep, including asking for help from family or friends, hiring a night nurse, or dividing the night duties so each parent could get at least one period of uninterrupted sleep per night. She wrote: 'It may be helpful to remind yourself that addressing your depression is valuable for your baby too, not just some kind of selfish personal indulgence.'

In Catherine Cho's book *Inferno: A Memoir of Motherhood and Madness* she described being sectioned with postpartum psychosis three months after the birth of her son, Cato, in 2017. She had never heard of the condition before being diagnosed with it. Cho and her husband, James, had taken Cato away from their home in London for a cross-country trip in the US to meet friends and relatives, travelling through six cities in a month. She barely slept and became so unwell that she could not differentiate between reality and fantasy. She became convinced that she could see devils inside her baby's eyes. In the book she wrote: 'Pregnancy had brought a list of worries – episiotomies, prolapse, pre-eclampsia. I was so preoccupied with the idea of losing my body, it had never occurred to me that I might lose my mind.'[17]

Postpartum psychosis affects about one in every 500 mothers after giving birth.[18] When we spoke, Cho said she did not know the cause of her experience of mental illness. 'It is impossible to know,' she said:

From my husband's point of view sleep was probably the number one factor, but for me it was probably more psychological, the shift in identity as a new mum and cultural pressure and expectation. I gave birth to my son and, because it was an induction, that was three days of not sleeping. Then

I spent an additional five or six days in a shared ward where I didn't sleep properly. And then throughout the time until the psychosis when my son was three months old, I never had more than a few hours of sleep at a time. Sleep and self-care wasn't something I prioritised.

She said her husband wanted to help at night, but she insisted on doing the feeds alone. 'I was the one who said, I'm not working, I'm breastfeeding, let me just do the night shift and you can help me when you're at home. That was how I'd always heard about it and assumed it would work,' she said. Cho repeatedly developed mastitis, painful swelling in her breasts that became worse when she slept for too long without breastfeeding. 'Everything was then compounding, and I couldn't sleep even if I wanted to sleep,' she said. 'So yes, lack of sleep was a significant contributing factor.'

Cho's descriptions of her temporary psychosis are terrifying. By the time her husband rushed her to hospital, after several days without her sleeping, she was convinced they were in purgatory. In the hospital's emergency waiting room, she was stripping her clothes and screaming. She was held in an involuntary psychiatric ward in New Jersey for two weeks and recovered with the help of close medical care and antipsychotic and antidepressant medications, which she took for a year. Her family returned to London, and she described the process of slowly bonding with her son again, while her husband took on the majority of the care during his first year:

I was so incapacitated when I came back that James had to do everything. He was the sole parent, taking care of Cato during the day, taking care of the nights and doing all the feeds, he was monitoring everything and he said he realised how much he had not been doing before. In that first year it was just him really and they really bonded. I think that's such a gift, and a silver lining of the experience is that James and Cato have such a great bond.

Cho's postpartum psychosis was extreme and there is no suggestion that the condition is in any way an inevitable result of lack of sleep or doing all the night feeds after becoming a parent. However, she and her husband have since had a second child, a daughter called Cora, and the experience made them rethink how they shared care for the baby. Cho did not have any mental health problems following Cora's birth. She said:

> The first time James took parental leave with me and he did that again, but this time he was very insistent that he did the night shift. I was still breastfeeding but he would wake up with Cora, change her and bring her to me to feed. He would sit with me while I fed her, I would hand her back to him, he would burp her and then put her back to sleep. That took a toll on him, but he would do it consistently. The idea was that all I had to do at night was feed her. With my daughter, the priority was to make sure I had sleep.

Cho, who is a literary agent, said her 'pet peeves' were the assumptions made about parents based on their sex:

> It frustrates me when people say that the mum is much better at putting the baby to sleep. Sure, because she's the one who has been doing it. Often guys I know very well as modern people, and who are willing, also don't realise that they have to take initiative. I have friends who say, oh he doesn't know where anything is, he doesn't know where the diapers are, where the clothes are or what to feed for dinner. Well, he should and why doesn't he? I'd go out for dinner with a

friend, and she'd be checking in to make sure her husband was okay because he never knows where anything is. And actually, he should just figure it out. He can learn. Because I'm a woman and gave birth to babies the assumption is that naturally I am a better parent. That's, for sure, a myth. We're all learning at the beginning.

Cho said she finds it 'infuriating' when people say fathers need a full night of sleep to work because mothers can nap with their babies:

If a father is working in an office job, then they should be doing the night shift with their partners. Compared to staying home with a baby, I found going to the office a break. Commuting is a break. Not enough fathers understand that. As more and more of my friends are having kids, I'm shocked at how much my friends who are women are doing versus their husbands and how it is assumed that is what it should be. It is really dangerous, not just in terms of medical conditions like psychosis, but in terms of career progression, everything. I'd be really sad for my kids if that's their future.

There are many very serious problems associated with disrupted sleep. The bestselling book *Why We Sleep*, written by Matthew Walker, professor of neuroscience and psychology at the University of California, Berkeley, assessed the science. It is pretty depressing reading for new parents. Walker outlined evidence suggesting that routinely sleeping for less than six hours a night weakens your immune system and substantially increases risks of certain forms of cancer. Insufficient sleep also appears to contribute to all major psychiatric conditions and be linked to risk of developing Alzheimer's disease, problems related to cardiovascular disease, stroke and congestive heart failure. There are immediate consequences of existing on only a few hours of sleep per night, affecting memory, learning and logical thinking, skills that should be essential when learning to look after a newborn. Walker wrote that sleep:

> enriches a diversity of functions, including our ability to learn, memorize and make logical decisions and choices. Benevolently servicing our psychological health, sleep recalibrates our emotional brain circuits, allowing us to navigate next-day social and psychological challenges with cool-headed composure.[19]

There are quick consequences for the wider body as well. Walker wrote: 'Inadequate sleep – even moderate reductions for just one week – disrupts blood sugar levels so profoundly that you would be classified as pre-diabetic.'[20] With this in mind, fathers should be doing all they can to ensure the night shifts are shared.

About three months after Solly's sleep regression, the relentless dummy runs and my fury at Robin for sleeping through them, I was woken up by Robin getting back into bed. By this point Solly was sleeping in his own room. 'Didn't you hear him? He was screaming,' Robin said. I had not heard anything. At first I did not believe him. I never slept through Solly crying. It was November by this point, and I had just gone back to work, with Robin starting parental leave.

Over the next few months, the same happened again and again. The anecdote seems too neat when I write it down, but it is true. Overnight, with Robin taking on primary responsibility for Solly's day-to-day care, he started waking first at the sound of crying while I snored next to him.

CHAPTER THREE

YOU'LL STILL GO TO THE OFFICE A BIT, RIGHT?

Reimagining Parental Leave

'Well, of course everyone is incredibly supportive,' Barry began, his eyes wide and the corners of his mouth pitched up in an exaggerated smile. 'We're delighted you'll be off for most of next year and getting paid for it while we're all working.'

We were standing by the canteen on the 14th floor of a glass office block overlooking the Thames, where *The Times* is based. He had heard that I was expecting a baby through surrogacy and would be taking extended parental leave. Barry is an older man, with children of his own. We are former colleagues, and I had bumped into him by chance while he was visiting a contact for lunch at my office.

He shifted his expression to concern. 'You do know what it's like, being with a baby all the time?' he asked. And then, almost to himself: 'I wonder if you'll just take the time off and then leave.'

I clutched my coffee and imagined spilling it onto his well-pressed, white shirt. Oh dear! Or chucking his massive Swiss watch out of the window and seeing how far from London Bridge it would land.

I have experienced a wide variety of reactions to my decision to take extended parental leave since I first started telling people that

Robin and I were expecting a child. While there have been a few Barrys, most people have been supportive, including a little army of dads I met on the front line during the first few months of Solly's life: the Goldman Sachs banker wearing his baby boy in a sling on wet mornings in the park; the prison officer who was the only other dad at the weekly 'mother and baby' music classes; a fellow male journalist on Twitter, sharing stories about being thrown up on. The new mothers I met for takeaway coffees and walks during the lockdown in spring 2020 seemed completely unbothered by me being a man. We mostly talked about the typical new parent stuff that everyone else finds excruciating: how well our babies were sleeping; nap times; when we would start weaning; how breastfeeding was going for them; the best bottles to use; the number of poos the babies were doing.

Some others found the idea of me being on leave with a baby either hilarious or totally bemusing. For the first year of Solly's life we lived in a flat in Willesden Green, north London. On my daily walks with him in his buggy, I started to get to know the local characters. My favourite was a pharmacist who would make Solly giggle and sing to him in Gujarati. She would also laugh out loud at the idea of him being cared for by a six-foot bloke with a growing lockdown beard and came up with a nickname that I quite liked. We would walk into the chemist and she would shout, 'It's MummyDaddy!' before giving me free supplies of nappy cream and apple sauce.

Solly and I would leave the pharmacy and do a loop past the Tube station and the bank before I'd get a takeaway coffee. There was a woman who spent her mornings chain-smoking outside the café. When I first told her that Solly had two dads and I was on leave from work with him she became determined. 'No, I can be his mother,' she informed me. Every morning after that she would stop us for a coo and offer me advice such as 'Make sure he is warm!' and 'Fresh air is good for babies!' while I tried to wheel him away from her trails of smoke.

Others, often professional men, quizzed me about why on earth I would choose to do something so, well, girly. It sometimes felt like playing a trick on them. After all the political-correctness courses, they had learned to be careful when speaking to female colleagues who were pregnant but forgot the act when talking to me. 'You'll still go to the office a bit, right?' I was asked by someone who had clearly never looked after any of his own children alone when they were newborn babies. 'You're setting a precedent, you're going to fuck us all, aren't you?' a male friend half-joked over a drink one Friday night.

Tom Whipple, the *Times* science editor and a pioneer of men taking extended parental leave in the newspaper's London office, wrote a piece about his experiences in 2014.[1] He described a similar array of comments, including from a friend who said, 'Tom, Tom, you've let yourself down,' and 'Some people might say – not me, some people – that you should grow a pair.' A colleague asked him, 'But what is your wife doing?' When Whipple explained that his wife was going back to work while he was on leave for five months, the colleague shook his head, saying, 'It's the end, the end.'

Whipple wrote that the only comments he minded, though, were the ones from fathers who said they would love to do the same but, alas, their employers would not allow them. In fact, it has been legal in the UK for more than a decade for dads to share parental leave.[2] The problem is, only a tiny proportion of fathers do so.[3] Despite theoretical change to encourage equal parenting and women's equality at work after having children, it is still very unusual for fathers to take anywhere near as much leave from work as mothers do in order to share the responsibility for caring for their babies.

Couples in the UK are entitled to 50 weeks of shared parental leave after having a baby. This can be split between them however they see fit, on top of two weeks of paternity leave specifically for the father. For instance, a mother could take the first six months off work, with the father with her and their baby for the first two weeks, and then he could take the second chunk of the year. Or she could go back to work temporarily for a specific project for a few months, while he takes over with the baby, before swapping back. Couples can choose to take their stints separately or to be off together. Some might choose a more traditional approach, with a mother taking her full allocation of maternity leave and the father only using his two weeks of paternity leave. These rules apply to employees who are new parents regardless of their gender or sexuality, and parents through adoption or surrogacy get the same entitlements.[4] The government pays new parents on leave for nine months of the year, but the rates are very low – the weekly amounts are equivalent to less than half of minimum wage.[5] The two weeks of paternity pay are also paid at this rate. Some companies top up the pay, but the packages vary massively.

Robin and I split our year of parental leave. We had both spent the previous 15 years building up our qualifications and dedicating a huge amount of time to our careers. Why should only one of us take the risk of being away from work for months? Why should only one of us get the once-in-a-lifetime experience of dedicating so much time to bonding with our newborn son? As we have often found since having Solly, being a gay male couple freed us from usual expectations. Neither of us came to parenthood with typical assumptions about gendered roles so we could just focus on practicalities.

We were lucky as we both worked for companies that topped up the state-funded parental leave pay. My work's policy offered more weeks of fully paid leave to the parent who took the time off from birth (usually the mother) than Robin's did, while his work offered a better stretch of fully paid paternity leave for the other parent (usually the father) than mine did, six weeks rather than the typical two. Our companies' policies were relatively good and, financially, it was a no-brainer. We would be off together for the first six weeks of Solly's life – me on shared parental leave and Robin on paternity leave – and then at about seven months, after my stint of parental leave and some holiday, we would swap, and Robin would take most of the second half of shared parental leave. We worked it out so we were both off work for the same number of days in total.

Whipple came to a similar arrangement with his wife. In his *Times* article on shared parental leave he wrote of being asked why he felt the need to take so much time off with his newborn when so few other fathers in Britain did this. He wrote:

> Well, I replied, if nothing else, because I couldn't really think of a good reason not to. Given it was possible, how precisely should I explain to my wife that, purely by virtue of her gender, she should be the one responsible for the bulk of childcare?

In wealthy developed countries, we like to think we are on our way to achieving sexual equality but, really, we have only done half the job, if that. Over the past century, equality campaigns have pushed governments and employers to try to establish conditions that allow women equal opportunities in education and at work. However, men are still typically not working as hard as women at home. This was demonstrated clearly during the pandemic, when researchers found that women took on much more of the housework and childcare during periods of lockdown, even when they were also doing more professional work than fathers who had lost their jobs.[6] Ed Miliband, the former Labour party leader in Britain, made this point about men not doing enough at home in his 2021 book *Go Big*, writing:

> Too often gender equality is framed as only being about how to extend to women the chance to compete on the same terms

as men but in a society defined in the traditional image of men's lives – centred around work. Our ambition should be to build a world where men engage equally in the caring that has historically been done by women, and in so doing reorder the values of work, family and love so that work does not always come first.[7]

Despite well-intentioned reforms to parental leave in the UK, very little has changed. In December 2021, the Institute for Fiscal Studies (IFS), an economic think tank, published a report which concluded that there had been almost no progress towards closing the gender pay gap in the past 25 years when improved education for women was taken into account. It found that the average woman earned 40 per cent less than her male equivalent and inequalities in earnings between the sexes 'increase vastly after parenthood'.[8]

While it has become more common to see men looking after their babies – pushing buggies and bottle-feeding in parks at the weekends – the number taking extended time off work to do so in the UK is still tiny. In the US, there is rarely paid maternity leave for new mothers, let alone for their partners.[9] The scientific studies referenced earlier in this book indicate that men are biologically suited to caring for babies, as long as they are present, putting in the time and actually doing it. So what needs to change? How do we ensure that women, after dedicating their early lives to building up qualifications and careers, do not then feel they have to make almost all the professional sacrifices after having children? And how do we encourage fathers to do their share at home?

The solution suggested by an array of leading economists, social policy academics, authors, charities, campaigners and political reformers is that both mothers and fathers should be offered fairly paid 'use-it-or-lose-it' parental leave. Instead of giving parents a year to share between them, fathers should have dedicated leave that only they can take, alongside mothers' maternity leave. This approach accounts for the fact that most women want and need their own dedicated leave in the months after having a baby, but that also it is incredibly valuable for fathers to have this time as well.

Nordic countries are, typically, progressive in this area and have already had these policies in place for decades, with dramatic results. When a child is born in Iceland, each parent is entitled to six months' leave from work, regardless of their gender or sexuality, paid at 80 per cent of their salary up to a maximum of ISK600,000 (about £3,500) per month. Each parent can transfer up to six weeks of their allocation to the other if they wish, so women can take more if they feel like they need this time. Single parents can take 12 months' paid leave, whatever their gender or sexuality. The average new father in Iceland takes 91 days of parental leave.[10] In total, fathers in Iceland now take about 30 per cent of all parental leave,[11] compared to 0.1 per cent in 1995 when there was no paid paternity leave.[12] It is extraordinary when you think about the change already; a new generation of babies in Iceland is having months of direct care from their fathers when this almost never happened in the same country fewer than 30 years ago.

Decades of countries experimenting with parental leave policies have shown that new parents only routinely decide for the fathers to take proper chunks of leave from work if there is an allocation earmarked specifically for them and it is paid at a reasonable rate. Sweden experimented with shared parental leave similar to the current UK policy in the 1970s, but 20 years later only ten per cent of the leave was taken by fathers.[13] The country switched to a 'use-it-or-lose-it' system and fathers there now also take about 30 per cent of all parental leave.[14]

The experiences of parents who are already sharing caring responsibilities suggest that when men do more at home, there are widespread benefits for the whole family. Mary Ann Sieghart, a broadcaster and former national newspaper columnist and senior editor, explored these issues in her book *The Authority Gap: Why Women Are Still Taken Less Seriously Than Men, and What We Can Do About It.*[15] When we spoke, Sieghart said:

> The real gender pay gap isn't just how much less women get for their paid work but how much more work they have to do at home. Women on average do 60 per cent more unpaid work than men do. This is the childcare, chores, ferrying children or elderly parents around, shopping for food, all those sorts of things. Counter-intuitively perhaps, when a woman earns more than her male partner, she does even more of the unpaid work. You'd think it would be less if she is earning more. It's almost as if it's a way of salving his ego.

The crucial time to redress this imbalance is following the birth of a child, when the gap in earnings between men and women really starts to widen. The hours and hours at home set a parent up for a lifetime of confidence in looking after their children alone and there are benefits for the whole family. Sieghart told me:

> There is a huge amount of academic evidence showing that it is so much in men's interest to do an equal share of this unpaid work, particularly the childcare, and to take as much parental leave as possible. In general, in more gender-equal relationships where the men and women share the chores, not only are the women happier and healthier and the children happier and healthier – they do better at school, they have fewer behavioural difficulties, the girls are more ambitious and the boys are less likely to be violent – but also the men are happier and healthier, they are twice as likely to say they are satisfied with their lives, half as likely to be depressed,

much less likely to get divorced. On average they drink less, they smoke less, they take fewer drugs, they get better sleep at night and here's the absolute clincher – they have more frequent and better sex.[16]

Sieghart had her two daughters before shared parental leave was a possibility. However, while working full-time as an editor at a newspaper, she often had to be in the office on Sundays, meaning her husband, Dai, regularly had sole responsibility for their children:

> My husband, unusually for the time, which was in the early 1990s, had sole charge of our baby and toddler for at least a day a fortnight. As a result, he was as aware of their needs as I was. So when we were together looking after them at weekends I didn't have to ask him to 'help' me; it was a joint team effort. So I didn't have to say, 'Can you please make up a bottle?' Or to change a nappy, or whatever; he had already started doing it. That was a huge burden off me. But it also meant that the children were just as likely to turn to him, as to me, for hugs, cuddles, food, whatever it was. That was really bonding for them. Whereas, if you're a flaky dad and occasionally you give them a ride on your back but otherwise they're always going 'Mum, Mum, Mum', you don't get that sense of being needed, which is part of the bonding process. My female friends were very envious because they had husbands who expected them to do most of the childcare even though they also had jobs.

Sieghart said men in senior positions at work needed to set the example to younger employees by being vocal about taking proper leave after having children. 'I think it's very important at work that as well as men having use-it-or-lose-it parental leave, which is reasonably well paid, there also need to be relatively senior men in the organisations doing it,' she said. 'Employers have to actively say it will not be held against you if you take this time because a lot of men are terrified that if they do, they'll be penalised for it.'

Sieghart added one note for mothers who may struggle to share parental responsibility entirely:

> What I did learn, which I think is very important for women, is that I used to come back sometimes after their days alone with dad and all they had eaten was deep-fried food all day and I would start criticising him. And eventually he said: 'Look, if you want me to take responsibility for the children, you've got to let me do it my way.' And I did. And that was transformative.

Sometimes the smallest details matter most. In April 2021, Jess Brammar, now editor of the *BBC News Channel* and *BBC World News*, tweeted about sharing parental leave with her partner, Jim Waterson, the *Guardian*'s media editor. She wrote that, crucially, this meant he knew where all the baby things were without having to ask:

> I've never felt more like A Mother than when I developed [the] uncanny knack of being the only person in the house who could locate anything related to our child. 'Where's the other sock/toy rabbit/nail clippers/Calpol?' yelled down the stairs repeatedly, as in houses across the land. Turns out a few months of having to look after a baby day-in day-out means you have to get across all of that. And it's transformative, and sticks when you are through the other side.[17]

The post prompted other mothers who had shared parental leave with their partners to post about similar experiences. Alexandra Topping, a journalist at the *Guardian*, stated that sharing the time off work with a baby means the domestic care burden is shared, setting the pattern for the child's whole life. 'It means that children have BOTH parents fully engaged in all aspects of their upbringing – including buying socks,'[18] she wrote.

Waterson took three and a half months of parental leave during the pandemic from when his son was seven months old. He told me that the key to him growing in confidence was being allowed to fail:

> I found the toughest period was when we had three weeks of crossover, with one parent who had been doing this full-time for six months and one coming in to prepare to do it solo. I did have to go, look, you've got to let me fail and you've got to let me leave things behind at home. You've got to let me make all of the mistakes you made in the first month or two so that I learn. It meant that, at the weekend, rather than me being vaguely aware that there was a bag that I needed to grab that had already been prepacked, it was on me to know where those things were. I had to get the wash through, to know when they need the nap and everything else.

He said he was welcomed among mothers on leave at the same time as him and invited to the WhatsApp groups, which made the experience much easier. As a bonus, he got 'enormous congratulations for taking substantially less time off than the woman' and was 'made out to be this brilliant dad for taking a kid that was already past the most challenging bit of being a small baby'. He said the reality for men sharing parental leave is that 'you are neither extraordinary, nor are you brilliant, nor are you tortured or wacky, you are just looking after your kid'.

The biggest challenge Waterson faced during this time was navigating the UK government's incredibly complicated shared parental leave policy. After returning to work, he posted about it on

Twitter, writing that take-up among men was 'a piss-poor national embarrassment' and that if anyone wanted advice, they could send him a direct message. He said:

> I am someone who gets excited about policy documents, who likes understanding loopholes, how to get the cheapest rail fares or maximise your return on something, I am immersed in this world. But I struggled to understand what exactly I was allowed to take and when. Groups of friends would come to me and say, you've got 36 weeks in this pot and 39 weeks in that pot and my company has this and I don't understand.

Waterson said the response to his tweets was 'crazy', with men across the country sending him private messages asking for advice and saying they wanted to take the leave but that they had googled and found the information confusing. Many also were unable to take the time off because the statutory pay is so poor, and they were the higher earners in their couples. Given that a myriad of societal reasons means women usually still earn less than men, even before having children and potentially in anticipation of having children, families often come to the conclusion that it makes no financial sense for the mother to share leave with the father. Waterson said:

> There were people who DMd me saying, 'It made me happy that you got to do this but I work in a factory and the idea of being able to afford to take the time off is so unimaginable. The idea that we would have enhanced parental leave policies is laughable.' If there is not money coming from the government, most people can't do it. It is an elite policy.

With government support for parents on leave lacking in many countries, some big companies have taken it upon themselves to overhaul the benefits they offer to their employees who have children.

Aviva, the British insurer, is typically cited as a positive example. In November 2017, the firm began offering to pay the full salaries of staff on parental leave for six months, both for mothers and fathers. Usually when you take shared parental leave in the UK, companies' enhanced pay policies only apply to one supposed 'primary parent' who takes the first period after the child's birth. In my case, I got my work's enhanced pay because I took the time from Solly's birth (I was, essentially, treated like a mother). What Aviva has done is pledge to allow all employees to take the full enhanced rate, whatever their gender and irrespective of whether they have a partner also on leave.

The results have been transformative for new parents at the company. In a press release from June 2022, Aviva reported that in the four years since it started its equal parental leave policy, more than 2,500 Aviva staff in the UK had used it and almost half of them (1,227) were men. Four in five new dads at the company have taken at least five months out of work to care for their babies in the first year of their lives. In total, mothers were taking more time for parental leave – at an average in 2021 of 43 weeks, compared to 24 weeks for fathers – but the gap had been bigger and was gradually closing. Aviva said it introduced equal parental leave entitlements 'to help remove barriers to career progression, challenge traditional gender roles and level the playing field for women and men at home and at work when a new child arrives'.[19]

While this is great for new parents at the company, and for equality, it is also useful to reflect, five years after Aviva launched the policy, on how this change appears to have affected productivity at the business. Danny Harmer, Aviva's chief people officer, said it was impossible to assess exactly how much of an effect it has had on profits, given there are many different shifting dynamics in a big business. However, bosses have not noticed any negative consequences, which is encouraging. 'It is frustratingly hard to quantify,' she said. 'But a lot of employees have now used the policy and I have no data that suggests negativity from a productivity perspective.'

At Aviva, managers typically do not hire parental leave cover for the time new parents are off but cover the extra work internally. It costs to find new people and train them up, and the managers find that they do not tend to be fully up to scratch for six months anyway. Harmer, a mother of three, said it was important to have a long-term perspective about the benefits for companies that can afford to offer enhanced policies. Mothers can leave work to have children after building up years of experience and then never come back. By supporting parents during these years, they are more likely to stay with the company and keep progressing into senior roles many years later:

> The way we view it is much more about how we keep hold of our people. How do we get them to come back from parenting, and to understand that you can combine parenting with a really successful career? Why would you ever want to find someone new, rather than keep the people you have who know what they are doing?

Other big businesses across the world have started offering similar, or even more generous, equal parental leave schemes. In 2015, Netflix announced that it would allow all of its employees to take off as much time as they want during the first year after their child's birth or adoption.[20] Goldman Sachs, the investment bank, has also announced a new global paid parental leave policy of at least 20 weeks for all parents.[21] Accenture, the consultancy and professional services firm, offers 32 weeks leave at full pay to either parent in the UK.[22]

This is all great if you are among the few people to work for one of these huge companies. While lots of employers now top up statutory parental leave pay in some form, there is huge variation in generosity and whether they are willing to do so for fathers as well as mothers. The 2021 IFS report into the gender pay gap in the UK referenced a survey of 375 employers. It found that 63.5 per cent of them topped up maternity pay in some form, and more than one in five paid new mothers their full salaries for at least six months after the birth. In contrast, only 25.1 per cent offered to top up pay for those taking shared parental leave and 20 per cent paid fathers the same amounts as mothers when they were on parental leave. The IFS report stated:

> Overall, the results of this survey indicate that far more mothers will be entitled to enhanced pay than fathers, implying that many couples will lose out financially if transferring parental leave from the mother to the father.[23]

Jo Swinson, a former leader of the Liberal Democrats, was the government minister responsible for getting the current shared parental leave policy passed as law in the UK. In her book, *Equal Power*, she described the response from the business world as 'intriguing'. She wrote:

> Most business groups welcomed the changes. Some grumbled about the additional burden, which given we hadn't in the end been able to increase the overall amount of leave parents could take, I thought was an illuminating argument... the subtext was clear: some bosses felt that men taking leave was more of an inconvenience than women doing so. They basically thought the men were more indispensable, more important.[24]

She also described research into men being enthusiastic about the policy but sharing their concerns about the impact on their careers. 'Discussing views on taking shared parental leave with men was like watching the penny drop, as if the workplace consequence of parenting had never before been appreciated,' she wrote. 'Welcome to the world of the working mother, guys!'[25]

While she wrote of being proud of the work she did on shared parental leave when she was in government – and described the joy she feels when she hears about families who have benefitted from it – she said there needed to be further change to ensure more fathers took it. As she wrote in her book in 2018:

> The scale of pregnancy discrimination in the UK is shocking: some 54,000 women each year are forced out of their jobs as a result. In an antenatal class of nine women, one of them will be sacked, or treated so badly she is forced to leave her job as a result of her pregnancy. It's a shameful situation for 21st-century Britain, and it's getting worse.[26]

I met Swinson and her husband, Duncan Hames, also a former Liberal Democrat MP, at a café in south London on a spring afternoon. As we spoke, over cheesecake and a pot of tea, the café was playing a cracking soundtrack of 1990s power ballads. They sat opposite me, and both described how they had tried to parent equally. They have two sons, Andrew, eight at the time of writing, and Gabriel, aged three. Andrew was born when both of them were MPs, and they did not feel it would be fair for Swinson to have to make most of the sacrifices simply because she was a woman. When Swinson was pregnant with Andrew, she was a government minister in the Department for Business and Hames was Parliamentary Private Secretary (PPS) to Nick Clegg, then Deputy Prime Minister. The updated shared parental leave policy she worked on had not been completed yet. Hames decided he would cut down his hours at work anyway, by resigning as Clegg's PPS. He said that when he told Clegg and Don Foster, the Liberal Democrat Chief Whip, they did not seem to understand his decision. He felt it had not occurred to them that his responsibilities might be about to change – even though they, of course, knew his wife had an incredibly demanding job as a government minister:

> It was quite telling. Whilst they were both quite happy for me to do what I wanted to do, I don't think either of them thought it was necessary. But it's an unpaid position. It is 8.30 a.m. meetings in Whitehall during the week, a lot of speaking to MPs in what would otherwise be downtime at the end of the day. It was obvious to me that it was going to make a difference.

Swinson described how shared parental leave allows men to be open and visible in making sacrifices after having babies, rather than quietly trying to juggle work and childcare. Mothers have no choice, with their bodies announcing their change in responsibilities. 'Part of it is a very visual thing. They [bosses] literally see you as a mum being pregnant,' she said. 'But it's not just that, it is also that they're not doing it themselves. If your bosses are men who did not share these responsibilities after having children, then they don't consider that other people might be doing things differently to them.' Swinson said there should be no shame in men proudly being equal parents:

> Men who have lots of children, but it seems to have no impact on their lives whatsoever – because they make no time to spend with them – what message is that sending about the role of fatherhood and how important it is in our society? Moving to a situation where there is an expectation that if you have a new baby that will have, as a dad, some impact on your availability, would be a much better thing. If you said, 'No, nothing's going to change at all,' people should

be saying, 'What? How come?' In the same way that for a
mother people would think that was strange.

Alongside progressive policies, Swinson said there also had to
be cultural change. This included, in her words, 'everything from
people being role models at work, senior leaders being open about
when they take time to go and pick up the kids, to soap operas
and films. Even the conversations men have with each other.' She
described the difference in how men and women prepare to have
children from a young age:

> As a young woman I think it is quite common for you to think
> you're going to have children. And I also think it is probably
> common to think about how that is going to have an impact
> on your career before it actually happens, and perhaps on
> whether to opt out of opportunities you could pursue. But
> a real thing I noticed when talking to Duncan about it was
> it wasn't an issue he had given much consideration to. How
> will my career change when I have a family?

Even though having a baby through surrogacy takes a huge
amount of dedication and planning, many years in some cases,
Robin and I had not spent much time worrying about the impact
a child would have on our careers. We thought about the practicalities of the surrogacy process and of having a baby. We thought
about parental leave and the first year of our child's life. However,
we definitely did not lose sleep over the potential impact on our
careers long term. We just assumed – perhaps naively – that we
would juggle the responsibilities and deal with challenges as they
came. I shared this with Swinson and Hames, and he nodded in
agreement, clearly having felt similarly. Swinson said:

If you went out into the street and spoke to 20-year-old women, I think many of them will have given that some thought. I don't think that thought process happens in the same way for most men. And there is no reason why it shouldn't. The conversations that men have with each other, that parents have with their sons, all of that, is the mood music for how you start to change it, but some of that change happens very slowly.

She described fathers who took shared parental leave and did primary caring for their children as pioneers, setting the example for their young colleagues, family and friends: 'In many organisations they are the first. And that is a little bit different to women in the workplace trying to break through a glass ceiling but there are a lot of parallels as well.'

Hames was a pioneer in one very specific way – he was the first MP to vote in parliament while looking after a baby. In the weeks after Swinson returned from maternity leave, Hames's parents looked after Andrew one day and then dropped him off with Hames at 5 p.m. Swinson was on the front bench in the House of Commons debating a piece of legislation. Hames said:

They weren't expecting votes and then suddenly there was a 7 p.m. vote called, and we both needed to be there. No one had voted with a baby before. I realised Jo wasn't going to be able to help so I put him in a sling and went to vote. Michael Gove had recently been made Tory Chief Whip. Confronting him alongside the rest of the flock in the government lobby was Andrew at less than seven months old.

Hames said Gove and some others looked surprised, but no one objected. He was not criticised even though female MPs have since been chastised for bringing their babies to the House of Commons. 'People are not in the habit of telling men what they can and cannot do, and they are very much in the habit of telling women what they can and cannot do,' he said.

When Andrew was ten months old, he was in nursery part-time, and Hames would look after him on Monday mornings before parliament formally started at 2 p.m. He would start at home and then take Andrew to his Westminster office, feed him lunch that he had mashed and frozen and then reheated. Then Hames would take him to nursery for the afternoon. 'For all that people didn't take into consideration all the choices I was making, it was very rare for people to tell me I was out of order,' he said. 'Frankly, in our public life there are a whole load of people, mostly men but not exclusively, who take it upon themselves to call women out and challenge their choices.'

By the time their second son, Gabriel, was born, Swinson and Hames were able to benefit from the shared parental leave policy she had spearheaded. Hames was no longer an MP by this point and took parental leave from his job as a director at Transparency International, the anti-corruption organisation, which had an enhanced policy that was equal for mothers and fathers. He took the leave from when Gabriel was two months old, for four months, spending the time in Scotland to be with Swinson in her East Dunbartonshire constituency. He would go for long walks overlooked by the Campsie Fells with Gabriel in a sling and a bag of nappies and expressed milk bottles on his back, while Swinson's mother helped with their older son. He said he found being the primary carer for Gabriel as a baby 'really challenging' and 'hard work' but that the time had enabled many crucial parenting responsibilities to stick, such as being on top of his daily schedule, sleeping patterns and preparing food, as well as helping them to form a close bond.

Reflecting on Britain's current version of the shared parental leave policy that she helped to pass eight years previously, Swinson said it had 'always needed to evolve'. She said the next stages needed to be longer dedicated leave for fathers and better rates of statutory pay. 'We were in a coalition at the time and couldn't get everything we wanted, which included a period of use-it-or-lose it leave for dads, which was going to be six weeks,' she said. 'There is a strong case for it being longer than that but that was the starting discussion point. That was ruled out on the basis that it would be deemed to cost more, it wouldn't get through.'

She also said any changes would have to involve close consultation with women's groups to ensure there would be consensus about the impact dedicated leave for men would have on women's entitlements. Other countries have accounted for this by allowing men to transfer some of their leave to their partners, if that is what they want. As described earlier in this chapter, parents in Iceland can transfer up to six weeks of their six-month allocations. In Sweden, one parent can also give their partner some of their 240 days of leave, although at least 90 of the days cannot be transferred. Swinson said her policy was 'imperfect', but it was essential to get it passed by 2015, before the next general election.

Lucinda Platt, head of the Department of Social Policy at the London School of Economics and Political Science, said better paternity leave policies are needed not just for reasons of fairness but because they benefit the economy. The fairness argument for sharing parental responsibility is obvious – clearly it is not right for mothers to be compelled to do more at home simply because of their sex. The economic argument may seem counter-intuitive. Surely employers having to cope with extended leave requests from employees of both sexes would not be better for their productivity? At most, would it not have zero effect if men and women took six months of parental leave each rather than women taking the full year themselves?

Scandinavian countries seem to prove otherwise. The gross domestic product (GDP) per capita, which measures national productivity relative to population size, is lower in the UK than in the Scandinavian countries, where it is more common for fathers to be off work splitting care for their children.[27] Currently, far too much female talent is lost from workplaces after years of them building up qualifications and experience. At the same time, men's careers do not appear to be negatively affected when they take a few months off to care for their children. Splitting work and caring responsibilities allows all parents to focus their time efficiently, rather than expecting mothers to do more caring and fathers to do more work, whether or not this fits with their interests, qualifications, experience and talent. Platt said:

> When generous paternity leave is implemented by employers, this makes financial sense because both parents can fulfil their potential better. Actually it is good for productivity – it's good for individuals' productivity but it is also good for national GDP – if both women and men are able to do the jobs that match their interests and skills and are able to do caring roles when they want to.

While it is clearly a good thing for equality – and wider society – for men to take more time off work in the months after their children are born, there is debate about how best this could be achieved while protecting mothers' existing entitlements. The Fawcett Society, the UK's leading charity campaigning for gender equality and women's rights, believes the best approach to parental leave is not shared parental leave, which, essentially, requires women to give up some of their existing rights. Instead, it advocates a '6-6-6' model. This would involve the mother being entitled to the first six months – the essential period for her recovery after pregnancy and childbirth, and for breastfeeding, if she chooses and can do so – and then the family having a further 12 months of potential leave, with one six-month chunk for the mother and one six-month chunk for the other parent. The charity does not believe that women should have to take the full initial six months of health-related leave, just that this should be reserved for them so they can choose to have this time if they want it.

In terms of statutory pay, the Fawcett Society believes mothers should have nine months of their 12-month entitlements covered, as is the current policy, plus partners should have another three months of their six-month allocation paid. In practice, this would typically mean that families could have a year of leave between them paid at the statutory rate (rather than the current nine months). The mother would be on leave for nine months and then the partner would be off with the baby for the last three months of the year. If they wanted, both the mother and father could take three more months unpaid each. The charity also wants flexibility in how couples could share the leave, so some could choose to do stints at the same time, and for it to be possible to take allocations at any point in the first 18 months of children's lives, rather than the existing 12, potentially helping with the financial burden of childcare.

Andrew Bazeley, who was policy, research and public affairs manager at the charity at the time of writing, took me through the proposals:

> Clearly the current shared parental leave policy does not work in terms of take-up. Imagining a world in which men equally share childcare and domestic responsibilities is quite a leap. That is not the world we live in at the moment for the most part. The system that we propose can help men to imagine that. If the system pays for you to have three months off to care for your child that helps men think, alright, I can be a more equal partner in this. My job is not to be the breadwinner and her job is not to stay at home; our job is to share this.

Systems can play an important part in creating the realms of possibility, and at the moment they don't really do that.

Bazeley also said the UK government's statutory pay for new parents was far too low, describing it as 'poverty wages'.

The Fawcett Society's proposals are not equal in terms of time off work for mothers and fathers. They reflect the reality of there being good health reasons to reserve the first period of leave for women, while also encouraging partners to share responsibilities for childcare more fairly in the longer term. Jemima Olchawski, chief executive of the charity, said its model aimed to acknowledge that extended maternity leave is incredibly important for many women and that they should not be made to feel pressured into sacrificing this time. Understandably, women's rights organisations do not want change in the name of equality to actually mean that women lose maternity entitlements that they already have. Olchawski said:

Sometimes there is a hint of criticism of women who are seen as trying to control the second part of the leave and do not want to give it up. You have been through this huge experience and gather this huge amount of knowledge and, as a society, we put a lot of expectation and pressure on women to be excellent mothers. We spend a lot of time implicitly telling them that you are naturally the good one and this is, ultimately, your responsibility, the buck will stop with you. So it is quite hard then for lots of women to be like, I am going off, back to work, and I'll see you at six o'clock tonight. It is quite a big shift.

Olchawski said there are plenty of other issues that need remedying to allow mothers to have equality, before we should take any of their maternity rights away, even to be shared within the family:

I am always really reluctant to be critical of women who are making the best decisions they can in a system which is really, really challenging. I don't think the biggest barrier, by any stretch of the imagination here, is that women won't let go. If we were to imagine the long list of things that should be addressed to improve equality at home, this would be a very long way down. Let's say it's as high as number 80. And so we could get into how this is another way that it is women's fault, because we're really controlling and we won't let go, or we could deal with all the other 79 things and then see what happens when those conditions are in place.

When I spoke to Waterson, he said he had also heard from a lot of men that they did not want to share parental leave if this meant taking from their partner's allowance:

> After I tweeted about shared parental leave, the pushback was often from men who said that my wife, girlfriend or partner has always dreamed of having that year with the kid. At the moment, you only have a 12-month window to share in the UK, so she could feel cheated or like a bad mother if she couldn't take it.

The finer details of fair parental leave policies will vary depending on the country. Women's groups have to be at the centre of their designs and the decisions as to whether it is felt best to have equal allocations for mothers and fathers, schemes that allow parents to swap some of their entitlements so women do not lose what they already have, the '6-6-6' model or another option. However, the evidence, fundamentally, is clear. Fathers are biologically primed to take responsibility for childcare, and to share this with mothers fairly, if they have time to establish these patterns as committed caregivers to their babies. They are also much more likely to take leave from work to do this when they and mothers have use-it-or-lose-it allocations of parental leave and these are paid properly at levels that acknowledge the importance of parents being with their children after birth.

The obvious immediate benefits are that this helps to mitigate the negative impact of childbirth on women's careers and encourages fathers to be with their children. This creates a ripple, with fathers continuing to share the domestic work for many years afterwards, which benefits everyone in the family. There are also compelling arguments that this has economic benefits.

It is encouraging that some big companies are seeing the benefits of investing in parents sharing leave after the birth of their children, but this is not enough. While there are some dads now wheeling their newborns around parks and changing nappies in branches of Gail's bakeries in north London, the vast majority of families have not been able to benefit from shared parental leave. There will be no proper change until governments pay up so families can benefit in countries and towns that are not full of people on London wages. We will know there has been progress when there are shopkeepers regularly saying hi to MummyDaddies on leave from work with their babies in Warsaw, Wyoming and Wellington, as well as in Willesden Green.

CHAPTER FOUR

WHICH ONE OF YOU IS QUITTING?

Returning to Work in the Nursery Years

I am sitting in my car outside Solly's nursery, and I am doing maths. If Solly goes to nursery four days a week and spends one day with grandparents, while Robin and I both carry on working full-time, is he still with us most of the time? And if the answer is no, does that make us awful parents?

Solly has just turned one and has been at nursery for a few weeks. Here are my calculations. We usually drop him off at 8.30 a.m. and one of us picks him up between 5.30 p.m. and 6 p.m. Let's call that nine and a half hours a day, so 38 hours per week. He sleeps for about two hours per day at nursery, so I knock that off otherwise we'll win on a technicality based on sleeping every night at home. Am I sounding crazy?

I keep going. He's awake at nursery 30 hours per week and awake at his grandparents' house for about seven and a half hours per week. Each weekday we are with him about one and a half to two hours either side of childcare – let's call it three and a half hours per day – plus 12 hours per day at the weekends. I get my phone calculator out. A total of 41.5 hours awake with us, versus 37.5 at nursery or with grandparents. We win, just about. It will be good for him. He seems happy. I drive off and try not to think about what happens when he drops his nap.

In the months that followed, this car park outside Solly's nursery saw a lot of action. With Covid restrictions, parents were not allowed to go inside. We sent him every day without seeing the classrooms or touching the toys or the mat that he slept on. He was meant to have a settling-in session with one of us on his first day, but it was at the height of the pandemic and the owner preferred for us not to come in even for that. Every day we were sent pictures and detailed updates, and we had a brief tour when we first signed up for the waiting list months earlier, but once he started going, we could not enter the front door. We got to know the other parents while waiting every day in a queue for the teachers to pop their heads out and give us quick in-person updates while we tried to stop our toddlers running down a few stairs and a path to the on-site playground, or towards the cars.

Initially, Robin and I were both working from home after our shared year of parental leave. We had wondered if we would spend a lot of the time battling guilt. In truth, we were both busy and the days passed quickly. It seemed a betrayal to admit it, but those hours focused on work while Solly was at nursery felt like a treat. Solly was being cared for by professionals. He was safe. He seemed to be having a good time. Work could be stressful, but the stakes were less high than when my full-time responsibility was caring for our tiny baby. And then it would be late afternoon, and I felt reenergised to get back to the nursery doors, grab Solly for a cuddle, take him home and appreciate our time together before bed.

As Covid restrictions eased, Robin and I both started going into our offices in central London more frequently. We would alternate days so if one of us was in the city, the other worked from home. Whichever one of us was going to the office took Solly to nursery on the way to the station, and the other picked him up at the end of the day. The commute, which used to be a drag, became something I looked forward to. I would listen to podcasts and music. I would write. In the office, I could switch off from the responsibilities of parenting, knowing that if there were a problem at nursery, Robin would be there for Solly. Working from home made life much more manageable – it would have felt impossible to balance work and childcare if we were both commuting five days per week – but the easier days for me have definitely been the ones in the office.

Solly was crawling when we first sent him to nursery but, surrounded by bigger children, he soon learned to chase after them. Up on his feet, his personality started to explode. We wondered what impact childcare was having. It seemed positive. He was becoming loud, fun and sociable, and rarely nervous in public. He jumped and danced and launched his head back in giggles when he played.

We saw other parents struggling with the drop-offs as their babies cried and clung to them with one hand, while clutching a comforter with the other. Solly rarely seemed upset. He was almost always happy to go in and then excited when he saw us at the end of the day. It was as if we had sent him early enough for him not to have understood the separation and then, by the time he understood, he had already formed bonds with some of the teachers.

As he got a bit older, there were exceptions – usually on a Monday morning after a long weekend break, or for a few days after a longer holiday – when he did get upset at the door, reaching back for me or Robin and crying. But we were assured by his teachers that he was happy again within a few minutes of us leaving. We learned that it was better to arrive late, so when we got to the door, Solly could see his friends inside and wanted to join them.

When we first sent Solly to nursery, we decided that we would keep open minds. If we could tell that he was not happy, or that being in childcare four days per week was not good for him, we would work out how to cut down hours at work or see if we could afford a nanny instead of nursery. One plan was for both of us to ask our employers if we could go down to four-day working weeks, or nine-day fortnights, if needed. We were determined that neither of us should make the professional sacrifices alone. But the signs were good, so we kept sending him for full days and both carried on working full-time.

One of Solly's first words was 'running', which he pronounced as 'wunin'. He refused to watch TV for longer than five minutes at this age and had little attention for sitting and focusing on a task for long. We were pretty exhausted balancing work with trying to keep up with his energy. When we arrived at the nursery doors to pick him up at the end of working days, he would fly out and sprint down the path shouting 'wunin, wunin'. When we went to soft play activity centres at weekends, he would climb fearlessly and, invariably, identify another toddler to be his new best friend, grabbing their hands and leading them to the slide with him. He could be rough but also seemed empathetic, knocking his new friends over, then saying 'sad' and softly touching their faces.

As his speech started progressing, we tried to encourage him to call me 'Dad' and Robin 'Daddy'. He was having none of it, shouting 'Daddy' for both of us, which then progressed to 'Daddy Pauly' and 'Daddy Robin'.

When I picked him up from nursery one day, a teacher nervously approached at the door. 'I hope you don't mind me asking,' she said, 'but when Solly gets tired before his nap, he's started reaching out to me and calling me "Mummy". What do you want me to do?' She looked relieved – and a bit disappointed – when I explained that he was probably begging for his dummy. As if on cue, Solly reached to me and shouted, 'Daddy Pauly! Mummy, mummy, mummy.' I gave it to him, and he shoved it in his mouth before sprinting down the nursery path towards the cars.

On another evening pick-up, I ran to chase Solly down the stairs towards the playground and turned my ankle. It was agony and I shouted out to a teacher for help. She found Solly and led us both through the front door. Finally, I was inside. It was lovely and clean, with small, neat baskets of toys, wooden furniture and white walls. The teachers got a cold compress for my ankle and looked after me like I was one of the accident-prone toddlers. I was able to drive so we left, but within a few hours my ankle was massive and purple. An MRI scan later confirmed that I had managed to tear two ankle ligaments during that fun episode of wunin.

The nursery doors also became a hive of whispered chatter in the days after the owner sent an email stating that she was having to increase the fees. With energy prices rising sharply during 2022, the nursery, an independent Montessori franchise, was struggling to meet its costs. The fees were barely affordable as it was.

After concerns were raised by parents, the nursery re-evaluated and increased the fees by less than had been initially suggested and with more notice. The nursery had been charging us £320 per week for Solly to be there for four days, but this was rising to £348 – the increase was still almost nine per cent. And, of course, we were all facing the rises to energy bills as well.

This is the other maths that parents will be very familiar with doing when planning to return to work after having a child. With full-day childcare for working parents often ludicrously expensive, how much money do you have to earn for it to be worth all this time away from your child? Should you, essentially, work for free for a few years just to make sure you do not lose your career and the income long term? It might be reasonable to assume these questions would also include ones about which parent in two-parent families should cut down their hours, or whether both should do so to a lesser degree. However, in most families it seems to be assumed that the mother should put her career on hold. You often hear the same explanations for women who have had children with male partners sacrificing their careers – her salary did not cover the nursery fees. But why is only her salary considered? What about the other parent, if there is one? Should families not be assessing the costs against their total income and then deciding what is best for all of them long term?

In Britain, full-time, state-funded education begins when children start school, usually between the ages of four and five.[1] There is an implicit assumption that from the age of one (after parental leave) and four or five (school starting), a non-working mother will mostly be around to look after her children, while her husband's single salary covers most of the family's costs. There is some earlier state support, which I will discuss in more detail in this chapter, but this properly starts for most parents only after their children turn three and is not enough to ensure women have equal opportunity to continue with their careers.

As with parental leave, government support during the nursery years is designed for the realities of life in the twentieth century, with a dad at work and a mum at home. This makes no sense now. The reality is that the economy relies on parents going back to work after having children. However, at the same time, families can barely afford childcare. It is usually mothers who take the hit to their careers – staying off work longer than they want to, reducing their hours, rushing off early for the school run and passing up promotion opportunities – to keep the system just about functioning.

Figures reported by *The Sunday Times* in June 2022 showed that the number of women in the UK not working so they could look after family had risen five per cent in the previous year, the first sustained increase in 30 years.[2] Based on surveys with thousands of parents, Save the Children, the charity, has estimated that about half of all stay-at-home mothers in England – more than 870,000 – would prefer to work if they could afford to do so.[3]

The burden of childcare costs for parents varies massively across countries. International comparisons show that in some countries the average two-earner couple spends almost a third of their income on childcare, while for others it costs almost nothing.[4] In Germany, parents with children in public childcare centres can have fees heavily subsidised, or even be exempt from payments altogether.[5] In April 2022, Sharmaine Lovegrove, who works in publishing in Berlin, shared on social media that it cost €46 (£38) per month to send her twins to nursery for seven hours per day, five days a week, adding: 'In the UK we'd be paying £3k a month!!'[6] The fees included lunch and two snacks a day, all made with organic food.

In Estonia, where the education system has been rated as the best in Europe and the government invests heavily in early years kindergartens, parents never pay more than 20 per cent of the minimum wage on childcare, the equivalent of less than £500 a month.[7] Were we to send Solly to his nursery full-time, five days per week, it would cost £19,750 per year. This is almost the full take-home pay of someone on a salary of £24,000 per year. The average UK worker's earnings are not much more, working out at about £26,000.[8] Robin and I just about afford Solly's nursery fees while both working full-time but absolutely recognise that we are among the lucky few with jobs that are well paid enough to get by without making life-changing sacrifices. We have also been able to stretch to afford a nursery that gets decent inspection reports, has less turnover of staff than most and offers good, varied food. The same is not possible for many parents.

In March 2022, a survey of 27,000 parents by Pregnant Then Screwed, a British charity that campaigns for better policies for parents, found that two thirds paid the same or more for childcare as their rent or mortgage, with one in four parents skipping meals or forgoing heating to afford it.[9] Parents in the UK pay the second-highest amounts in the world for childcare, behind only Cyprus, with it costing the average couple 29 per cent of their income. There are three other countries where parents, on average, spend more than 19 per cent of their combined income on childcare: the US, Ireland and Czech Republic.[10]

While childcare fees can be ludicrously high, the money often does not go to the staff actually doing the caring. The people who look after our children while we work – soothing them when we drive away, distracting and teaching them with games, showing them how to share and care for other children, calming them to sleep for naps, feeding them, changing their nappies and cleaning up their mess – are among the lowest paid workers in the UK. The average nursery worker earns less than the legal minimum wage. There is a loophole that allows nurseries to fill teaching spaces with apprentices, who are expected to gain experience while working long hours for almost nothing. About 13 per cent of childcare workers earn less than £5 per hour, little over half of the minimum wage.[11]

Many nursery owners are also struggling. In 2021, a petition launched by Pregnant Then Screwed and *Grazia* magazine called for reform of the childcare sector and gained more than 100,000 signatures in a week. This sparked a debate on childcare in parliament, during which it emerged that there had been 442 nursery closures in a year, a 35 per cent increase from the year before. Most of the closures were in the most deprived parts of the country.[12] The pandemic had wrecked much of the sector, with Covid relief on business rates insufficient to keep them afloat.

Nurseries like the one Solly goes to are having to increase fees and beg for donations if they want to survive. With limited nursery places, parents have to put deposits down to be on lengthy waiting lists for a chance of getting a place. For some, you have to get your name down while pregnant. We enquired about a space at a ridiculously popular nursery when Solly was a few months old, about six months ahead of him needing a place. We got a call back when he was 18 months old – long after we had found another – to say the place was available.

High-quality childcare is expensive, with strict and necessary guidelines to protect children, such as having at least one carer for every three children under two.[13] Parents are paying their way and nurseries are doing their best to get by, but the government is not contributing anywhere near as much as it needs to if it wants people to go back to work after having children.

In March 2022, I went to an event at the House of Commons celebrating single parents hosted by Gingerbread, a charity. One of the speakers was Carly Newman, a 36-year-old single mother to Ezra, who was almost four at the time. She told of her struggle to support her son alone, having balanced work over the previous three years with the almost completely unaffordable costs of childcare. A government minister, also speaking at the event, stood silently a few metres away from her, bowing her head. After the event, I got in touch with Newman, wanting to hear more about her experiences. With her son almost old enough to start school, she would soon stop having to pay for childcare. 'It's only when I look back now that I think, how did I do that? How did I afford it? How did I manage?' she said.

After maternity leave, Newman, who is a manager for a charity, went back to work on part-time hours. Initially her mother could cover the time looking after Ezra, but when he was 18 months old, this was no longer possible. Newman was just about able to balance the almost £900-per-month cost of her son being at nursery three days a week, their £1,300-per-month rent for a basic, small flat in south east London and living costs by topping up her wages with universal credit, the UK state benefit. While the nursery fees and her rent had to be paid up front, the universal credit only started being paid into her account after five weeks. She had to borrow money to get through this time, including taking out a universal credit advance to cover the nursery fees, which was then deducted from her future payments. Newman said:

> I was just trying to set up very basic situations – a home for me and my son and childcare while I went to work I was just trying to go back to work. These are normal, acceptable things. I had just finished maternity leave and I still felt like a shell of myself. I was very much still in survival mode. I was still breastfeeding. I had lost confidence. As a single parent, I was trying to do this alone and it felt like such a battle. At the beginning I just muddled through. The up-front costs were brutal. It was that thing where you feel like, is this worth it? What am I even working for? I am still paying financially for that time, I am paying off the credit cards.

Throughout those early months navigating life as a working single mother, Newman faced repeated hurdles. Her nursery and rent bills had to be paid at the beginning of the month but her salary was not enough to cover both, and her universal credit payment only came into her account on the eighth of the month. She tried to steel herself against any feelings of shame and asked the nursery if she could change her monthly payment date but was told this was not possible. She also asked her tenancy agents if her rent payment date could change and the answer was the same. There was also no movement on the universal credit date. 'There was this dilemma,' she said. 'If I can't pay both my nursery and my rent on time, what do I choose? How do I choose? I chose nursery at the time because I was more embarrassed about it. Can you imagine me going there in the morning and them saying Ezra couldn't come in because I hadn't paid the fees?' Newman decided instead to pay her rent a few days late every month and see what happened. She got repeated late payment emails in the days before she paid every month but was not evicted.

During one particularly difficult period, Newman tried to pay her rent and found that her universal credit money was not in her account. While on a train station platform on the way to work, she phoned the government helpline for claimants. It turned out that a one-off payment she received in lieu of holiday from work had confused the system, which assumed her earnings had increased and she was no longer eligible to claim. The official on the phone said they could not simply restart her account. Instead, she had to be set up with a new one and wait another five weeks for the first payment. 'I was at this station, crying on the phone, sobbing. I kept thinking, how am I going to pay our rent? I have never felt so helpless and vulnerable,' she said. Newman had to take out another advance payment to get through the month. She added:

> In many ways, I am one of the privileged ones. I was fortunate enough to be able to muddle through because I have a level of support. I have parents who helped with childcare. They have their own home. It is the mentality around knowing I had that potentially to fall back on. I work for a charity that helps people claiming universal credit and managing debt and I have experience with consumer issues, and I still felt like I could not navigate through this system, and I work within it. How many people are not in that scenario? If they had similar experiences to me, how would they cope?

In various ways, Newman's experience of returning to work during the nursery years encapsulates how the system fails parents.

The way public funding for childcare works in Britain is complicated. These are the basics. After a child turns three, their parents can claim 15 hours per week of free childcare for them. This doubles to 30 hours per week if the parents work for at least 16 hours per week on or above minimum wage and neither of them earns more than £100,000 a year.[14] Children from very low-income families are entitled to the 15 hours of free childcare one year early, from after they turn two.[15] Lower-income working families can receive support through the benefits system, with those on universal credit potentially having as much as 85 per cent of their childcare costs paid for by the government. However, there is a cap on this of £646 per child per month,[16] which would have covered just two days of fees at Newman's nursery in south east London. Universal credit claimants also have to pay out up front for the nursery costs and then apply for the money back – and people having to rely on universal credit do not tend to have bags of spare cash lying around. Newman said she found it incomprehensible that state help for nursery fees starts for most people when their child is three years old: 'I have never understood it. What is supposed to happen when your child is between one and three? You want us to all go back to work, but childcare is so unaffordable. It is so backward.'

There are also important caveats to the state support for families. The full 30 hours of free childcare after a child is three are available for 38 weeks per year, rather than the full 46 or 47 weeks that most jobs require full-time employees to work. The funding also does not start from a child's third birthday. Instead, there are three set term dates during the year, and children qualify from the beginning of the term that comes after their birthday.[17] This does not massively affect some people, like us, whose child was born in March, a few days before the new term date at the beginning of April. If you have an April baby though, you have to wait until September for it to kick in. I asked Newman about her experience of this, and her answer was almost inevitable: 'Do you know when Ezra was born? The first of April. So I had to wait until he was three and a half.'

There are some additional schemes to help cover childcare costs. Working parents can get some money off childcare fees through the tax system. You can set up an online government account for your child and for every £8 you pay in, the government adds £2 to pay your provider. The government will contribute up to £2,000 a year and this is possible as long as the child does not have a parent earning more than £100,000 a year.[18] However, the scheme is so badly publicised that as many as 800,000 families who are eligible have not been claiming the money.[19]

As well as this all being incredibly confusing for parents, nursery owners say the current system is the cause of their problems. In particular, the 30 free hours of childcare for working parents is crippling providers because the government is not paying them enough. On average the government pays them £4.43 per hour per child for these places for three- and four-year-olds, which is less than they need to cover their costs (and much less than parents are charged). The shortfall for each child is reported as more than £2,100 per year.[20] As a result, nurseries have to make up for these losses by increasing their fees for everything outside of the free hours. So parents may get 30 hours' free childcare per week at some point after their child turns three, but they pay much more when their child is two to allow nurseries to make up for it. It is an added cost that is presented as a giveaway.

Many nurseries also now charge for food and other extras, such as nappies and wipes. There have been reports that at nurseries which charge extra for lunch, children from poorer families are having to make do with packets of crisps while their friends have hot meals.[21]

Pregnant Then Screwed, the organisation whose work sparked the parliamentary debate on childcare, was founded by Joeli Brearley after she was sacked from her job at a children's charity the day after she told her boss she was pregnant with her first baby. Pregnant Then Screwed campaigns for reform of the childcare system in Britain, as well as for the government to fund all new parents, whatever their sex, having 90 per cent of their salaries paid for a minimum of six weeks of their parental leave. When we spoke, Brearley emphasised how parenting roles are established and then reinforced because of government policies:

One of the reasons women will step down from their careers – even when they're earning more money – is because of the way the system is set up in terms of parental leave and childcare support. It means women tend to be the ones to take long periods out at the beginning of a child's life. So they are the main carer. They are the ones who know how to do bedtimes, to get the child to sleep, they are the ones who know which way to slice the piece of toast so the child doesn't have a meltdown. They've learned all of those techniques so that the dad tends to look to the mum when things go wrong, and they haven't learned on the job by themselves in the same way. So a woman, even if she was on more money before, when she returns to work she feels that child is predominantly her responsibility. And it is impossible to do a full-time job and do all of the domestic labour, so she has to take a reduction in her hours and therefore pay.

Brearley's charity supports families struggling to cope with the costs of childcare in Britain, with many parents reporting having to go to extreme measures such as skipping meals so that they can pay for nurseries and keep working for some basic income. Brearley said:

If you look at what is happening with childcare it makes me want to pull my eyes out. It is a massive contributor to poverty, the fact that the UK's childcare system is the second most expensive in the world as a proportion of income. You go on parental leave and bring in £157 per week which won't even cover your rent or mortgage and then you've got to navigate the childcare system, where most people pay more than they do on their rent or mortgage, and they're already in enormous amounts of debt. It is no wonder fewer people are having kids now.

Brearley, who has two sons, aged eight and six at the time of writing, spoke of the importance of dads having proper time in sole charge of their children, without the mother there as well. Robin and I have also learned that it is crucial that we each have times in sole charge of Solly. Otherwise, one of you seems naturally to take on the role of main carer, while the other acts like a sort of sous chef, working hard but generally responding to instructions rather than taking initiative and sharing the mental load of parenting. Brearley has come to the same conclusion:

> If you do it together in heterosexual couples, the dad will become sort of a carer for the mum, rather than for the baby. So they will be making the cups of tea, doing the laundry or making dinner. They don't do much of the hands-on care with the baby, so you need to have that separate time with the baby. It's really complicated how you look after a child, it's really difficult. Different children have different rhythms and different things they need. You tune in after a certain period of time to what they need, and you just don't get that without individual time.

Two of our closest friends, Deborah and Paul, are a married couple with two daughters, Penny and Margot. Deborah and Paul both work in London in finance for the same employer, Investec, which has an equal parental leave policy for mothers and fathers.[22] They have shared parental leave and continue to split responsibility for balancing their careers and childcare, alternating who does early pick-ups from nursery and bedtimes. At dinner at their house on a Friday night, over a Brazilian takeaway, Deborah explained to me the concept of having a 'key person risk', which I had never heard of before.

'It's a thing at work,' she said. 'In an organisation, only they can do their job and so, if they leave, you've got a problem. It's the same at home. Both of us have to know how to clean, feed, put to bed, do the nursery drop-offs and pick-ups, everything.' Paul said this principle also took the pressure off him to be a traditional breadwinner. 'We both work, so if one of us loses our job it doesn't all come crashing down,' he said. 'It would be tight, but we wouldn't have to panic. I love that, as a man.'

Deborah said a key turning point for them was switching roles during parental leave for their first daughter. She reminded Paul how she was anxious for the first few months of Penny's life. 'I would talk every day about being worried about Penny and you would be like, can you just chill out?' she said. 'And then we switched, and within a week, you started doing that. I was the first to wake up if there was a problem in the night whilst I was the main caregiver. But once we switched and I was back working, it seemed to also automatically shift over to you waking up first.'

I sat back and listened to them talking to each other. Paul said he had no choice. 'When you switched to being back at work, you really switched to being back at work, and I felt that,' he said. 'You would go in the room and shut the door and be like, I'm in meetings, don't come in.' Paul turned to me. 'I'm a better dad because of that. It was a brilliant thing. It meant the buck stopped with me. I got into the routines. I was all over the routines.'

Deborah's advice to other women who want to share responsibility for childcare is that sometimes you have to just shut the door and leave it to the other parent:

As a woman, you really have to want this. If you want to take all of the parental leave and be the one to cut down hours at work, that is fine, lots of women want to, but then I don't think it is a surprise that they are then always doing more at home. I know women who say it is so hard, my husband can't put the kid to bed by himself. If you both sacrifice a bit, you both gain a bit. We both sacrifice a bit, so we both get to spend time with the kids, and we both get to work.

For women who go back to work full-time after having children, many describe a constant sense of pressure to cut down hours and remain semi-available for childcare emergencies at all times, whether or not they want to split the responsibility with a partner. There remains a huge imbalance in the way mothers and fathers are often expected to behave at work after they have children. Working mothers can be dismissed as being overwhelmed with other priorities, while working fathers are viewed as they were before, with no expectation that their responsibilities will have changed at all.

Research by Pregnant Then Screwed has found that 62 per cent of women who returned to work after having a child did so for fewer hours because of childcare costs, while 17 per cent had to leave their job for the same reason.[23] UK government figures have also suggested that fathers are almost twice as likely as mothers to have requests for flexible working turned down by employers.[24]

Going back to work after a large chunk of leave can be daunting. Robin and I both felt this after our stints on parental leave. In the weeks before the end of my parental leave, I worked in the evenings as I was paranoid about being written off as someone who was no longer committed and could not bear the thought of starting again with a totally blank slate. I felt I needed to be producing investigations for the newspaper as soon as I was back. I put this pressure on myself; it came from the insecurity you feel when you have completely prioritised family over work for six months.

Later, it turned out some of this insecurity was justified. As a print journalist, your work, or lack of it, is very visible. If your name is not on the front pages for a while, colleagues and competitors wonder what has happened to you. My mum loves to joke about this. 'Haven't seen your name in the paper for a while. Have you been sacked?' she will ask, knowing exactly how to wind me up.

Shortly after returning to work following parental leave, I was told that someone senior at another newspaper had asked one of my bosses what had happened to me and whether I was still employed by *The Times*. The suggestion was that I must have been underperforming. They did not know I had been off on parental leave, but it stung. It took a few months to readjust and regain my confidence – and to prove to my mum, myself and others that I had not entirely lost it. Long term, though, I have not felt that my career has suffered because I am a father now. It has become obvious to me that the same is often not true for women at work.

When Solly was almost two, I had to go away for two working weeks (I came back home briefly for a weekend in the middle). No one asked me what childcare I had planned to cover the time I would be away, or how Robin was going to cope without me. When I spoke to my friends Deborah and Paul about this, Deborah described the experience of a female friend of hers who is a barrister and has two young children. 'After she had her second child, a colleague said to her, it is really hard to be a mother and a barrister, particularly with two children. She thought that was interesting. No one would be saying that to one of her male colleagues,' Deborah said.

The issue of women being viewed differently at work after having children also came up in my discussions with Mary Ann Sieghart, the author of *The Authority Gap: Why Women are Still Taken Less Seriously Than Men, and What We Can Do About It*. 'Employers assume once you've had a baby, you're not really interested in your career any more,' she said. 'You're not really committed, are you? So you'll want to work part-time, you won't be interested in promotion, you don't want extra responsibility. Well, maybe she does. That really holds women back.'

The disparity in how men and women are often treated at work after having children does not only come from employers and colleagues. Nurseries and schools often phone mothers when there is a problem, even when a father is listed as the person they should contact in emergencies. Specific instructions not to call working mothers are ignored because of assumptions that it could not possibly be the case that a mother would not be primarily responsible for her children at all times. There is no suggestion that nursery or school staff would do this intentionally or with malice – the instinct to call only a mother when a child is unwell must surely be unconscious and deeply ingrained.

Raina Brands, a professor at University College London, had a huge response when she wrote about this issue online in March 2022. She and her husband both work but she was repeatedly called by their son's nursery, even though he was listed as the point of contact. 'Today they called and I asked them to always call my partner first and 2 hours later THEY CALLED ME AGAIN,' she wrote on Twitter. 'What makes this more absurd is the fact that my partner has always been the main point of contact! He filled out all of the forms, he did all of the settling-in sessions, and he drops our son off every morning. But they are incapable of viewing him as a primary caregiver.'[25]

Brands' tweets got thousands of likes from equally exhausted working women across the world and from fathers who were primary caregivers, prompting many to share their own stories. One mother wrote that she was working abroad with a medical team in Haiti and had repeatedly warned her daughter's school to call her father in emergencies that week. She added: 'The team was ascending a mountain 2 hours north of Port-au-Prince when I received a call from them.' Another wrote that her husband was the point of contact for their children's schools, adding: 'He and I were hanging out one day – my phone was upstairs. When I finally got it, there were THIRTEEN MISSED CALLS FROM THE SCHOOL. My kid had thrown up and instead of calling him, they left increasingly hostile messages.'

My favourite of this genre of tweets was from Lucy Greenwood, who specialises in overseeing major commercial and investment legal dispute cases. In March 2022, she wrote: 'Yesterday: daughter ill at school "don't ring my mum she is in hearing and won't pick up, please ring my dad". School rings me. #BreakTheBias'.[26] The tweet was liked by more than 104,000 people, but one account, named realBREXITnow, was displeased, suggesting she should have answered the phone. The account wrote several critical responses, arguing that if she was in a legal hearing, she could have asked the judge for a break. Eventually, Greenwood responded: 'I was the judge.'

When we spoke, Greenwood said she had been fighting against sexist assumptions about work and childcare for two decades, despite her seniority in the legal world:

> When our oldest was in nursery, my husband, Paul, and I were both working full-time and we had this deal. Two days a week I would run out of the office at half past five, two days a week he would run out at half past five and on the fifth day we would ring and see who could leave. It was really interesting how if ever he had to leave early to pick up our son, he would be lauded, whereas I would get so many comments: 'Oh, leaving early again are you, Lucy?' After I tweeted, there were all these mental gymnastics that people were trying to do to work out how I could and should have answered the phone instead of addressing the point, which is that the school should be thinking

about calling the father, particularly as they had been asked to by my daughter. It should not be unusual.

Greenwood said these continual assumptions about women having sole primary responsibility for their children resulted in them often carrying a far greater share of the 'mental load' of parenting, even when both parents worked equal hours. She described an anecdote her husband gave while making a speech for a women's group at his office:

> Part of it was reading out an email I had sent from the airport when I was going away on business. It was basically 'do this, do that, pick up swimming things, she needs to be here', a great long list of what was happening, which I sent as I was getting on the plane. He read it all out and said: 'That's what Lucy sent me when she left on business. When I go away on business I say: I'm off, see you next week.'

Greenwood said that when her daughter was unwell at school and they failed to get her on the phone, they eventually listened to her daughter and called her father. 'What happened with my daughter's school is just a snapshot of what is replicated all over the world. I do not blame them,' she said. 'That summed up so many situations over the past 20 years since I've had children where these assumptions have been made.'

The ingrained expectation that women who go back to work are also their child's primary carer at all times has lasting impact. The 2021 IFS gender pay gap report suggested that prohibitively expensive childcare mostly affected women's careers because they were likely to be earning less than their male partners and to be less active in the labour market before having children, making them more likely to sacrifice work afterwards. However, it also found that even when mothers earned more than their male partners before childbirth, they were still more likely than the dads to reduce their hours of work in the years after childbirth.[27]

When I spoke to Lucinda Platt, head of the Department of Social Policy at the London School of Economics and Political Science, she homed in on this point. 'Even if the woman earns more, she's still going to be the one to drop out. It is not a logical economic decision,' she said. 'It shows that these are very strong norms that shape the way people behave. We are socialised into this.'

Platt said it was crucial that government policies encouraged parents to share responsibility for work and childcare equally, so women could fulfil their potential. 'It is hugely wasteful that we are seeing women getting more and more qualified and then working part-time, dropping out and going into jobs which are below their qualification levels,' she said. 'It is a waste of all that investment in their education and training. But there's also equally the point that if men are prevented from doing caring, this is bad for family relationships.'

Where could we start in trying to fix the childcare crisis? One good place is Estonia, which is rated by the OECD as having the best education system in Europe.[28] Almost all children go to high-quality nurseries, which they can attend from when they are 18 months old until school, which starts at seven. Like in Germany, the Estonian government heavily subsidises nurseries so they are always affordable for parents. In Estonia, the nursery teachers have to have a university degree and there is a curriculum to prepare children at nurseries for school, with them all given a school readiness card describing their development and offering referrals to specialists for those who need extra support. While the Estonian government spends a relatively large amount on early years education, it spends relatively little on its education system overall. Well-funding the earliest years is an investment, which means underprivileged children catch up quicker, children are set up for learning when they are toddlers and less money is needed later for schools.[29]

By comparison, in Britain there has been shown to be a significant gap in attainment between 16-year-olds depending on their socio-economic status, and 40 per cent of this gap is already established before they start school.[30] The Finnish system is similar to the one in Estonia, with nurseries heavily subsidised so that nobody pays more than about £240 a month, while low-income parents pay nothing. There is a focus on outdoor play, whatever the weather, and on improving outcomes for disadvantaged children before they start school.[31] The education system in Finland is rated as the second best in Europe.[32]

Over the next few years, equality campaigners will also be watching what happens in Canada, where the government has pledged as much as $30 billion (£18.6 billion) to ensure families pay no more than $10 (£6.20) per day for early years childcare from 2026. There are plans for about 250,000 new childcare spaces throughout the country.[33] The nationwide strategy follows evidence from the Canadian province of Quebec, which implemented a low-cost childcare policy in 1997 and has since been shown by economists to have easily recovered the costs because of the resulting increase in women going back to work.[34] As a bonus, children have benefitted from high-quality nurseries. In Canada, the education system is already one of the best in the world.[35] 'They've done that because they can prove it is good for the economy,' Brearley said. 'They've crunched the numbers and figured out that for every dollar you invest in childcare, you get $1.50–$2.80 back into the wider economy.'

Failing to fund early years education properly is a false economy – because investing in children in their first few years has lifelong results, for them and their families, and provides huge returns for the economy long term. Quality, affordable childcare is also absolutely central to sexual equality and equal parenting. It allows mothers, as well as fathers, to continue to contribute to the economy by not having to sacrifice the careers that they have worked so hard to have before children, enabling them to split their time at work and caring at home as they see fit.

Will there ever be a time that nurseries, schools and workplaces do not automatically assume that when there is a problem with a child it is the mother who will have to go and sort it out? Almost everyone I interviewed for this chapter asked me the same question: Who does our son's nursery call when there is a problem? I had not thought about it much before. We gave both of our mobile numbers to the nursery when we signed Solly up and sometimes they call me first, sometimes they call Robin first. If they cannot get hold of the dad they called first, they try the other one. With the options being two men, it has genuinely seemed random and fair. It can be as simple as that.

CHAPTER FIVE

WHO IS THE REAL DAD?

Why Parenting Is Active, Not a Genetic Condition

The first time I was asked who Solly's real dad was he was not even born yet. It was about 7.30 p.m., after work, and I was at a pub near London Bridge station telling a group of acquaintances why I was not drinking alcohol. A bottle of red wine was being shared around as five of us stood in a circle. I explained that Robin and I were expecting a baby through surrogacy, we had just had the 12-week scan, and we had pledged not to drink alcohol in solidarity with Rachel, our friend who was going through a surrogate pregnancy for us. I have a vague memory of doing something cringeworthy like pushing my tummy out, patting it and saying: 'Look! I'm already showing!'

I can picture them all around me, smiling widely, mouths open and eyes pushed right out, and starting to congratulate me. One of the guys, short, older and posh, with a permanently red face, looked confused about the booze thing. One of the women, an intense brunette with a veiny forehead, gave me a high five. The group in the pub were not my closest friends; I knew them through work, and it was a one-off event. It was fun telling them about the news.

They were intrigued by the details, in awe of Rachel's generosity and happy for us. Most said things like 'That's brilliant news. Good for you' or 'You and your – your partner must be so happy'. They asked questions and I answered them, grinning, being as open as possible.

The posh man with the red face then lurched forward. 'Well,' he said, and then put on a booming American accent. 'Who's the Daddy?'

Robin and I had discussed how to deal with this question. We knew people would be curious about how we decided to become parents and which of us would have the genetic link to our child. We thought most people would not ask and would just quietly wonder to themselves. I took a breath and very earnestly explained to Posh Face that we would both be our baby's fathers. He raised an eyebrow. 'Yeah, yeah,' he said. 'But who is the *real* dad?'

In the weeks that followed, Robin and I were asked again and again about who our child's real dad would be. At dinner one night, a friend listened to me and Robin describe the IVF process and then asked: 'So who won?' We always answered that we would both be our baby's fathers. If they pushed, we explained in as matter-of-fact a way as possible that Robin would be the baby's genetic father, if that was what they meant. We did not want the 'who's the daddy?' question to be some kind of mystery. If we did not think it mattered, we should be confident about being straightforward about it. We did not want the question to bother us, but it was asked so frequently that it became exhausting.

We asked other gay fathers if they had had the same experiences, and everyone had similar stories. Just as people are obsessed with gender roles in parenting – and the idea of men being inherently less able to care for children – people are also obsessed with genetics. Who does the baby look like? Whose nose does she have? Will she be loud like her mum or bookish like her dad? Genes are obviously important when it comes to children's basic traits. But are they actually relevant in terms of parenting and outcomes for children?

Many women feel guilt believing that, as mothers, they should be around for their children most of the time. But do they need to worry if they share childcare with others? Earlier in the book, I explored studies into whether men are biologically capable of being equal parents, and the findings suggest they absolutely can be, through committed caregiving. But what about the most important thing – the impact this has on children? Is the key to raising well-adjusted children who you are or what you do?

One of the world-leading experts in outcomes for children in all kinds of family set-ups is Susan Golombok, professor and former director of the Centre for Family Research at the University of Cambridge. Since the 1970s, she has been studying children in non-traditional families, including those born through sperm and egg donation, adoption and surrogacy. Her earliest research was instrumental in convincing judges in family courts to allow lesbian mothers to keep custody of their children, when they had previously been seen as threats to their welfare.

In Britain, during the 1970s, mothers who had come out as lesbians were repeatedly denied custody and separated from their children even though heterosexual women were almost always awarded custody after their marriage breakdowns. The reasons given at court included: fears that children raised by lesbian women would act inappropriately for their gender, with their sons preferring toys and games supposedly meant for girls; fears that the children would be bullied at school and therefore develop psychological problems; and lesbians being seen to lack the capacity to be sound mothers.[1]

In 1976, Golombok was a master's student and decided to carry out an objective study into the wellbeing of children being brought up by lesbian mothers to see if the claims made during these court cases were supported by research. She decided to compare families with single, heterosexual mothers to those in which the children were brought up by a lesbian mother and a female partner after being born into a heterosexual marriage. In all cases the children were being brought up by women, some gay and some straight.

She interviewed all of the mothers and used a procedure designed at the Institute of Psychiatry to assess what each of them said and how they said it, to try to understand the quality of the relationships between the mothers and their children. She underwent intensive training in the interviewing techniques by experts at the Institute of Psychiatry. Transcripts of the interviews were analysed by an independent psychiatrist who was unaware of the family backgrounds. The children's teachers were also asked to complete questionnaires about their behaviour, and the children were asked questions about their favourite toys, games and activities.

The findings may seem obvious now but were revolutionary to many at the time. The lesbian mothers were found to be just as warm, committed and involved as the other mothers, and their children were no more likely to have emotional and behavioural problems.[2] Two other similar studies carried out in the US around the same time supported her conclusions.[3]

In her 2020 book *We Are Family: What Really Matters for Parents and Children*, Golombok reflected on how it took many years of studies producing similar findings for them to be seen as definitive. Research on families cannot be as precise as studies into, say, drugs. You cannot randomly allocate children to straight or gay mothers to see how they develop. Golombok wrote:

> Family researchers have to work in alternative ways, slowly building up a picture based on a series of investigations that focus on different questions, and repeating these investigations with new groups of families to find out whether the findings remain the same. It is only when several studies, ideally by different research groups, produce similar findings that confidence can be placed in the results.[4]

Over the past five decades, Golombok and her colleagues have used various in-depth studies to assess the outcomes for children born to all kinds of parents. One of the studies involved them revisiting the children from the original lesbian-mother study in 1991, almost 15 years after they were first assessed, and by which time they were in their mid-20s. They interviewed more than 60 per cent of those who had previously taken part. The young adults who had been raised by their mother with a female partner (a step-parent without a genetic link to them) were no more likely to have suffered with mental health problems than others of the same age. They were no more or less likely to identify as lesbian, gay or bisexual than anyone else, not that that should have mattered.[5] One criticism of the work at the time was that those who took part had volunteered – potentially meaning lesbian mothers with children experiencing problems would not have come forward.

Golombok has since studied mothers from the Avon Longitudinal Study of Parents and Children, in the west of England, which recruited more than 14,000 pregnant women in 1991 and 1992 so that they could continue to be researched as they raised their children. Golombok assessed the outcomes for children aged seven from the study group who had mothers who were either lesbian, single or raising the children with their father in a more traditional set-up at home.[6] The conclusions were the same as before – that the outcomes for the children brought up by lesbian mothers were as good as those for children in traditional families – and these findings have been replicated by researchers in the US studying even larger groups of children aged 14.[7] The key challenges these children with lesbian mothers appeared to face were from society, with them often having to cope with stigma from their schools and their peers.

Golombok and her colleagues continued to study outcomes of children growing up in various families with non-genetic parents, including those born through egg donation, sperm donation, adoption and surrogacy, both to heterosexual and gay male parents. Their studies have repeatedly and consistently indicated that sex and genetic connections are not crucial to parenting; what is most important for children is having positive relationships with their parents, whoever they are.

One of the studies involved 40 gay-father families through surrogacy and 55 lesbian-mother families through sperm donation. At least one parent in each family was not genetically related to their children. The children showed very low levels of emotional problems relative to other families, and the gay fathers were assessed as having just as positive relationships with their children as the lesbian mothers had with theirs.[8]

Robin and I read Golombok's research papers when we were considering whether or not to try to have a child through surrogacy. I can picture myself at Willesden Green Tube station early one weekday morning in 2018, waiting for the train to work while using my phone to read research about outcomes for children born through surrogacy, pinching the screen to zoom in on the tiny text. At the time, I found the results reassuring. A few years later, having gone through the experience of being a non-genetic parent, I find them completely unsurprising. I am obviously biased, but I could not believe more strongly that parenting is about what you do – the day after day of showing up to love and care for your child – rather than the proportion of genetic material you share with them, whether you are a man or a woman, or what some sperm once did with an egg. Here is how I became Solly's real dad.

Robin and I met in early 2014. We were living in flats close enough in London that our profiles were visible to each other on Grindr, the gay dating app. A few days after chatting for the first time on Grindr, we also matched on Tinder, another dating app. It must have been destiny.

After a first date at a restaurant in Covent Garden on 15 February (Robin refused to have it on Valentine's Day), we became inseparable pretty quickly. We must have discussed how we both wanted children very early on as I do not remember ever not knowing this about Robin. We got married in 2017 and opted for a civil ceremony in an old building that was once a chapel, which went down really well with our Jewish families. Afterwards, there was lots of food, a soul band, Israeli dancing and, as is tradition at Jewish weddings, we were hauled into the air on chairs.

At some point during the next year, we started seriously discussing how we would try to have a child. Initially we were against exploring surrogacy. Wasn't surrogacy something that celebrities did in America? Didn't it cost hundreds of thousands of pounds? Didn't it involve picking eggs from a catalogue of women based on crude categories like academic achievements and eye colour? But then a friend told us that he and his husband were expecting twins through surrogacy in Britain. They had developed a genuinely close relationship with the woman who was carrying their children and were certain they would remain friends for life. They went to every scan together and were spending weekends visiting her and her family.

We learned how in the UK surrogacy is legal but not commercial, which means you cannot pay surrogates a fee for carrying your child. Instead, you cover expenses such as train tickets for medical appointments, loss of earnings, maternity clothes and medication. Essentially, you have to make sure she is not paying for you to have a child. The ban on surrogates earning money for doing this in Britain is intended to avoid exploitation; so no woman decides to carry another person's baby out of desperation or because she is being forced to do so by, say, a desperate couple or an abusive partner looking for financial gain. Women in Britain carrying surrogate babies do so altruistically.

It all sounded so lovely, if slightly bewildering because such extreme altruism can be so hard to comprehend. We also did lots of detailed research and found out that it was becoming an increasingly common route to parenthood. About 450 babies per year who are brought up in England and Wales are born through surrogacy – not far off four times the number recorded a decade ago.[9] We read authoritative studies about the outcomes for children born through surrogacy, and the results were positive. I use the term 'surrogate' rather than 'surrogate mother' because every surrogate in the UK I have met and asked has preferred this wording and their preference should be respected. It is understandable given that they do not see themselves as the child's mother.

Robin and I briefly looked into adoption but also applied to join Surrogacy UK, a not-for-profit organisation that hosts social events and an internet forum for surrogates and 'intended parents', a term used for couples like us in the surrogacy community. While every podcast or article on adoption seemed to focus on negatives – lack of support from local authorities, violence and trauma – we also listened to surrogates talk about the joy and pride they felt after creating a family and the lifelong friendships they had formed with the parents they had helped. We were drawn to the idea of having a child through surrogacy in Britain.

In our teens, in bedrooms only a few miles away from each other in north London, Robin and I had both separately gone through a kind of mourning process, coming to terms with our sexuality and the idea that we would never get married or have children. But the law changed, and we had got married. And now we allowed ourselves to imagine something that we had not thought was possible – sitting by a hospital monitor and seeing the little clouds of limbs at a first scan, picking names, holding our newborn baby, whinging to friends about sleepless nights. All the clichés.

The first Surrogacy UK social event we went to was in the summer of 2018 at a pub near Stroud. We booked a B&B nearby for the weekend and tentatively walked in, expecting some kind of speed-dating event for wannabe parents and surrogates. We soon discovered that there were no 'active' surrogates there (surrogates currently looking to meet intended parents), but it did not matter. We met a gay couple and their adorable son, pushing a toy car on a ledge and humming to himself. Among about 30 or 40 other people, we also chatted to a straight couple who had miscarried repeatedly for a decade before joining Surrogacy UK but now had twin girls. We ended up spending most of the day with a powerhouse woman just over five feet tall with a blonde bob and a Brummy accent who had carried twins for a gay couple. She talked about the pride she felt in having been a surrogate and still travelled the country for surrogacy events even though she was not able to carry any more children. This was not some kind of matching event – it was a loud and lively community, like any other but with a bit more chat about sperm counts and uterine lining.

The following week we got the train to Macclesfield for another Surrogacy UK social event in a park. I immediately had one of those moments that makes you want to jump off a cliff – 'She's only a month old – you look incredible!' I said to a new mum holding her baby. She looked at me like I was insane. We got on particularly well with two straight couples who were also new to Surrogacy UK. One of the women spent a lot of the day running around after her daughter, an energetic two-year-old toddling around and trampling on paper plates. 'Don't waste your time chatting to me!' the mother had said early on, pointing to her stomach. 'This doesn't work any more. Hysterectomy.'

Early in the process we learned that there are two types of surrogacy: gestational and traditional. Gestational surrogacy involves fertility treatment and a woman carrying a baby that is not genetically linked to her. One woman's egg is fertilised with a man's sperm in a lab and then a resulting embryo is transferred to the surrogate. From our experience, creating embryos and transfer, if successful, costs about £15,000 in Britain. Traditional surrogacy involves artificial insemination (we learned about this from drunk dads in pubs). In practice, this typically means an intended father discretely masturbating into a pot in a locked toilet upstairs at the surrogate's home while the surrogate and their partners share tea and biscuits downstairs and talk about the weather. The intended father then comes downstairs looking sheepish and the surrogate goes upstairs and does what she needs to do with the pot and a syringe. They track ovulation to make sure they do this at the right time of the month. When it works, it means that the surrogate is also genetically related to the baby. Without IVF, it is much more affordable.

We decided to try gestational surrogacy as it made more sense to us at the time that a gestational surrogate could be pregnant without feeling a maternal connection to the baby (although we have since become friends with traditional surrogates who say they see it as egg donation and feel no maternal bond with the babies they have carried through surrogacy). We signed up to a fertility clinic in London and a separate organisation that finds altruistic women who want to donate eggs.

Crucially for us, the egg donation agency did not have lists of donors for couples to choose from. Instead, we were interviewed, our details were sent to potential donors and then we were chosen three months later by a woman who liked the sound of us. We were sent some non-identifying details about her, a passage she had written on why she wanted to help us and two pictures: one of her as a newborn baby and one of her as a little girl at primary school. We could have said no, but we knew we would say yes before reading her profile. This woman chose to remain anonymous, but it is Solly's legal right to be able to have her details when he is 18 and we will support him in trying to find her if he wants to (and give her the biggest hug imaginable). She was only paid expenses as egg donation also must be altruistic in Britain, but we bought her a small, inexpensive present and wrote her a card for when she went to the clinic for her procedure.

We ended up with six good quality embryos, which were frozen. Four of the six that made it were created with Robin's sperm and two with mine (Robin was praised by the nurses for his excellent sperm quality – 'the best count and quality we've seen in ages!' – and gasped when they told him the results. He has cerebral palsy and said, 'This is the first time I've ever been praised for a physical exam! I feel so sporty!'). Clinics can grade the embryos, judging which are most likely to lead to pregnancy by how they have developed in the laboratory for the first few days. We made the simple decision that we would use the embryo they thought was most likely to lead to pregnancy when the time came.

After about six months of going to surrogacy events around the country, we met Rachel and James at a pub overlooking the River Derwent near Matlock in Derbyshire. They were nervously chatting to each other by the bar, and we went over to say hi. We did not know if she was a surrogate or they were intended parents. We were all wearing stickers with our names on them, and one of the surrogates' sons had drawn a robin on Robin's one.

We spent most of the day talking to Rachel and James. James told Robin he looked like Tom Hardy, which went down very well. We found ourselves going into great detail about our fertility clinic visits, mimicking the awkward man with a clipboard who led us, one by one, to the deposit rooms and describing the awful leather chaise longue and the picture of a female glamour model on the wall – 'Not much use to us!'

We carried on going to events and then, a few months later, went back to Derbyshire for another one at the same pub. Rachel was there, this time with her sons Charlie and Jack, then seven and five. Jack has autism and can feel anxious in loud, busy places and with new people but saw me and inexplicably jumped up to give me a hug. Charlie was colouring and Robin got involved, helping him out and giving him drawing challenges.

A few weeks later we got a call from Surrogacy UK to let us know that Rachel was keen to get to know us better. At Surrogacy UK, intended parents are not allowed to ask surrogates if they want to carry a child for them. Rightly, surrogates are in control. The phone call we received is known in the community as 'The Call' and starts an official period of at least three months, during which time the surrogate and intended parents are encouraged to see each other as much as possible. You also receive paperwork outlining different awful decisions you might have to make during a surrogate pregnancy so you can discuss them and see if you agree. Would you all agree to abort if you were told the baby would be so disabled they would have no quality of life? How do you feel about home birth? How often do you want to be in contact during and after the pregnancy?

We spent the next few months travelling up and down the M1 to Rachel's home, spending the days with her and her family and the nights in a Premier Inn. We bonded over a shared love of Chinese takeaway, true-crime documentaries and countryside walks. Rachel told us how she had been inspired to become a surrogate by her sister, who had carried a boy for a couple with fertility problems. They came to London, and we went to the zoo and on an open-top tourist bus. They slept on sofas in our two-bed flat. We also went through the dreaded paperwork and were relieved that we agreed on every discussion point.

After this initial three-month period, the surrogate or intended parents can choose not to continue without hard feelings, or you sign an agreement. In Britain this is not a legally binding document, but it makes your intentions and the decisions you make together really clear. After our three-month period of officially getting to know Rachel and her family, we all agreed we wanted to continue, and so we signed the agreement and had counselling separately and then together, as UK fertility clinics require (although the use was questionable given the counsellor asked Rachel and James if they knew why Robin and I could not have children naturally. 'They're both blokes,' James said). And then, in July 2019, our first frozen embryo was thawed and transferred to Rachel's uterus, while her legs were in stirrups, and she reached out behind her to hold both of our hands.

Robin and I were at a friend's wedding in Cornwall five days later when Rachel did the first pregnancy test and sent us a video with the result. She was pregnant. We called her and all screamed in excitement down the phones like teenagers.

In the weeks that followed, Rachel felt exhausted and nauseous – a combination of typical early pregnancy symptoms and side effects from fertility treatment drugs. We felt awful. We called and texted, probably driving her mad, and sent her favourite caramelised biscuit spread in the post. She never complained, but we would have. We also started to get our first glimpses of the variety of ways people respond to gay parents.

At our three-month hospital scan, we were told one of us should hide on a bench near the scan room and sneak in at the last minute so others in the waiting room would not know they had let three of us in (these were the days before Covid stopped partners coming to appointments). We stared at the screen as we saw the little outline of our baby's head and body and his limbs driving the sonographer mad with all their waving and kicking.

We have a WhatsApp group with Rachel and James, and every day during this time it was a continual stream of funny nonsense, like the best groups always are. One night Rachel messaged to say that Jack had kissed her stomach before bed and told the baby that it was a goodnight kiss from me and Robin as we could not be there. He made it a ritual. There was no confusion – he knew that his mum was pregnant with a baby for us because men cannot carry a baby in their tummies and she wanted to help us. Children can be so much more accepting than adults when they are just told the truth in a straightforward way.

One weekend afternoon, following repeated 'who is the daddy?' conversations with friends and acquaintances, we went to my brother Josh's house. He has three children and the youngest, Eva, six at the time, skipped towards me as we walked in the front door, her long, brown hair swinging. 'You're having a baby!' she shouted, reaching up for a cuddle. Then she looked serious for a moment. 'Do you know? That's going to be my new baby cousin.'

As Covid-19 changed the world, Rachel hit her due date, and then kept going. We had rented a cottage nearby and helped her with the school run and looked after her boys when she needed to rest. Again, we felt awful. She had her own family to worry about like everyone else – were her kids going to be off school? What was going to happen at hospital? We had the crib ready by our rented bed.

The hospital where Rachel had planned to give birth had been supportive and made arrangements with Rachel to allow me and Robin to be at the birth along with Rachel and James. But as Covid started to spread alarmingly across the world, the midwifery team changed their minds and said we could no longer come. During lengthy discussions, we explained the importance of us being there for our son from birth – for us to care for him that first night, while Rachel could rest and not have to look after a baby that she did not ever view as her own. They listened, spoke to Rachel independently and agreed that she and James could come in together until she was in established labour and then we could join. We were incredibly grateful and know we were lucky it was so early in lockdown as restrictions would prevent many fathers from being at births in the weeks that followed.

We would have done anything to have shared the pain Rachel went through in labour. After going nine days overdue, it was relatively quick in the end – just a couple of hours in hospital before Solly was born – but the contractions were relentless. I remember thinking that what Rachel was doing for us was utterly inexplicable. I could just about get my head around her enduring morning sickness, hormone changes and tiredness for us to have a family. But this much pain?

Robin and I were perched on a windowsill at the side of the delivery room, giving Rachel space. She was supported by James, who stood by the side of the hospital bed holding her hand and talking to her. Robin was holding a water bottle, which he had been told by the midwives to keep filling – to make sure Rachel could drink regularly but also, we suspected, to make us feel involved. I dug into a bag we had prepared for Rachel for the time in hospital and pulled out some foot cream. Robin looked at me like I was mad. 'Does she look like she wants a fucking foot rub?'

As the time came for her to start pushing, Rachel lurched back on the hospital bed, ripped the gas and air tube from her mouth and shouted: 'Stop!' James clung tight to her other hand and two midwives, low beneath her legs, looked up. 'Can someone please get my phone?' she asked between quick breaths out. 'I need a photo [breath] of the moment [breath] the guys [breath] meet [breath] their son [breath].'

James reached for the phone and in moments it was all captured: our son, Solly, born; me cutting the cord; me holding him for the first time and staring at Solly's tiny blue eyes; Robin holding him close while Solly sucked his thumb; Rachel and James cuddling the child that their family had helped to create, altruistically, for ours.

The rest of us cried more than Solly did. We held him in disbelief. We named him Solly, a shortened version of Solomon, just because we like the name, and his middle names are Bertie, after my great aunt, and Ezra, which is Hebrew for 'help' to honour Rachel.

In the days after Solly's birth we stayed in the cottage we had rented close to Rachel's family. We wanted to have Solly's first community midwife visits near to the hospital where he was born. We kept checking in on Rachel, and she came to visit Solly, but she insisted she felt fine and was delighted to be at home with her family. We still text each other regularly, send pictures and videos and stay with each other a few times a year. Rather than paraphrase Rachel's thoughts about being a surrogate, here are some words she wrote about her experience of carrying Solly:

After our sons Jack and Charlie were born I knew I did not want more children. But I felt excited about the possibility of being pregnant again. It is something about the bump. When I am pregnant, I lift my T-shirt up and have my belly out while walking around the house. I rest my hands on it while snuggling up in front of the TV and feel the little kicks, rubbing my tummy to get the baby to move more.

I first heard about surrogacy almost a decade ago. My older sister, Leanna, announced to the family that she was going to be a surrogate. Seeing her go through the pregnancy – and then the happiness she felt afterwards – inspired me.

Being pregnant with a surrogate baby is totally different to being pregnant with my own children. Right from the beginning – before conception – I knew the child wasn't mine. I felt connected to the baby but in a very different way. When I was at 14 weeks and in the bath and felt him move for the first time, just a little flutter at that stage, I wasn't excited for myself, I was excited to get out of the bath and grab my phone so I could tell the guys. I loved seeing them buying the cot and the dresser and the Babygros. I loved seeing pictures of them building things for the baby, putting the furniture together, like James and I did for our boys. Our sons have understood surrogacy in a way that many adults are not able to. I wondered whether they might find it confusing when I was pregnant. In the end it was never a problem – they knew the baby was Paul and Robin's and that two men can't grow babies, so I was helping them.

In the end, the labour was quick. My first contractions were after 6 p.m. and Solly was born before 10 p.m. When you have your own baby, you cherish that magical first picture of you with your baby. They are memories you need captured because it's all such a blur at the time. I wanted that for Paul and Robin. I looked down at Solly as I held him and it was just like I thought it would be – like cuddling a nephew, or the baby of your closest friends.

It is a strange feeling, being proud of yourself. As you go through the day, you do not often take a moment to give yourself praise. But when I see photos of Solly with his dads, or videos of him laughing when he is playing with his grandparents, I think to myself: 'I did that. I had a part in bringing that happiness to them.'

Rachel and James were initially Solly's legal parents even though he was in our care from birth, neither of them have a genetic link to Solly and they did not want this status. This is the law in Britain. In practice it did not affect our daily lives as Solly was living with me and Robin. But we had to go through a six-month 'parental order' process through the courts and social services for Rachel and James to transfer their theoretical legal rights as parents to us. This meant that, technically, they had legal responsibility for a child who was not in their care for half a year. The biggest concern for us during this time was what would happen were Solly to have had a medical emergency. Treatment could have been delayed if a doctor demanded consent from Rachel and James and we could not get hold of them in time. Thankfully that never happened.

Before Solly's birth, we were asked a few times whether we were concerned about his surrogate wanting to keep the baby. Hi, random acquaintance, thanks for probing me on a Monday morning in Starbucks about whether I am worried about being separated from my future baby! The truth is we never gave it much thought. It was so clear to us that Rachel wanted to be a surrogate rather than a mother again. If she wanted another child, she could have tried for one with her husband. Surrogates can also worry about intended parents abandoning them before the birth, changing their minds and leaving them with a child they never planned to keep. It was crucial that we built a really strong bond before starting fertility treatment. We trusted each other throughout.

The UK's surrogacy laws, which were written in the 1980s, are in the process of being reformed, and surrogates have been central to calling for the changes. In 2019, the Law Commission, an independent body that reviews the law, published its proposals, including parents through surrogacy in Britain having legal status from birth, while maintaining surrogates' rights to object to this if they want to for a specific time period. With the interests of the child at the centre of the proposals, there would also be a national register of surrogacy arrangements to ensure anyone born through surrogacy would have access as adults to an impartial legal record of how they were conceived, including the identities of the woman who carried them and any other donors, such as an egg or sperm donor.

The proposals also have important caveats. Parents would only be able to have the legal status from birth if they adhered to new strict safeguards and regulations before conception, including involving a licensed fertility clinic or surrogacy organisation, all of those involved having independent counselling, legal advice and criminal record checks and the completion of a professional assessment of the welfare of any child that they hoped would be born. The changes would also only apply to those going through surrogacy in the UK. If not, they would have to go through the full parental order court process involving social services.[10]

In some parts of the world, particularly in developing countries, surrogacy can be exploitative, with women coerced, sometimes by abusive partners, into carrying babies for rich foreigners. Some parents in Britain who have gone abroad for commercial surrogacy have done thorough checks and have been convinced that the agencies they used were ethical ones and that the women were making independent choices. There is clearly a range of experiences, but the general risk of women in poorer countries being coerced into surrogacy, or doing it through desperation, is very real.

At the end of the six-month legal process following Solly's birth, Robin and I became his official legal parents during a quick hearing on video call and could then apply for a new document to replace his initial birth certificate, with us now listed as his two parents. In the days afterwards, a court official sent Solly a small brown teddy, with a little blue-and-white-striped bow around his neck, in the post. We called the teddy Judge Jonny. He still sleeps with Solly, alongside two monkeys, a sheep, Peter Rabbit, a dog called Monty and a dinosaur called Whitney. While our route to parenthood has not been the most common, I believe that what we have experienced and learned is relevant to other parents, or anyone thinking of becoming one – because of what two-father families suggest about anyone's ability to be a parent with primary or equal responsibility, whatever their sex or genetic relationship to their child.

I met Golombok – the scientist whose work had helped convince us to try surrogacy as a route to parenthood – on a sunny afternoon

at her office in Cambridge. I asked her about the conclusions she had
come to after more than 40 years of studying non-traditional families.
She said she and her colleagues had assessed 'high in the hundreds,
if not more than one thousand' families during this time, including
those with straight, gay, lesbian, genetic and non-genetic parents:

> The kinds of families that I have researched, not one could
> have had children by accident. Often they had gone through
> years and years of infertility, fertility treatment or faced
> hurdles such as adoption or surrogacy. They had children
> against the odds, and it was such a struggle that when they
> did eventually become parents, they really appreciated it and
> were really committed and loving. It is about the motivation
> of the parents, not biology.

Golombok described her team's study involving 40 gay-father
families through surrogacy and 55 lesbian-mother families. The
lesbian-mother families had used sperm donation, so all the children
were born through assisted reproduction. The idea was that comparing
gay fathers with lesbian mothers would show clearly any differences
that existed between men and women as parents, rather than comparing gay-father families to traditional families which would also
have had a father in the home. The study used similar methods to
Golombok's previous work, assessing the relationships between the
parents and the children, as well as the children's emotional wellbeing
and their likeliness to have mental health and behavioural problems.

The researchers assessed the gay fathers as having just as positive
relationships with their children as the lesbian mothers did. In a
surprising finding, they also reported that the gay men's children
showed lower levels of emotional problems than the children of
lesbian mothers.[11] 'In both groups they had very low levels of emotional problems, but in the gay-father families they were even lower

for some reason that we haven't been able to explain,' she said. 'To put it another way, they were just extremely well-adjusted children.'

As with children of lesbian mothers, the children of gay fathers experienced some negativity from peers. In *We Are Family: What Really Matters for Parents and Children*, Golombok wrote of this study that 'our findings clearly refuted the idea that men are less capable parents than women'.[12]

The study's results should come with caveats. It was the first of its kind, so much more similar research is needed. The parents who took part were volunteers, so it is possible that only the fathers with the most positive experiences would have come forward. Given the high costs involved with fertility treatment, the children in gay-father families would also have been likely to have been brought up in relative wealth (although those with fathers on lower incomes seemed to be doing equally well). One academic reviewer of the study questioned whether men might be less attuned to emotions than women, thus skewing the results in their own favour during interviews. Golombok said the alternative explanation was that gay fathers who had spent years planning to have children and persisting despite challenges may just make good, dedicated parents. She said this possibility was supported by the very positive independent assessments written by their children's teachers.[13]

Even with all of the caveats in mind, the study's key finding is hard to dismiss. All of these children – in 40 families assessed by these expert researchers alone – were being brought up exclusively by men and they were doing as well as anyone else.

Another of Golombok's team's studies into the outcomes of children adopted from the care system showed those who had been placed in gay-father homes were doing just as well as those with adoptive mothers (in this study, many of the children, across all family types, showed emotional and behavioural problems, but this was expected with children adopted from the care system, and this was no more likely when they were brought up by adoptive gay fathers).[14] Golombok said the researchers were particularly impressed with some of the gay parents they observed who had adopted children with severe emotional problems and developmental delays. 'They were just amazing, dedicated parents,' she said.

One key finding of Golombok's, which has informed our parenting, is the importance of openness. Her team have found that, at aged seven, some of the children born through surrogacy showed higher than average levels of emotional and behavioural problems.[15] These issues then disappeared by the time the children were ten.[16] In their teenage years, the children through surrogacy were 'flourishing', according to Golombok.[17]

One possible explanation for the challenges some of these children faced when aged seven was that, at that age, they understood more about surrogacy than previously and, potentially, they had to cope with issues relating to identity at a younger age than other children. It is important that these children are not misled in any way about their origins. When children through donor conception were aged seven and ten, parents who had told them about their origins had more positive relationships with them than those who kept secrets from their children about their genetic origins.[18] It would clearly be impossible for us to pretend to Solly that one of us carried him. We already talk to him about how he was born – if you ask him whose tummy he grew inside he says, 'Aunty Rachel!' It is reassuring for us to know that openness is best for him. Golombok said:

> Our findings have shown the children do just as well when raised by fathers as they do when raised by mothers. What my research tells me is that if fathers are highly involved in parenting then they have just as good relationships with their children and the children are just as likely to flourish as those brought up in traditional families. From our research, gender

and genetic connections matter less in parenting than the quality of parent-child relationships.

Molly and Sam, who are both 28 years old and from Yorkshire in the north of England, have two children, a daughter aged five at the time of writing and a son who is a few months older than Solly. Their daughter is genetically related to both of them, and their son is adopted. I came across Molly's profile on Instagram – where she posts about her family – and wanted to speak to her for this book given that she and her husband are among very few people who know what it feels like to be parents to both a genetic and a non-genetic child. They asked me not to use their children's names. 'The love is no different in terms of amounts. I couldn't love my son any more,' Molly said. 'For me, DNA has meant diddly squat.'

While the couple had no previous family experience of adoption, Molly had been inspired to adopt from a very young age. In particular, she remembers the impact of watching *The Story of Tracy Beaker*, a BBC TV adaptation of a Jacqueline Wilson book about a girl in the care system:

> It sounds really silly, but I used to watch Tracy Beaker and I was obsessed with fostering and adoption. I was probably about ten years old. I used to come home from school to watch it – when you couldn't record, and it was on at five o'clock so I'd have to get home in time. As an adult, I always had adoption at the back of my head.

Molly, who works in marketing, and Sam, a teacher, had their daughter when they were both 22. The baby was five months old at their wedding. While Molly loved being a mother and her relationship with her daughter, she had a traumatic pregnancy and labour. Despite feeling anxious about having to go through the experiences again, she and her husband soon started trying for another child. She then had two miscarriages. Before leaving hospital after her second miscarriage, she had decided that she did not want to try anymore:

> To set the scene, we were in the early pregnancy unit confirming our last miscarriage. We were in the consultation room waiting for a doctor. And I remember turning to Sam and saying, 'Do not make me do this again.' He knew I was interested in adoption and he said, 'Mol, we can adopt, I'm so done with this as well, we don't need to do this.' I honestly left that hospital and I was fine. Knowing I didn't have to be there again was amazing. It was weirdly positive for me; it was like a door closed and a cloud lifted knowing that I could actually do adoption.

The couple began a period of research, attending adoption information evenings, reading articles and watching videos posted by adopters online. Sam had worked with children in care previously so was concerned about whether they could cope with bringing a child who had suffered trauma into their family, particularly because of the potential impact on their daughter. Molly felt confident that it would be fine. 'There were also lots of positive stories,' she said. 'We were reassured that we had a lot of control over what child we would adopt and what needs we felt we could meet. I trusted our gut.'

They were matched with their son before his first birthday. Initially they had a two-week transition period, during which they spent 14-hour days at the baby's foster home, gradually becoming acquainted with him, initially just being in the room without touching him so he could get used to their presence and voices, then gradually starting to get involved with playing and nappy changes. Towards the end of this period, their daughter was allowed to visit so he could get used to her. And then, at the end of this period, he came home with them.

Molly and Sam were warned not to expect to fall in love with their son straight away. They were told he might appear to reject them but that they could build trust, day after day, by being there for him, over and over again. Molly explained to me the differences between how she bonded with her two children, and it reminded me of how scientists explain the different ways this usually happens for mothers and fathers:

In terms of building an attachment, it is very natural and instinctive with a biological child. But with a child through adoption there is none of that natural, hormonal, chemical – when it is as if you are programmed to attach to that child and them to you. There is no breastfeeding. The bonding is harder. You have to make it happen. With my son, there was a lot more toddler wearing [wearing him in a sling], cuddles, feeding him bottles, eye contact, it was like going back to scratch with him, skin-to-skin at bath time and bedtime. It was meeting every single cry and us being there. Two years on now, I couldn't adore him more. Sam is obsessed.

Molly said she felt intensely protective of her son, and in awe of how he is developing:

We are so proud of him. From his perspective, seeing how much he loves us and trusts us now. I look at him and think, everything you have been through, which should have programmed you to not trust any adult in the world, but yet you love us and want us here with you. We find it so weird that we did not know him before he was with us.

She said her son and daughter were like any other siblings, adding, 'They love each other. They fight. They play. It is no different to any other relationship. But she is so protective of him.'

Mirroring Golombok's findings about openness, Molly has listened to many adoptees speaking about the importance of knowing about their birth families and she wanted this for her son:

> I would never want to replace my son's birth mother. That is so important to him. That's who he looks like, that's who he grew in and that's his genetics. I am his mum, but it is so important for him that he still has his birth mum as well. Even though adopted children might not see their birth parents or have them in their lives, that connection is always there, and you should not try to rob that from them.

As with many non-traditional families, they have had to deal with some irritating comments, even when apparently well meaning. For Molly, one moment stands out:

> I was in the middle of the supermarket. Someone who had heard we had adopted and was curious about it stopped me and said, 'I think you've done an amazing thing. But I could never do it. I could only have my own children.' To which I said, 'That's funny, because he is my own child, and I couldn't love him any more' – and then I walked off down the freezer aisle. It is hard for some people to understand but we have honestly found that DNA doesn't matter.

When a child is born, the people around them often become obsessed with genetics. Parents, friends and family members peer over a buggy, searching the new baby's face to work out who they look like. I do it as well. It is hard to resist. I sometimes look at Solly and get flashes of Robin and it can feel genuinely thrilling. 'He just smirked like you do! Look at his eyes – they're exactly the same as yours!' Robin cannot see it so does not find this game as fun as I do.

When Solly was a few months old, we went for a just-about-legal lockdown walk and saw a friend's parents. We stopped to say hello and the mother leaned towards Solly's buggy. 'Oh, he is gorgeous,' she said to me. 'He has Robin's eyes and your mouth!' I smiled, said thank you, and wondered what she had been doing during her biology classes at school.

When Solly was close to two years old we were at a kiddush (a Jewish celebration for a new baby that usually involves a synagogue's congregation descending on the new parents' home, drinking whisky and eating pickled herring and a disgusting-looking but incredibly tasty beef and bean stew called chulent). A couple who knew my parents and remembered me as a child said hello and the mother was fascinated by Solly. 'He is such a Bentley,' she said, referring to my parents' surname. 'He is identical to you.' I then introduced her to Robin, and I think she realised pretty quickly that Solly was much more identical to him.

While there is nothing wrong with this game of look-a-likes – it is just a bit of fun, and, of course, lots of characteristics are passed down to children through genes – Golombok's team's research over the past five decades suggests that the key to bringing up well-adjusted and happy children is not about what you automatically share through biology but about what you do. This is central to equal parenting because it shows that anyone can take on primary or equal responsibility as a parent and do a good job of it, if they put in the time and effort, whatever their sex.

Solly has two fathers and was born because of the extraordinary generosity of two women, an egg donor whom he may want to meet when he is older, and Rachel. He is developing into the most wonderful little boy, who is clever and funny and exhausting and makes friends wherever we go. Every day he makes people happier than they were before they saw him.

I am sure Robin and I have made countless mistakes as parents, but no more or less on average than anyone else. When Solly runs towards me, flinging himself into my arms, or calls out for 'Daddy Pauly' in the night, or nestles into my shoulder in front of the TV, he is not thinking about my genes or my chromosomes, and neither am I.

CHAPTER SIX

DADDY-LED WEANING!

How New Fathers Can Share the Domestic Load

It is 8 p.m. on a Sunday evening, and I have to be in south Wales for work in 12 hours' time. It is at least a three-hour drive, and if I leave now I should get there before midnight. I am going to be away for at least a couple of weeks but plan to come back for the weekend in the middle. Still, Solly, who is almost two now, has become clingy to me in the past few weeks. If Robin and I are both bathing him and I leave the room, Solly stands up and shouts for me. He bangs on the bathroom door when I am in the shower. He calls for me to get him from his cot in the morning and wants me to change all of his nappies. It is horrible for Robin and exhausting for me. We know it is probably just a short phase but this work trip away feels like it has come at the worst possible time. As I say goodbye and shut the front door behind me, I try not to think about how hard the next few days are going to be for Robin.

Fast forward five days and I make it back in time for Solly's bedtime on the Friday. He is happy to see me and gives me a big cuddle but does not seem upset. I bath him, read him stories and put him to bed.

The next morning Solly wakes up and calls for Daddy Robin first. We all have breakfast together, and then I have a shower in peace while Robin and Solly watch TV on the sofa. I come back to the living room and Robin is changing Solly's nappy, while Solly holds a chocolate brioche roll in either hand, taking bites from each, one at a time. 'Daddy Robin chocolate bread!' Solly says. This is new, I think, trying to ignore the stains on the sofa that I hope are just chocolate.

Over the next few months, Solly goes through occasional phases of becoming clingy to me again, but it mostly seems to happen when we are all together for his bedtime. It is partly my fault; I cannot stand it when he screams for me and I end up taking over, which makes things easier in the moment but undermines Robin. On days when I am in the office until late, Solly has a great time with Robin and goes to bed easily. The most important lesson we learn during this period is that it is good for us to have separate one-on-one time with Solly. Sometimes, if I find myself taking on more of the workload at home, the best thing for all of us is for me to just bugger off for a few hours and let Robin get on with it in his own way.

I may be wrong, but I imagine that my experience of the domestic load of parenting is probably more similar to those typical of mothers, rather than fathers – because I took the first half of parental leave in the first year of Solly's life. Of course, I was not breastfeeding or recovering from pregnancy and childbirth, so my experience was very different to most mothers in lots of ways. However, given that I was the parent dedicating all my time to looking after Solly in the first few months, when Robin and I were trying to work out how to care for a newborn, I made a lot of the decisions. When Robin was not working, he always split the feeds, nappy changes, night waking, bottle cleaning and putting Solly down for naps. Robin definitely did his fair share. But I was the one who primarily worried about what we were doing and when.

Before having Solly, I assumed I would try to be an intuitive parent who responded naturally to his cues, feeding him whenever felt right. Within a few weeks I did a massive U-turn. Essentially, I became a male Gina Ford. I was obsessed with the strategy of parenting: organising a scheduled system of bottle feeds, gradually reducing naps, always focused on what changes could be made to encourage Solly to sleep for the longest possible period during the night. This meant I had soon developed my own ways of parenting and, generally, Robin was happy for me to take the lead.

That all changed when Solly was around six months old. Robin was about to take over parental leave and, among everything else, he took charge of weaning Solly onto proper foods. He made the decisions about whether to puree vegetables or to let Solly try to feed himself with big chunks of food, and figured out when and how to introduce solids in between bottle feeds. It felt natural that he should be primarily responsible for this while off work.

In the weeks before we started, Robin read baby-food books and bought a steamer, a blender, baby bowls and freezing pots. By the time I finished my share of parental leave, pandemic-related restrictions were still tight so I was working from home. This meant I could take breaks to get involved with the actual feeding and loved seeing Solly with a face full of puree, begging for more of the mysterious colourful food. But I did not generally have to worry about what food Solly was eating and when or preparing it – that was primarily Robin's responsibility.

When I have conversations about the possibility of fathers being parents with equal responsibility, the subject of breastfeeding often comes up. Naturally, women who breastfeed take on more of the direct responsibility for the hands-on care for newborn babies, feeding them during the days and nights. Whether or not to breastfeed is, clearly, a deeply personal choice – or a decision taken out of women's hands because it is not possible for some – and it is not something Robin and I had to think about. In a way, we felt glad to be freed from the guilt that surrounds decisions about breastfeeding. With Robin and I both doing bottle feeds, it was easy for us to split them. It meant we could share the exhaustion of waking at night but also both benefit individually from those gorgeous moments, holding our son in the quiet, watching him gently suckle and hearing the little sounds he made.

In the UK, three in four mothers do not exclusively breastfeed by the time their baby is six weeks old,[1] and many choose to express milk as well as breastfeeding directly. In the US, one in five babies has been given some formula milk before they are two days old, and just over half of mothers do not exclusively breastfeed by the time their baby is three months old.[2] In these cases, if the mothers have partners, I can see no reason why they should not be doing their full share of bottle feeds during the nights, including all the prepping, cleaning and sterilising.

But what about the millions of mothers who do breastfeed? Can partners of any of these women really take equal responsibility for parenting during this time? Through reading and listening to others, I have come across some ideas that might help.

In an earlier chapter, Catherine Cho, the author of *Inferno: A Memoir of Motherhood and Madness* – about her experiences of postpartum psychosis with her first baby, Cato – described how she tried to do things differently when she had her second child, Cora. While she breastfed during the nights, her husband, James, was determined to take on the mental load. So he would take responsibility for waking up when Cora cried at night, changing her nappy and then taking her to his wife. After feeding, he would burp Cora and put her back down to sleep.

In Gideon Burrows' book about fatherhood, *Men Can Do It!*, he wrote about how he and his wife, Sarah, would take turns having primary responsibility for the nights as new parents, even though she was breastfeeding. He described how on every other night, when he was in charge, 'when the baby cried it would be me that got up blurry eyed. I'd lift the baby from the cot, change the nappy and sodden baby grow and replace with new ones, and then I'd take the baby to my wife.'[3] After Sarah breastfed while in bed and half asleep, Burrows would then 'burp the baby, check the nappy again and carefully (gratefully) place them back in their cot to sleep. For another couple of hours. Until the whole thing would start again.'

While these tactics may well help – and I can see why they might, given the importance of the mental load of parenting being shared – there has to be some acceptance that during the time when one parent is breastfeeding and on leave from work, they are bound to be, mostly, in charge.

For many fathers, weaning can be an important turning point, and a key way of them sharing the domestic load long term. The best-selling baby-food book in Britain when Solly was a newborn in 2020 was *Wean in 15*, a plan from Joe Wicks, the young father and fitness coach who got the nation doing PE lessons on YouTube during the first lockdown.[4] Ella's Kitchen, the UK's number-one baby-food brand, which fills the shelves in baby sections in stores across the world, was started by Paul Lindley, a father of two who had become passionate about making healthy food for his children. This trend for fathers to get involved in weaning makes a lot of sense. While breastfeeding can often mean it is impossible for fathers to take fully equal responsibility in the early months of parenting, anyone can steam and puree a swede. Often fathers who manage to take shared parental leave do so from about six months after their child's birth, which is the typical age that weaning starts. While milk feeding is absolutely central to caring for babies, it does not actually last very long, whether by breast or bottle. But if you gain confidence in preparing food for children, it is a skill that lasts throughout their upbringing.

In her book *Equal Power*, Jo Swinson, the former government minister, wrote about how feeding their babies had become a key area of equal parenting for her and her husband, Duncan Hames:

In the first six months of our son's life, my husband and I had a rough rule that I did inputs, he did outputs. Of course, sometimes I changed nappies and Duncan gave Andrew bottles of milk, but I spent a huge amount of time breastfeeding and Duncan certainly perfected a much slicker nappy-changing technique than me. When I went back to work, however, Duncan took responsibility for the pureeing stage: cooking, blending and freezing cubes of various fruit and veg for the weaning process.[5]

When I met Swinson and Hames at a café in south London, they said he still did most of the cooking for their children. They believed this was linked to him being in charge of weaning when their sons were babies. When their first child was ready to start solid foods, Swinson was going back to work as a minister after maternity leave. She said:

It was a great idea from my sister. I was chatting to her and saying, how are we going to do this? And she was like, get Duncan to do weaning, it is an absolute pain in the arse, all of that pureeing and mashing, and I was like, that's a really good idea. It was one of the best decisions we made.

Hames was determined to be a father who took on his share of responsibility for his children. He described an almost obsessive dedication to weaning, which he did for both of his children. 'I had a whole factory production line going at weekends for purees,' he said, gesticulating with his arms like a celebrity chef at a chopping station.

We had these little tubs, and I would fill each one and freeze them all. I was in charge of all of it. You had ice cubes of puree and different bags, and I would dip into a number of different bags eventually to make a balanced meal. They would all start off as different cubes of frozen puree and it was only after a good heat that they would start to resemble something you might eat.

Swinson and Hames came to the same conclusion as me and Robin: that the best way for them to parent as equally as possible was for them both to have specific areas of primary responsibility, such as Hames doing more weaning, as well as them both having one-on-one time with their children when they were fully in charge. This gave them both the space to do things in their own ways. In her book, Swinson wrote:

It's not about achieving a precise 50/50 split every day. What's more important is genuinely sharing the responsibility rather than one person being in charge and directing the other, and being able to share frustrations when this isn't quite working out, rather than letting them fester.[6]

During our interview, Hames turned to his wife and reminded her of a key breakthrough they had with their second son, Gabriel, when he was about six months old. He had been sleeping in their bed, almost attached to Swinson and being fed during the night. But Swinson had to go away for work for a weekend and Hames was on shared parental leave. While she was abroad, Hames managed to get Gabriel sleeping through the night in his own room. Swinson said, 'I went to Paris, he had been sleeping every night in our bed. I came back and that was it, he was in the cot. I was like, wow, that was impressive.' Hames said the key was his wife being away:

I do think that there is something to be said, if you are taking over, of having the space to do it yourself rather than being in a situation when they [babies] know if they scream loudly enough they can get their other parent back. It was a unique occasion when I was doing everything for him and there was no crying out for mummy. And, very easily, surprisingly easily, he took to staying in the cot all night long knowing that he was not going to be able to lie down in bed with his mum. We obviously did not intend to go back after that.

Before having children, Hames had been recommended the book I mentioned earlier, Gideon Burrows' *Men Can Do It!*, which encouraged men to take their share of responsibility for parenting, including the domestic work at home:

A good piece of advice in the book, which I started repeating to Jo when I was looking after our first baby, Andrew, was saying: 'It is fine that you do it like that. But more than wanting me to do it like that, you want me to do it. So you need to let me do it the way I'm going to do it.'

Hames took responsibility for various key areas of parenting their two children. With their second son (the one he got sleeping through the night) Hames came up with schedules of naps and feeds to encourage him to keep sleeping well. He said:

I guess I had enough space and autonomy to try something and because it was me on shared parental leave at the time, I was looking after him. That was indicative of the autonomy that I felt, that shared parental leave had given me.

After about an hour of our interview, Hames quietly reminded Swinson that she had to leave to pick up one of their children and take him to a swimming lesson (he was clearly still in charge of schedules). Hames had a bit longer until he had to go and get their other son from his nursery, so we continued talking. He said:

All of these things, you think it is all about the baby but a lot is about the parents. It is good for your confidence as a dad when no one is looking over your shoulder, you can just calmly deal with the situations as they arrive. You're not being held to your partner's standards. It is quite possible the mother has already worked out how to do everything if you've had a long period in which she has been on leave and the father has not been on leave from work. If you allow that to establish a teacher-pupil relationship in relation to the parenting, whereby the mother has all the answers and the father has to learn them from her, psychologically you are never going to get into an equal parenting approach.

He said he believed that fathers needed to take independent parental leave to develop their own routines, responsibilities and techniques, rather than following instructions from their partners, adding:

There are plenty of parents I know where at the weekends that is what the father is doing. He is being helpful, he's giving her a bit of a rest. He's taking the kids out to do something – but the parenting isn't shared in the same way. They don't have shared ownership of how they parent. The mother has determined how to parent and he helps out.

One of the things Hames did before their first child was born was to reflect on how he and his wife were splitting domestic work at the time. It was clear to him that he had not been doing enough. He decided that if he could not do his share of the basic domestic work before children, he would have no chance of doing so afterwards. So he made a determined effort to do more laundry and cleaning. He said these domestic duties had stuck, long term, as well as him doing more of the cooking. 'I should recognise, though, that Jo still responds to the kids at night more than me,' he said. Hames was really keen to get across to me that none of this had come particularly easily to him:

> We are very glad about how we have gone about parenting our boys, but what I don't want to do is sound like a salesman for it on the basis that it is easy and it is great. I want to be frank that it is hard and just because we were very committed to it does not mean that I found it easy. Before Andrew was born, I probably believed that some men were better at this than others, or at different ages parenting is more your thing, and the truth is it is not about how good you are at any of this, it is about how committed you are to doing it.

Hames said some fathers could find the challenges of adapting to fully involved childcare particularly difficult if they were used to doing well in their careers:

> If you have been successful at work by the time you become a dad and you are used to an environment where you are very competent, or even accomplished, at what you do – and now you are faced with a challenge which is completely new and you start off lacking any confidence in it at all – if you believe that it is meant to be easy, then you can very quickly decide that it is not for you. I want to acknowledge that both times, in different ways, I found it very hard. And, actually, it is only by persevering with it that you will find your own techniques and feel comfortable with it.

To me, this point feels essential. It is so tempting for some fathers who spend long hours at work, and do not get involved much with domestic work, to dismiss what their wives are doing at home with their children as easy. There is this idea that parental leave is all coffee breaks, mindless baby music classes and pushing swings in the park. Yes, being with your young children can be wonderful and fun and fulfilling. There are some hours in coffee shops. But it can also be exhausting in a way that makes your whole body ache.

After one day working from home when Solly was nine months old, I walked into the living room and found Robin lying on the floor in front of the TV, half asleep, his head inches from a nappy bin, while Solly joyfully used his body as a climbing frame and watched *Madagascar*, the animated film about zoo animals who end up in the wild. Yes, I took a picture and tweeted it.

I am currently writing on a Sunday evening. Robin was away for work on Friday and Saturday, and during the last three days alone I feel like I have had all of the moments – from utter glee to exhaustion, bewilderment, fury and almost everything in between. I try to remember them.

Leaving work at 4 p.m. on Friday to be at nursery in time for pick-up, feeling terrible about how early it was and then logging on after Solly was asleep to carry on, mostly out of guilt. Trying to keep calm while Solly threw all the washing I had just folded onto the floor while shouting 'Daddy pants!' Grabbing a knife from his hands in a pizza restaurant. Laughing while he dipped his pizza slices into his apple juice before sucking them dry and throwing his head back in giggles. Sprinting after him when he made a run for the road and then getting a smack in the face for stopping him. Snuggling on the sofa watching eight episodes of *Bing* on BBC iPlayer together. Making up a story before bedtime, using a book about animals for cues, and watching Solly fighting sleep, rubbing his eyes, but shouting, 'Again! Again!' Cheering Solly on at a football class on the Sunday morning as he won a race. Trying to keep him concentrating and not running off in the wrong direction – and then losing it with Robin for distracting me by saying one of the children looked like Michael McIntyre (this may or may not have been influenced by a build-up of resentment for him being away for the two previous days).

For many people, parenting is not easy, and, for many people, taking responsibility for parenting – proper, no one else is going to do this but me responsibility – is not easy. Housework is not often very fun either. But if a mother wants a career and to be at work as much as her partner, it is just unfair for the partner to do anything other than make sure the domestic workload is shared as well.

In reality, we have a long way to go before fathers do as much as mothers at home. A study published by the University of Bath in 2022 looked at the way mothers and fathers shared housework after having children. It used data from another study of more than 6,000 heterosexual couples in the US between 1997 and 2017 and analysed how they split chores such as cooking, cleaning and other housework. It found that even when the mothers earned more than their spouses, they still did more at home. In fact, the more the mothers earned in comparison to their partner, the more housework they did. Joanna Syrda, the lecturer in management who authored the study, wrote that parenthood seemed to cause families to become more traditional at home, rather than incentivising a more efficient division of labour. Speculating as to why women who earned more than their spouses did even more domestic work, she wondered whether society's ideas about parents' gender roles made women in high-earning jobs feel like they had to compensate at home.[7]

This problem of women doing unfair amounts of housework and childcare was particularly clear in the earliest days of the pandemic. In August 2020, the Fawcett Society, a charity that campaigns for gender equality, published a study with academics from Queen Mary

University of London and the London School of Economics into how families split childcare during the height of the first Covid-19 lockdown in Britain. The academics studied data from a survey of 1,424 parents of children under 11 and diaries written by 70 to 100 women each week. The findings included that mothers in couples were more than one and a half times more likely than fathers to say they were doing the majority of childcare during school and nursery closures, and three in four mothers said they were doing most of the domestic work.[8]

Another analysis by the Institute for Fiscal Studies (IFS) highlighted how even when both parents were at home, mothers' attempts to work were more interrupted. The IFS reported that during lockdown, mothers were combining paid work with other activities at home half the time, compared with a third of the time for fathers.[9]

In Britain, researchers from the University of Bristol also found that during the first lockdown in 2020, even though parents were at home together, women typically did much more of the childcare than men (roughly ten hours more per week). The results, from a survey of more than 4,000 people, also showed that women did more at home irrespective of their employment status. Women who worked from home during the first lockdown still did more childcare than men who had lost their jobs or were on government-supported time off work.

There was one glimmer of hope for equality. Compared to similar studies from before the pandemic, men appeared to be doing a larger share of the housework and childcare than they had done previously, even if it was still nowhere near enough.[10]

Anna Machin is a professor of evolutionary anthropology who specialises in the science of fatherhood. Her 2018 book, *The Life of Dad*,[11] was based on more than a decade of her research into fatherhood while at the University of Oxford. When we spoke, she said there were no scientific reasons that men could not be equal parents or do just as much of the domestic load of parenting. To state the bleeding obvious, having two X chromosomes does not make you better at the laundry, or at hoovering, or at spooning some mashed carrot into a baby's mouth. It also does not mean you are automatically better at comforting children. Like many other experts I have spoken to while writing this book, she said the key was fathers actually doing it, getting involved in childcare and taking on specific areas of primary responsibility.

'The science backs this up very strongly,' she said. 'Fathers are as biologically primed to parent their children as mothers are. We always talk about mums being the instinctive parent, or mother's instinct. It is absolute nonsense.'

Machin explained how, for men, a key biological change that happens after becoming a father is a drop in testosterone. Machin said this is caused by interaction with their baby, as the only fathers seen with testosterone matching pre-birth levels are those who are totally absent and have no contact with their children:

> This drop in testosterone is absolutely critical to parenting. Testosterone weakens the impact of dopamine and oxytocin on the brain, two of the key bonding hormones, so when it goes down, you bond more easily with your baby. It is linked to being more empathetic towards children and more motivated to care for them.

During our discussion, Machin spoke about the assumptions around parenting that she found most irritating, starting with the caricature of the useless father. I immediately thought of Daddy Pig, Peppa's stupid, clumsy, lazy father. He is grumpy about losing his glasses and then realises he has been sitting on them all along. Silly Daddy! He tries to put up a painting and wrecks the wall. He tries to cook. Oh dear, Daddy Pig's barbecue is on fire! Machin said:

We have this view of dads as inept and not capable of doing anything domestic. It absolutely winds me up. It is this idea that we can get rid of dads, that they are dispensable. Sometimes they are more of a hindrance than a help at home.

She said mothers had to fight against these societal expectations and see their partners as equals at home if they wanted to be freed from carrying the weight of domestic responsibility. 'What gets me really annoyed is when mums go out and they leave the dad a list of things that have to be done in a particular way,' she said. 'And the thing is, dads are not male mums. They are individuals. They will get it done, but they might get it done in a different way. Just let him do it. He's not stupid.'

Machin said that it is beneficial for children to experience that different adults do things differently:

It is really important for children's development because they have to understand that the world is full of individuals and you have to deal with the individual ways people do things. It is not about splitting stuff down the middle and saying I have done five nappies today, you have to do five nappies today. It is about coming to a comfortable relationship where you are each doing hopefully an equal bit of the load, but that load might be slightly different.

Reflecting on the alternative, she asked: 'Can you imagine how deeply dull it would be if you had two parents who did exactly the same thing all the time?'

Machin's research has led her to believe that men taking independent periods of parental leave is crucial for sexual equality. She is among those who have witnessed, first hand, how some men who take this time off, typically from when their baby is around six months old, assume primary responsibility for weaning. She said:

> This has been the case particularly when their partner has been exclusively breastfeeding. Breastfeeding is wonderful in many ways, but it is, of course, also excluding for fathers. I have seen several fathers who have then really stepped up when it has come to weaning, and it has become their thing. They can suddenly be involved and feed their child.

Machin said taking extended time off work to care for children had profound effects on the men she studied:

> The dads I speak to who have taken shared parental leave, they have got such confidence by the end of it in their ability to parent that child. They no longer feel like their partner is the primary parent and they are the secondary parent who is just there to take over if the mother wants to go out. They don't need lists.

Michael Lamb, emeritus professor of psychology and former head of the Department of Social and Developmental Psychology at the University of Cambridge, is one of the world's leading experts on fatherhood. For the past five decades he has specialised in the study of children's social and emotional development, particularly in their first years of life, and has concluded that there is no reason fathers cannot be as nurturing, caring and involved as mothers. He has given testimony in court in support of gay fathers and lesbian mothers having custody of children. He also believes in the importance of fathers having prolonged one-on-one time with their babies so they can learn to parent in their own ways, form unique bonds, feel the weight of primary responsibility and, crucially, prove to themselves that they are capable of looking after their child independently.

In the immediate post-war period, academics researching babies' development focused almost entirely on their relationships with mothers. This was most clearly seen in the 1950s with the emergence of British psychiatrist John Bowlby's hugely influential attachment theory. Bowlby argued that babies were genetically programmed to seek and form an attachment to their mother and that separation from mothers had devastating effects on their development. His views on fathers' roles in families were typical of the time, focusing on them as breadwinners and emotional supports for the mother so that she could parent,[12] with little or no attention given to the possibility that fathers might also affect their children's development directly, through loving and caring for them, talking to them and educating them – or even, in worst-case scenarios, by maltreating them. Lamb wanted to change this, writing in 1975 that fathers had been the 'forgotten contributors to child development'.[13]

Searches of studies that Lamb has authored or co-authored show repeated conclusions that sex or gender is not key to parenting. In 2012, he had a paper published which assessed hundreds of scientific studies into childhood wellbeing and adjustment over the previous four decades. He wrote that it had been well established that both men and women had the capacity to be good parents and that the key was men actively caring for their children. 'Nothing about a person's sex determines the capacity to be a good parent,' he wrote. 'Nor is there evidence that children *need* relationships with parents of both sexes in order to develop normally.'[14] He wrote that it was clear that 'mothers and fathers influence children's development in the same (non-gendered) ways – promoting psychological adjustment when they are caring, loving, engaged and authoritative.'[15]

Lamb also wrote that there was a substantial and growing body of research on parents who had chosen to raise biologically unrelated children (like me!) and that these papers 'consistently show that these children tend to be as well-adjusted, on average, as children raised by their biological parents, and that such parents are at least as competent as parents raising their biological children.'[16]

A decade later and the evidence is still building. Among Lamb's most recent studies was one published in January 2022 that he co-authored with academics from universities in Swansea, Amsterdam, Groningen and Paris, examining similarities and differences in the sensitivity of parents to their first-born children. The parents were from Britain, the Netherlands and France and included those who were gay, lesbian and heterosexual. Among the parents, 147 were defined as primary caregivers, with 102 mothers and 45 fathers fulfilling these roles. All of the children assessed were conceived through fertility treatment and they were on average four months old. The parents were video recorded at home while they looked after their children – playing with them, feeding them, bathing them and changing their nappies. The authors wrote: 'Our findings do not support presumptions that mothers are more capable of providing better quality care than fathers.'[17]

I spoke to Lamb on video while he was at his home on the east coast of the US. After I explained the premise of my book, he said that he agreed absolutely that fathers could be parents with equal responsibility, from the moment their children were newborn babies:

> I have been arguing for 50 years or so that there is no evidence that males and females differ in their capacity to parent children. At the time that a baby is born, most new mothers and fathers are pretty clueless. We live in a world where most of us have relatively little opportunity to participate in looking after children – some may have some experience babysitting, but even that is quite a constrained experience. The reality is that when you face this newborn baby both new mothers

and fathers are thinking 'holy shit'. The great thing is that babies are great teachers. Their signals are very clear. You do it right and they go back to sleep, or snuggle, or they calm down, and if they are a little bit older they give you a smile. And if you do it wrong, they grumble at you, and if you keep doing it wrong, they will grumble even more loudly. And so basically those skills are all learned on the job.

Given that women and men have the same potential to look after children successfully, why is it that women are so often assumed to be more naturally suited to the skills, and why do they usually do more than fathers domestically? Biology is important as a starting point, with mothers not only automatically getting the hormonal head start with boosts of bonding hormones from pregnancy and childbirth, but also taking the time off work immediately after having a baby partly because of physical recovery and the possibility of breastfeeding. There are also social, political and economic reasons, including policies such as parental leave and society's expectations of what women should be doing and should be good at, which combine to mean women are the ones who almost always spend more time with their babies in the weeks and months after birth. Lamb said the result was that, while men and women usually begin parenthood equally clueless, the mother has more direct time with the baby after birth to learn the parenting skills quicker, reinforcing the idea that parenting is women's work.

'There is this basic expectation either that mothers should know it, that they naturally know it, or that they will naturally learn it. And there aren't the same expectations that apply to men,' Lamb said. 'This creates a web of factors that guide parents into a division of labour, channelling mothers into doing more at home, and slowly becoming more skilful with their children.'

I asked Lamb about the theory that it was important for fathers to take time off work and be on parental leave for a period by themselves, as the primary caregiver. He said:

That is absolutely right. It is so easy to defer and for a lack of self-confidence to allow you to hand over responsibility for decision making and so on. You need to be the one who is there to manage it and to learn the critical lesson – that you can. And you may be doing it differently. Your partner may have mashed the peas with a fork, and you put them in the blender and, you know what, it goes just fine either way. The kid likes it both ways and doing it in the blender becomes your thing. That is so critically important to what I see as the essence of parenthood – feeling that this is a really special thing that we've got, that's unique to us. That's really critical for the child too, to have different relationships to learn that adults are different and do things differently. One does a nappy change really quickly with cold wipes and the other one is very gentle. All of those things are part of forming the essence of a relationship. That is critical for the child's long-range development.

He said that, as a bonus, taking time off work from when a child was about six months old – when dads on shared parental leave tend to take their portion – was an incredibly rewarding time to be a primary caregiver. 'Between six and 12 months, yes, it is tiring, but it is also so rewarding. Every day it is a new child and a new challenge. You see their little minds whirring away. It is magical.'

Many fathers bond with their children at home through physical play. Chucking them in the air and catching them while they shriek. Rolling around on the floor together. Tickling them. Lying on the ground and lifting them up in reps, ten at a time. This is not true of all fathers and many mothers do this as well, but lots of people will recognise this from their own families. I do it, and it has been a real source of bonding between me and Solly.

On days that Robin picks him up from nursery and I am working from home, they will come inside, and I will crouch down low, waiting for Solly to run to me, so I can catch him and then roll around with him on the floor, cuddling him and shouting, 'My Solly Bolly!'

As I mentioned earlier in the book, Robin has cerebral palsy, which is related to him being born prematurely and having a stroke when he was a few days old. It means he is weaker on one side of his body, walks with a slight limp and can struggle with balance. Robin's disability is relatively mild, and people often do not notice, or just assume he has had a sports injury, but he can find physical activities challenging. Still, he has naturally developed his own versions of rough-and-tumble play, wrestling with Solly on the sofa and nuzzling his neck until they are both giggling uncontrollably.

Machin discussed this kind of play at length in her book, *The Life of Dad*. While it may not help to clear the growing piles of laundry, or to feed a hungry toddler, this type of interaction has benefits for children's development – so I think it is useful to consider it as one of the ways parents uniquely interact with their children at home.

Academics argue about the reason men seem to spend more of their time with their children playing in this way. Is it due to biology or society? Is it because when you see your child less, say because you work more, you find ways to get quick boosts of bonding, and physical play is a really good way of doing this? Machin said that while men and women can adapt to different styles of parenting, the fathers she has studied tended to play with their children in this rough way more than the mothers did:

If you look at fathers, they tend to be the one who pushes the child physically. It is still very nurturing but there is also an element of challenge. They tend to be much more relaxed about the child climbing to the top of the tree – yeah you can do that, now let's push you a little further. With the dads who I have studied, when the kid is starting to do things, like crawling, they are always looking for the next thing. They will say, 'I am trying to get him to walk now.' It is always pushing. And it is cross-cultural. If you look at any society, it is not just a Western thing – that seems to be what dads do. This is crucial. It helps children go out into the world and explore, build relationships and deal with life's challenges.

Machin said the most recent data seemed to show that fathers are often the key parent when it comes to underpinning their child's mental health in adolescence and onwards,[18] adding: 'It is about mental resilience and being able to deal with life's knocks and challenges and failures.' However, Machin stressed that just as men could be as nurturing as women, there was no reason at all that women could not fulfil this physical role with their children if they wanted to:

What is amazing about the human brain is that it changes and adapts. When people say there is a female brain and a male brain, well there isn't actually. It is not set; it may be moulded through experience. It is so important that our brains are open to changing to make sure that the baby receives what it needs, regardless of who you are.

Lamb was among the scientists who first studied rough-and-tumble play between parents and their children in the 1970s. A key finding was that a greater proportion of the time that fathers spent interacting with their children was in the form of play than was true for mothers, and that when they played it tended to be this more physically stimulating kind of rough-and-tumble play.[19] When we spoke, Lamb wanted to be clear about the detail of these findings.

Firstly, while this kind of play was more characteristic of father-child relationships, actually babies played more with their mothers than their fathers because they spent so much more time with their mothers. In other words, dads spent a greater proportion of the limited time they had with their children playing. In their short windows of time after and before work, they were more playful. But mothers, who were with their children so much more, played with their children more than fathers did in total – and they also did this more physical type of play more than fathers did. He said:

> The second misunderstanding, which perhaps I made as well initially, was people assumed that because the fathers we studied did it more, that they needed to do it more, that it was a necessary part of father-child play and that it was what made fathers important. There has never been any evidence that this is what is important about father-infant interaction.

Lamb said fathers who do not feel comfortable with this kind of play should not feel like they have to do it – and mothers should absolutely do it if it comes naturally to them:

> In my opinion, it does not matter whether the dad is, or is not, somebody who does that with their child. What is important is that they do things together, that what they do together is emotionally rewarding to both of them and that it be authentic. If you are an active, sporty dad, yes, you should interact with the child this way. But if you are not a guy like that then do things that really matter to you. Rough-and-

tumble play is not essential for the child – it does have value and can work well – but you can be a great father without it.

I immediately thought of Robin. Sometimes he can feel like he is missing out on stereotypical dad play with Solly. But they have so many other ways in which they bond. Robin is an author and creative play comes much more naturally to him than it does to most other people. He makes Solly laugh hysterically while reading him stories, doing different voices and actions.

When I first met Robin, one of the many things about him that I fell in love with was how he made any situation fun. Being at an airport together became just as exciting as landing in a new, exotic country for a holiday. He is obsessed with finding very vague ridiculous lookalikes in public and a game that involves shouting out names at people in case you fluke it, guess the right one and they turn around. I often find Robin and Solly playing some absurd game that I never would have thought of.

At a playground recently, Robin was pushing Solly on a swing and Solly started mooing like a cow, first loudly and then very quietly. I came closer. Robin had been giving him instructions. What does a loud cow say? 'MOOOOOOOOOO,' Solly replied. What does a quiet cow say? 'Mooooo,' Solly whispered. A three-year-old girl on the next swing and her mother soon joined in. What does a loud duck say? 'QUAAACKKKKK,' the kids screamed. What does a quiet duck say? 'Quaaacckkk,' they whispered.

At home, they have a game when Solly is in the bath involving a dinosaur and a lot of splashing. In front of the TV, Solly only really watches cartoons with me but sits with Robin to share his love for old musicals. *Annie*, *Mary Poppins* and *The Sound of Music* are their current favourites. Robin is very clever – straight A stars, first from Cambridge clever – but also totally unintimidating and the most lovely, warm presence to be around. He is the opposite of pretentious.

'You would never know he is such a genius,' my brother, Josh, once said about him, which he meant as a compliment.

Robin has an instinctive way of slightly adapting his behaviour and conversation depending on who he is around, making them feel comfortable and at ease. Whether through genes or by nurture, Solly also already has an effortless way of bonding with people. Adults and other children seem to fall in love with him almost everywhere we go. It would be ridiculous for Robin to spend his time with Solly forcing himself to try to play rugby, go rock climbing or to balance him on his shoulders. That is not him. Robin is authentically himself as a father.

What Lamb said about one-on-one time with children also made me think of my own parents. I grew up as the third of four children in a loud, busy house in an Orthodox Jewish community in north west London. While I am not religious now, my parents, Esther and Simon, still are. This may seem to some like a contradiction, but they are also among the most open-minded, fun, socially liberal people that I know.

Growing up, they had typical parenting roles. My dad worked long hours and was the breadwinner, and my mum mostly looked after us, while doing part-time teaching, specialising in educating teenagers about the Holocaust. When I think back to my relationship with my father as a child, the one-on-one moments are the ones that I remember most clearly.

As religious Jews, we kept the Sabbath. For 25 hours between an hour before sundown on Fridays and when there were three stars visible in the dark sky on Saturdays we did not drive, use telephones or watch TV (apart from if it was the FA Cup Final, or the first night of a new series of *Big Brother* – don't tell the rabbi). This meant that while my dad was not around until late on weekdays, we would have his undivided attention at weekends.

We played an anagram game together with Scrabble pieces after Friday night dinners and walked to and from synagogue together on Saturday mornings, me stretching my legs to try to keep up with his long strides. We all talked and fought over grand meals that my mum cooked for two days before, and then my dad cleared away. After the Sabbath, my dad would watch me play football on Sunday mornings. We would get Chinese takeaway on a Sunday evening. Then he would be off again.

The moments with my mum that come back are skimming the foam and chocolate off her cappuccinos when we went out to cafés and staying up late on Thursday nights to join her on the sofa watching back-to-back episodes of *Friends* and *ER*. She did most of the domestic work, and he did most of the professional work. They both seemed happy with that arrangement, and that was their choice – a fair one for them, typical of the time. But I find it hard to relate to wanting to have either one of these distinct roles, rather than doing a mix of both.

I wonder how my parents would split the responsibilities if they were a couple in their twenties now. My mum was much more academic than my dad when they were younger. She got top grades at school and university, while he came into his own at work, a few years later. If they were young adults now, would she be as content to give up working full-time after having children? Would they be able to survive mostly on one income, while he is still establishing himself in his career? Would she keep working but also doing much more than her share at home, because that is what women tend to do now? Would they be able to buy a house, like they did? Would my dad split parental leave and do more domestically? Would they still have had four children?

Times have changed dramatically since my parents became parents just over 40 years ago. But you would not know that, judging by the latest package that Robin and I have received in the post.

At the time of writing, Solly is just over two years old. While we think he is not quite ready for potty training, Robin bought a popular book that is well recommended online so we could start planning how we want to do it. In a question-and-answer section of the book, the author offered advice to a mother who asked about whether she should start potty training her toddler on holiday because she had a newborn baby as well and, while off work, her husband would be around more to help. The author replied that she would recommend doing it at home and at the weekend, so the husband could take care of the baby while she focused on potty training. The author also suggested that the father have a trial run of caring for the baby alone beforehand so she would not be interrupted.

I generally try not to be someone who is permanently offended. But I had lots of questions. How can a modern-day father of two need a trial run to look after his second baby by himself? Is the author assuming that most women never work professionally? Why is it the mother's responsibility to make sure he knows how to do this? Why assume the dad will not be doing any of the potty training? The mother may well be on maternity leave, with the dad working full-time, but still, why is he only expected to do anything at home at the weekend? Why does the mother put up with this? How does a parenting expert, who must have seen so many families in her career, still have such low expectations of fathers?

This might seem like an extreme example, but even now in families with two working parents who want to split the workload equally, mothers still seem to be the ones who are much more likely to be burdened with more of the mental load of parenting.

I see it in my female friends' eyes. They carry it with them, when they are at work, when they are out for dinner with friends, whenever they are away. The stresses of parenting occupy a larger space somewhere in their brains compared to their husbands. Hopefully most fathers do not need trial runs to look after their own babies. But they are still often given instructions by their partners for when they are on their own with the children. This may be a WhatsApp message with a schedule of times for naps, meals or after-school activities. It may be a reminder of where the socks are, what food the children should eat, or how to make up a bottle at the right temperature.

At home, Robin and I have fallen into a pattern of me doing slightly more of the hands-on chores – the laundry, the cleaning, washing-up and taking the bins out – which is partly related to Robin's disability and things such as folding sheets being more of a struggle for him. To compensate, Robin does almost all of the planning, making sure we have enough nappies, wipes and cleaning products and that Solly's weekends are full of activities. We both get involved with the bills, but Robin is more on top of our accounts than I am. Traditionally, many dads take on more of the mental load for family finances – this has come up repeatedly in my discussions with friends about equal parenting and should, absolutely, be in the mix when considering the split of domestic responsibilities.

Robin and I have also started writing an email once a week to set out who will be at home early enough in the coming workdays to pick Solly up from nursery, to try to keep this split as equally as possible. It is not always seamless – we still have rows about things like the washing-up and who is doing more bedtimes – but we have settled on a division of domestic responsibilities that, generally, works for us.

We can also see how the early responsibilities that we took on at home after Solly was born have shaped us as fathers. Two years on, I still tend to be the one who obsesses over when Solly is going to nap during the day and how long the nap should be to ensure his nights are not affected. But I rarely worry about food. Robin does the online food shops and plans most of Solly's meals. When we go out for a picnic, Robin and Solly will prepare the sandwiches together, with Solly standing on a stool and spreading butter all over the counter and his face. Of course, Robin and I both do a bit of everything – Solly does not starve when Robin is away – but, in general, we find ourselves deferring to each other in these areas.

The way we split responsibilities was not intentional. When Solly was born, we would have said that we wanted to do it all equally. As it turns out, for us, equal parenting has not been about doing half of everything. It has been about taking the lead in different areas, or on different days depending on work commitments, so that overall the weight of responsibility feels shared.

CHAPTER SEVEN

SORRY, IT'S JUST FOR MUMS

Why Dads Need to Be Seen at Baby Appointments

When Solly was 11 months old, I got a phone call while waiting in a socially distanced queue outside a café.

'Hi, is this Rachel?' the woman on the other end of the line asked. 'I am calling to organise your son's one-year health check.'

By this point, Robin and I were used to the UK's health system not being able to cope with the realities of surrogacy. We had also recently moved home and expected that we might have to explain to our new local health visiting team how Solly was born and that his parents were me and Robin, rather than Rachel, his surrogate, and her husband, James. I did this as quickly as I could while approaching the barista at the café's window and mouthing: 'Skinny cappuccino, ah yes semi is fine, oh go on with chocolate on top.'

The health visitor was apologetic and said she would change the records on her system. She asked whether she should put down my name and number, or Robin's details. When I requested that she list both of us, she had to apologise again.

'I'm really sorry, I actually can't,' she said. 'We usually just have the mother's details. It only asks for one.'

Over and over again since Solly's birth, we have found that UK health service systems only usually list a mother as the person responsible for a child. This is why it is usually the mother who gets all of the medical calls about baby check-ups. The idea that there would be two parents listed as potential contacts has repeatedly stumped health staff when we have arrived for appointments for Solly. The mother is not here? There is no mother? What is his NHS number? You want a dad listed? You want two dads listed? Computer says no.

One of the many times this has happened was at a hospital Accident & Emergency reception desk after our most terrifying (and humiliating) evening as fathers. Solly was 18 months old and had a bad chest infection. He was off nursery, and on the Friday he woke up from his afternoon nap wheezing. He was groggy and his whole stomach was sucking in and out with every breath. Robin and I got him into the car and drove to the nearest hospital.

At the reception, a tired man took Solly's name and NHS number and then said, 'Rachel?' without looking up. I calmly said no, I was his dad, and when I explained the wheezing and Solly's age, we got seen quickly without many more questions. We were given an inhaler with a mouthpiece to give to Solly, but he refused to take it, so we had to restrain him while he screamed and fought and two nurses got ten puffs into his mouth. It was horrible. We did the same 20 minutes later and at regular intervals after that.

After an hour or so, his breathing got much better. We stayed in for a few hours, so Solly could be observed. It was during the pandemic, so Robin and I were only allowed to be inside the ward one at a time, while the other waited in the car.

After a couple of hours, the drugs made Solly hyperactive – something the doctor warned might happen – which was actually quite funny and a relief after the grogginess. He ran into other patients' bays by sprinting straight into the thin privacy curtains that hid them and then disappeared inside, before running back out with his arms up. I chased after him, apologising as I went, then gave up and watched as he pushed the hospital unit's wheelie bins around and squealed in delight. Eventually, a doctor said we could go home but gave us a plan involving giving Solly the inhaler repeatedly over the next few days. We had to wake him up every four hours during the night to do this and were under strict instructions to come back to hospital if we were worried that Solly's breathing was getting worse again.

The four-hourly inhaler sessions during the nights were tough. By the time one of us went to get Solly from his room, he would be breathing heavily again but, after waking him, he refused to take the inhaler. So I would have to pin him down on our bed while Robin quickly got the mask over his mouth and did the puffs. Solly was distraught, but then his breathing would calm again and he would go back to sleep.

On the Sunday evening, I checked on Solly as he slept in his room before Robin and I went to bed, and he was very hot. Robin got the Calpol and passed me the syringe as I gently woke Solly up. I tried to give him the medicine, but he started coughing and then threw up, a lovely purple mess – blueberries at dinner – all over me, him and the room. I carried Solly to our bed and started taking off his sleeping bag and then the white vest he was wearing underneath. On his chest, there was a large mark, like a dark rash. I looked at it and stretched some of the skin to see if it would blanch – a test to rule out possible meningitis – but it stayed dark. Robin and I both freaked out. Robin called the ambulance while I held Solly and tried to cool him down. The panic was rising fast, and I held Solly on the bed, hoping not to faint, trying to give him some water.

The ambulance arrived quickly, within 15 minutes. By this time we had gone downstairs and put on *Little Baby Bum*, a series of cartoons and songs on Netflix. Solly was calm and bobbing his dummy in his mouth, but the rash was still there, and he had a high fever.

The paramedics were lovely but confused. 'Does the rash look like it's getting smaller?' one asked. 'I wouldn't expect the rash to be that colour.'

I started to panic again. Could it be a bruise? Had I been restraining him too tightly when we had been giving him the inhaler? Were they going to think we had hurt him?

The paramedic had an idea. 'Can you get a wet wipe?' he asked. Robin got one, passed it to me and I wiped the rash right off Solly's body. Yes, we had called an ambulance because Solly had been sick and a bit of purple vomit had got on his tummy.

The relief was like nothing I have felt before. Like the lightest breeze, or a dam breaking. I found myself crying and saying, 'I'm so sorry – we're such idiots.' Not our finest hour of parenting.

The paramedics left and told us to go to hospital in our own time to get Solly properly checked out, but they were not particularly worried or offering to waste any more of their time by taking us.

After driving to the hospital, still a bit concerned about Solly's temperature, we walked in, and the night shift receptionist took his NHS number. 'Are you… Rachel?' he asked. After a very long and emotional rant – which the receptionist dealt with very patiently – he said he would do his best to try to get the record changed. Of course, we all knew he was not going to be able to do that, but it was kind of him to say he would try.

The rest of our experience was fine thankfully – Solly had medicine, his temperature went down, we were discharged, and, at the time of writing, he has never again wheezed like that. I am sure his NHS record remains the same though. Even when a child has two fathers who dedicate themselves to his care, the health service's computer systems function on the basis that this should only be a woman's job.

Solly is two years old, and we have already seen this assumption play out repeatedly in different ways. At every one of his routine vaccine appointments as a baby, health staff were surprised to see us – not usually because we were gay dads, or dads through surrogacy, but because a man was present at all. The comments were not typically negative. In fact, Robin and I got used to being complimented for doing the most basic parenting, with nurses repeatedly greeting us with variations of 'It is so great you're here – we never see dads!' At one appointment the nurse said: 'Oh, wow, a dad! You'll be stronger than mums so better at holding him down!' A pharmacist once told me it was wonderful that I was so hands-on and picking up the medicine for my child.

The comments are well meaning but also ridiculous. No mother would be praised for bothering to get her child vaccinated against a deadly disease. At Solly's BCG injection, when he was 11 weeks old, I was asked where his mother was and when I explained how he was born, the nurse challenged me: 'What do you mean he doesn't have a mum? Is she not in contact with him anymore?'

Was she accusing me of kidnapping my son? I explained that he had two fathers but also an egg donor and a surrogate. Which would she like to know more about? Was she worried about inherited conditions from the egg donor or about Rachel and how she was doing after the birth?

The nurse seemed confused by my questions and moved on. I may be wrong, but it felt like she was not quizzing me for any medical reason; she just found the situation bizarre and fancied probing.

The previous chapter looked at fathers' domestic responsibilities. But if sexual equality is genuinely desired, we also need fundamental changes outside of the home. Fathers are now doing much more childcare than their fathers or grandfathers did, but institutions still expect this to be, primarily, a woman's job. Women cannot ever achieve equality in the workplace if fathers are seen as a rare and wonderful thing at their own children's doctor appointments, at children's play groups or at the school gates.

While researching for this book, I read and heard repeated stories from fathers and mothers about how they had been treated very differently while doing the same basic things with their children, and about the various hurdles that made trying to parent equally when outside of the home more difficult than it should be. A theme that came up repeatedly was how outdated attitudes and systems can be within national health systems, and how this reinforces ideas about women having to take on the majority of responsibility for parenting, even when they want to share this with a partner.

Our friends Deborah and Paul, a married couple with two daughters, shared parental leave. Paul was off work when their first daughter, Penny, was due to have her ten-month health check. Deborah got the call and said Paul was on leave so would bring Penny. The health visitor was surprised and asked her to come as well. When Deborah said she could arrange to come at another time if she also needed to be seen, the health visitor was insistent. Deborah said:

> In the end we both went. We had to weigh her so had to take her nappy off, and Paul did it. They could not believe it. They were asking questions about development and weaning, and they could not understand how Paul knew all the answers. Pincer grip. Schedules. Naps. They were shocked. I said I was back at work and Paul was on leave, and it was like it did not compute. The whole thing was ridiculous.

During a previous appointment, when Deborah was on leave, she told the health visitor she was going back to work after six months. 'The health visitor was so judgy,' Deborah said. 'She said, "Okay so when you go back, are you going to go part-time?" I was like, sorry?' There is not much hope for shared parental leave in the UK if medical staff treat you with suspicion and judgment for taking it.

During my interviews with Catherine Cho, the author of *Inferno: A Memoir of Motherhood and Madness*,[1] and Joeli Brearley, the founder of the charity Pregnant Then Screwed, they also spoke about their frustrations during medical appointments for their children. Cho had postpartum psychosis after the birth of her son, Cato, and her husband, James, did all of the hands-on care. She said:

> It's a societal thing. The first two years of Cato's life I was pretty useless at appointments, in that I didn't know anything about his vaccinations or medical history. He had some medical issues at the time and every time he went to the hospital they would look at me and ask me the questions. 'Oh, Mum, so when was the last time he was admitted?' James always had to chime in. It frustrated me. Why am I supposedly the fount of all knowledge?

Brearley said: 'When we had hospital appointments for the children, if Tom [her husband] would go, the first thing they would say to him is "Where is their mum?" but they never said to me "Where is their dad?"'

Sam Draper, a former teacher turned stay-at-home father of two, was among 20 fathers who shared their experiences for a book titled *Dad* in 2021. He described taking shared parental leave and having primary responsibility for his children, while his wife went back to work. Still, health staff ignored him at appointments. He wrote that the expectation seemed to be that he would always be a 'secondary player' in parenting, no matter what proportion of it he actually did. 'Who do doctors, midwives and health workers direct their questions to about the welfare of our child?' he asked rhetorically.[2]

The Fatherhood Institute is a charity and the UK's primary think tank focusing on men's involvement in caring for their children. It is run by a team of men and women who are all parents. Jeremy

Davies, its spokesman, said the NHS has failed to keep up with the way families have changed over the past 50 years:

> The increase in the amounts of hands-on caregiving that dads do has been enormous. They are spending much more time directly caring for their very young children and the proportion of dads doing drop-offs and pick-ups at schools has increased a lot. Nobody is making men turn up for the birth of their children, but they do in massive numbers now. That is a cultural phenomenon. My dad wasn't there when I was born and nobody made me go to my son's birth, but I went. You would have to explain yourself very well, wouldn't you, if you didn't turn up at your child's birth these days. All of this has happened just because that is what people have done, not because of government policy. I became a dad two decades before you and I would love to say that the way services see fathers has improved in that time, but it barely has.

In June 2022, the Fatherhood Institute released a report titled *Bringing Baby Home*, which assessed almost 800 pieces of research into fatherhood in the first year of children's lives.[3] The report, funded by the Nuffield Foundation, a charity aiming to improve social wellbeing, found that 'NHS maternity, health visiting and other family services are failing babies by ignoring their fathers during the first postnatal year'.[4] The charity behind the report stated that even though there is clear evidence that fathers' physical and mental health impact on babies' future health and wellbeing, NHS systems are still not set up to engage with and support new fathers, who are routinely 'treated as visitors rather than central members of a new family'.[5]

One finding of the report felt particularly personal to us. It confirmed that 'health records for babies in the UK only allow the inclusion of one adult (the mother)'.[6] Aha, I thought, while reading it. That is why mothers always say they get the medical calls. And that is why Rachel is still linked to Solly's records. Despite our society supposedly accepting families with gay male parents – and Rachel going through a legal process to transfer legal parental responsibility to us – the health system still cannot cope with the idea that a primary parent could be a man. But how can it be in Solly's, or Rachel's, best interests for his health records to ignore the law and list her as the person responsible for his welfare? And how can it be in anyone's best interests for the default to be that fathers are not a central part of the family after children are born? The Fatherhood Institute's report found that fathers in the UK receive little or no support to develop their caregiving skills, to keep babies safe or to help them understand child development. They are also not screened for stress, anxiety or depression after the birth of their children, even though this can have a profound effect on the mother and the whole family.[7]

Health systems have failed to keep up with how mothers' and fathers' roles are evolving in various countries, including those typically cited as progressive when it comes to gender equality.

In 2014, academics published a global review of how parenting programmes included or ignored fathers, assessing evidence from countries including the UK, the US, Australia, Finland, Sweden, Brazil, Canada, Germany, the Netherlands, New Zealand, Israel, Jordan, China and various others. The researchers considered details such as whether fathers were explicitly invited to appointments, whether practitioners were ready and skilled to work with co-parents as well as mothers, and whether the timing and the location of appointments appeared to be deterrents to both parents attending. They found that fathers were 'marginal to the bulk of parenting interventions' and concluded that health professionals should engage 'unequivocally with co-parents – rather than include just mothers and explicitly or implicitly marginalize fathers'.[8]

In Sweden, despite a reputation for being forward-thinking on gender equality and relatively high rates of fathers taking extended parental leave, a 2016 literature review of 62 relevant studies found that they often felt excluded and ignored at perinatal appointments. 'Expectant and new fathers felt torn between what society expected from them as an equal parent and the messages they received from the Swedish child health field,' the author wrote.[9] Similarly, in Norway, a study in 2021 reported that, for fathers, 'a feeling of being left out and excluded is predominant'.[10]

When I spoke to Davies, from the Fatherhood Institute, he said that health professionals were missing key opportunities to encourage fathers to have greater involvement in their children's lives, from as early as the midwife appointments during pregnancy. Typically, midwives ask only very basic questions about fathers during these appointments, such as what their names are and about family histories of genetic illnesses. The questions are often posed to the mother, even if the father is also in the room. Davies said:

Of course the focus of antenatal appointments should be predominantly on making sure the mother and baby are okay. But checking in with the father as well, particularly if he is in the room, does not take long. At the moment, opportunities are missed to find out about him, to help him make sense of his new role, to help him to be a good partner to the mother and to do a good job as a father.

Fathers and other partners in Britain have a legal right to time off work to attend up to two antenatal appointments[11] and the percentage of men who do so appears to be very high. Even though fathers are not usually explicitly invited to these appointments, studies suggest at least three in four expectant fathers go to at least one. One survey of more than 1,000 dads by the Fatherhood

Institute in 2018 found that 94 per cent had attended at least one routine antenatal appointment.[12] Davies said:

> Culturally that has just happened. The dad is in the room and that is without anybody actively inviting him. But they are routinely just ignored. It is as if the reality of many people's lives – that this is happening with a man in the same house, and one with a unique relationship to that baby and the mother – it is as if that doesn't exist or cannot be acknowledged.

Many parents describe similar experiences of the father being all but ignored during the births of their children and in the hours afterwards. Davies said those who spoke to the Fatherhood Institute told of being treated like an 'unwanted distraction' at hospital, even though their partners wanted their support and help with their babies. He said that mothers and babies absolutely should be, by far, the main focus of maternity care, but that a few minutes of professional interaction with a dad before discharging the family home could make a world of difference.

As an example, Davies described his experience 22 years previously when his son was born at a midwife-led unit in rural England:

> The midwife took me to one side and spent no more than three minutes showing me how to bathe my son. It was a really important and useful skill to have – how to hold him and bathe him safely. It made me feel like a valid part of the picture. It gave me a skill that I could take responsibility for and, when we went home, I became the one who bathed him. That was the first and literally only time in my son's entire life so far where a taxpayer-funded professional has ever met me eye to eye and taken me seriously as a parent. How ridiculous

is that? It took three minutes and had a specific impact on what I then did as a father.

Davies said this was not about taking any focus away from mothers or babies in hospitals:

In fact, if you care about children and women, you should care about the father for all sorts of reasons. The negative ones might be that midwives and doctors see he is an awful, violent, person, in which case they should want to know about that and deal with it. But we have this suspicion of men in society and overestimate how many men are like this. In the vast majority of cases, he just wants to be there and to help. There are huge positives to be gained from acknowledging him, supporting him, helping him make sense of what is a huge life event and getting him on the road to being a really good dad. Because if he gets good at that, the child will do better, the mother will do better and have more choices in shaping her life after having a child.

I mentioned to Davies how Robin and I had suspected that only mothers are usually listed on their children's NHS records. By coincidence, just a few hours before our interview, he had been speaking to a researcher about the same issue. He said they had discovered that in some areas mothers could request that their partners' details are added but that it involves extra paperwork, and they are rarely told they can do this.

'The NHS does not link father's records with their children, and we are a million miles away from achieving that,' he said. 'It is an example of one of the very basic but very important ways in which fathers get treated differently. It sets up and reinforces this idea that the responsibility for children is all down to the mother.'

The way health services ignore fathers' roles in families can, in some cases, have severe consequences. There is increasing awareness about postnatal depression in mothers. While cases are still missed and there is more that can be done to help mothers find help, health visitors look out for early signs so they can refer women to other services. There is also growing evidence that men get postnatal depression, with studies suggesting that this affects somewhere between two per cent and 25 per cent of new fathers.[13] Men are much less likely to get mental health support if they need this after their children are born. This is clearly bad for these dads themselves, but also for their partners and children.

Elliott Rae is an author, campaigner for equal parenting and the founder of MusicFootballFatherhood.com, a parenting and lifestyle platform for men. He also put together the collection of stories for the book *Dad*, mentioned earlier in the chapter. He and his wife have a daughter, aged six at the time of writing. Her birth was traumatic. Rae's wife was quickly referred for help in dealing with the experience, while his post-traumatic stress disorder (PTSD) was missed.

In the weeks before the birth, Rae and his wife were told she had tested positive for group B streptococcus, a common bacterium, which, in rare cases, can cause serious risks to the baby if passed on during childbirth. About one in 19 babies that are infected die, and, of those who survive, one in 14 will have a long-term disability. It was recommended that Rae's wife should have antibiotics during labour to significantly reduce the chance of this happening. The antibiotics did not work properly, and their baby caught the infection.

'When she came out, she was lifeless, she wasn't breathing, she was grey,' Rae said. 'On one side of the room she was being resuscitated, they were doing CPR, and trying to suck fluid out of her airways, and next to me, my wife was also bleeding loads and the doctor was talking about blood transfusions.'

Rae felt himself leaving his body. He was next to his wife, trying to support her, but felt numb and like he was not really there, watching the scene from above. His daughter was resuscitated and connected to antibiotics. He found himself walking after her, towards the neonatal intensive care unit. He tried to call his mum but could not get through. 'A nurse looked at me, she looked at me in the eye and was so assertive, and she said, "You need to come back here – get back in the room",' he said.

Rae got through the next two weeks with his wife, both focusing on each day and not yet able to dwell too much on what had happened while their baby was in the intensive care unit. For the first few nights, Rae was sent home alone while his wife recovered on a postnatal ward, before a room became available for them to share. It was October, and his memories are of their home being cold, quiet, dark and it feeling 'really, really horrible'. After two weeks, they were then given the good news that they could go home, but within hours a bump emerged on the baby's head and she was rushed for an MRI test.

'All we wanted to do was go home, and then we had that news and it all came out,' Rae said. 'We just cried, basically, all night, and prayed. I had no energy, no strength. I was worried, knackered, I didn't know what was going on.' The tests came back fine, and they were allowed to go home two days later. Their daughter was one of the lucky babies who survived the infection at birth and made a quick, full recovery.

Rae had to go back to work immediately after they were released from hospital as his paternity leave entitlement was finished. He had previously always been confident at work and calm in crises, describing himself as an extrovert, but he became increasingly panicked. When his turn came to speak in meetings, he would freeze, terrified of talking out loud, even when he knew he had crucial information that needed to be shared. He had never considered himself a particularly emotional person, but he found himself crying on the train home from work. At night flashbacks stopped him sleeping. He said:

> I was reliving the birth, over and over again. It was difficult to process what had happened and why it had happened, whether I could have done anything differently. And the anxiety. I was going to work, and my team would say hello and I couldn't even say hello back, I would just mumble. It was like my brain and mouth weren't connected.

Rae said the anxiety spiralled. He could not understand why he did not feel like himself and was terrified he would never feel normal again.

In the days after they were discharged from hospital, Rae's wife was referred for counselling. At the time, he did not think he needed any help and was not asked. 'My wife had midwife visits and they were asking how she was coping,' he said. 'She was diagnosed with postnatal anxiety and had counselling through the NHS, because she was referred. It all happened as part of the process, which was good.' When he was at appointments, he was not asked how he was feeling and did not speak up. He said:

> When you are at an appointment about your baby's health, it is very unlikely that a man is just going to come out with, 'hey, guys, just so you know, I can't speak'. I massively felt that as a man I had to be strong. Men are much less likely to go and seek help and be forthcoming about the help that we need. It is all about the ideas that you are a man, and you should not need it. You should not show weakness.

In the months after becoming a father, Rae started writing his blog and took time off work. When his daughter was ten months old, a woman who ran another parenting platform arranged a meeting with him. She asked him about the birth of his daughter, and he could not get through the story. By luck, she knew a birth trauma specialist, and he arranged private counselling, which enabled him to process what had happened and to recover. Rae's experience shows just how easily mental health issues can be missed in men, generally but also after becoming fathers. He said:

> I hope people know I am not coming to this from a place of men's rights activism. I am coming from a place that this is better for everyone. For me, gender equality and women's rights are at the forefront of what we do. This is not about taking away from women. If we support dads, we support mums better.

Without coordinated national or international government plans for public services to catch up with how fathers' roles are changing, there are some local programmes that offer a glimpse of what wider change could look like.

One example is the Future Dads Programme, which is run at some hospitals and community venues in London, and online. It is a one-day course on a weekend that focuses on practical skills, such as how to hold, feed, bath, change and bond with a baby. It also encourages expectant fathers to engage with their partner's pregnancy and to think about why fathers are important and what kind of dad they want to be. The programme, which is designed by Future Men, a charity, and has been running for just over a decade, is advertised to expectant mothers and fathers in the leaflets they get from midwives and on posters in waiting rooms before antenatal appointments. The charity also approaches people in the local communities where it works.

Owen Thomas, managing director and head of programmes for Future Men, said the charity wanted to challenge men's most basic assumptions about what they could and could not do as fathers. While men often go to regular antenatal classes, they usually come in a supportive role. The Future Dads programme is just for fathers so they can feel fully included and not be hidden behind their partners. The focus is on them.

'Some dads will say, why are you teaching me how to hold a baby? My wife will be doing most of that stuff. They will say, I am traditional. I will be there and love my children but I'm not good at that stuff,' Thomas said when we met at his charity's office in south London.

One guy I know was nervous around his new son because he was premature and tiny. He didn't want to hold him. I said to him, hold on a minute, your sport is basketball. If you and your partner were both in front of me and I threw a ball at you both, who would you back to catch it? Pick up your son, be confident, he is yours. He needs to get to know your smell. Put him on your chest and just lie down. You can do this, and you are missing out by not taking this opportunity. I hear this stuff from dads all the time. But if you do these small things, picking the baby up, bathing them, changing their nappies, holding them to your chest, you start to be part of it, rather than being a peripheral figure. That is why this Future Dads course is so important.

The programme also teaches men about shaken baby syndrome and how to try to manage the intense stress that can come with having a newborn baby. It encourages the expectant fathers to prepare to have people to call during negative moments and, if they want, to share their numbers with each other. Thomas said:

Generally women are more open with their friends and relatives and share how they are feeling, including their negative feelings. It can be easier for them to reach out in those moments, and to prepare before because they are warned that their baby will be beautiful and loved but will also do things to your brain when you cannot sleep at night. Men often just think they can cope. And then the baby comes, and it is three in the morning and who are they texting? Who are the friends they call?

Thomas said he enjoys watching the men on the Future Dads courses as the day progresses and seeing the quick changes in them. 'We have these dolls that they practise holding and changing. At the beginning of the day, some of the men will say they do not feel comfortable holding the doll, what is this little dolly, I am not playing with that,' Thomas said, laughing to himself:

> But then a few hours later you look over and they are focused on the course leader, holding their baby on their knee and rocking it gently, back and forth, without even realising that they are doing it, like they have been doing it forever. This idea that men are not good at this stuff, that it doesn't come naturally, it is just nonsense.

Another programme which has been widely praised is Family Foundations, a course for first-time parents held at US hospitals. The eight-class course focuses on how mothers and fathers can share childcare responsibilities as co-parents. It teaches them to communicate better so they can manage disagreements and stresses on their relationship following the birth of their child. Family Foundations was highlighted as an example of good practice by the 2014 global academic review of parenting programmes,[14] and as one that has repeatedly been shown to improve outcomes for families. It was developed by a team at Penn State University, which has conducted various peer-reviewed studies into the impact of the programme with excellent results.

In one, published in 2010, 169 couples were randomly assigned either to attend the classes or not. They were assessed throughout the three years after having their children and those who went to the classes were, on average, less stressed and less likely to be depressed. There was also evidence of 'significant program impact on the quality of the couple relationship, parenting, and child behavior problems at child age three years'.[15] The key to the success of the programme appears to be that rather than focusing responsibility on mothers, with fathers in supporting roles as secondary parents, the classes teach parents to tackle the challenges of parenting together, as a 'cooperative team'.[16]

In my conversations about maternity services, I have heard repeated frustrations that interactions with expectant fathers, or about them, tended to focus almost exclusively on their potential to be abusive. There are clearly very important reasons that midwives and health visitors are trained to look out for signs of domestic abuse, which is known to increase during pregnancy.[17] But those who work in perinatal services repeatedly told me they felt the balance was not quite right.

The Fatherhood Institute analysed a range of studies on domestic violence and childbirth. One study from 2005, based on a longitudinal study of mothers and babies in the south west of England, suggested that when their babies were eight months old, 1.8 per cent of mothers had experienced physical violence from their partner since the birth, and 7.3 per cent had experienced emotional abuse. Other studies of new mothers suggested that the proportion of women whose partner had ever used force was between 2 per cent and 3.6 per cent.

The Fatherhood Institute report stated that it did not share the statistics to minimise the seriousness of domestic abuse – with it linked to causing awful developmental problems for babies, as well as the harm it causes mothers. But it wrote that it was important to counter 'the exaggerated "father-as-risk" narrative embedded firmly in most health and social care services'.[18]

It is a controversial point. It is truly awful that studies have shown that up to as many as 7.3 per cent of women experience emotional abuse in the months after having a baby and up to 3.6 per cent experience physical abuse. I do not for one moment suggest that any focus should be taken away from maternity staff doing all they can to spot warning signs and protect women. But it is the case that the overwhelming majority of fathers are not abusers. Automatically writing off these dads, just in case they are criminals, and missing opportunities to engage with them and help them to become potentially brilliant parents and partners does not feel like the best way to serve their future children.

In the north of England, a programme called Dad Matters has been funded with a grant from the Health Foundation, a charity, to try to promote early attachment between new dads and babies and to ensure they get mental health support when needed. Dad Matters works within the NHS, so midwives and health visitors in the greater Manchester area are increasingly trained to refer cases to them.

Kieran Anders, the project manager, leads a team of volunteers who approach expectant parents waiting for pregnancy scans at NHS hospitals, so fathers know who to contact if they want support. Anders said it was crucial that health staff do not only interact with fathers as potential risks but treat them as a core part of the new family.

'Men don't ask for support until they are in crisis,' he said. 'Services have a safeguarding focus and see dads as a risk, rather than someone to be supportive of. We think about a baby as being the centre of a family, and we have to include dads in that.' He backed the Fatherhood Institute's call for fathers to be linked to their children's NHS records:

> That would be immensely helpful. We should be able to track that dad. If that baby is born and it was a traumatic delivery or the baby was very ill, we would then know we should speak to that dad in the same way that if a mum has had a traumatic delivery she is offered counselling or a debrief, or a referral to a specialist team. Without them being linked, when 12 to 16 weeks down the line the dads start to struggle, we can't link it back to what happened. It is also about helping dads to see themselves as part of the parenting team rather than a support for mum.

Dad Matters expects to reach as many as 9,000 new fathers through the NHS in the greater Manchester area this year. 'It is moving in the right direction,' Anders said.

One small change that could encourage fathers to feel more responsible for their children is health services simply inviting partners to pregnancy and new baby appointments if the mother is happy for this to happen.

Davies, from the Fatherhood Institute, described a small study of 31 sets of new parents in Lincolnshire in the north east of England. Health visitors in the area had drafted two different invitation letters to appointments, one standard one addressed to the mother and another including the father and a line stating that the appointment was for 'you both'. About half of the group of 31 new parents were sent one letter, and the rest sent the other one. Seven out of ten fathers who received the letter that included them came to the appointment, compared to two out of ten in the first group.[19] 'It was only a small study but indicates that small changes can make a big difference to how fathers feel involved,' Davies said.

There can be a reluctance to make changes like these for fears about domestic abuse and fathers being controlling during appointments, or single mothers and lesbian mothers being offended by the assumption of a father being involved. Surely a very simple solution is for health staff just to ask the mother during one of her many routine appointments on her own whether she would like a partner included or not in the future.

With parental roles gradually evolving over the decades, we are in a period of flux. The way services in our communities have been designed – around an expectation that children will be looked after by women – can often be at odds with how families are actually living their lives.

When Davies spoke about the huge changes in the involvement of fathers over the past few generations, I immediately thought about nappy changes. My father's generation of men rarely changed nappies but, 30 years later, all of the fathers I know would be embarrassed to admit if they did not do this. Despite this change, baby-changing facilities in the community are often still in women's toilets. Sometimes the baby-changing table will be in a disabled loo. I have only seen a baby-changing table specifically in a men's bathroom a few times, and one of these was on holiday abroad.

Generally, when Robin and I are out having lunch with Solly, one of us will ask a waiter where we can change him, and they will say something like, 'We've got one but it's in the ladies.' We then have to decide whether to try to change him in the men's, either while sat on a toilet in a cubicle while Solly stands in front with his legs apart, or to go to the women's and hope not to be accused of being a pervert. If he has done a poo, I always go for the latter option. I give the women's toilet door a quick push. 'Anyone in there?' If there is no response when I do this a couple of times, I then go in with Solly and say something like: 'I'm a man changing a baby, I'm really sorry, I had to do it in here. There's nowhere else.'

Inevitably a woman then comes in at some point in the next minute and I have to explain myself bashfully while Solly says, 'I do big poo poo!' and she awkwardly waits for me to finish and assures me it is no problem at all.

In Gideon Burrows' book *Men Can Do It!* he described attempting to change nappies in men's public toilets:

> There's a clever little balancing technique that I call the toilet squat. Men who take their baby to the park or to the shops have to learn it for themselves very quickly. The trick is to change the baby's freshly filled nappy without anything – the change bag, the new nappy, the baby's freshly washed clothes, your hands or knees, and especially any part of your baby – touching the filthy, pissy men's toilet floor.[20]

Many fathers will be familiar with this, and not just the ones who take big chunks of parental leave. Mothers might also be familiar with just accepting that when out and about as a family it is not worth the hassle of a dad doing any nappy changes.

While on a holiday in Israel in April 2022, we went to a café in a park and there was a changing table in the men's bathroom. It felt like such a novelty that I took a picture and tweeted it, writing that 'gender equality is impossible until men are expected to care as much as women'.

Some mothers shared the post and wrote about their own experiences. One wrote: 'This used to drive me insane when my kids were little and it was always me that had to change them. Bloody ridiculous.' Some others wrote about how they have seen changes, with modern shopping centres increasingly starting to install changing tables in men's loos. One woman wrote that where she works all new toilet installations have to include baby-changing tables in men's toilets, adding: 'Progress is happening, just slowly.' An account dedicated to celebrating fatherhood, wrote: 'One loo by one, we're getting there… but this should be happening much quicker.'

On a Saturday recently in an English town, Robin and I had a really positive experience, with a changing table in the men's toilets in a Marks & Spencer and a parents' room in a John Lewis department store, with a large nappy-changing section not restricted just to women. How could we encourage faster change, and for this to happen not just in the big-name High Street stores?

Under a similar tweet from a father who complained of 'the number of times I had to change my son *on the bathroom floor* because only the women's bathroom had a changing table', an American woman offered some advice. 'The local mall where my dad shopped had a "mum's room",' she wrote. 'He changed my sister's nappy on the floor in protest in front of the security guard. It said "parent's room" the following week.'

The stories Robin and I hear from other parents about these kinds of inequalities are typically similar to ours, involving dads gleefully enjoying lots of praise for doing very ordinary tasks, or occasionally being seen as a novel, curious thing. It would be misleading to suggest that most of the comments from other people that Robin and I get really bother us. We have both had our share of ridiculous questions when out with Solly – including the typical 'Are you babysitting today?', 'Where's Mummy? and 'Is it lads' day out?' while walking Solly in his buggy. Mostly, though, we just go about our days and face much more friendliness and acceptance than hostility.

There cannot be many people who still automatically assume that a man out with his children must be a widower, as they might have done 50 years ago. The differences in the ways mothers and fathers are treated by others in the community are now more subtle. The comments tend to be a bit patronising, irritating, not massively troubling, but you hope they will gradually disappear as time goes on. Like flies at a picnic. You have to flap them away a bit, but it is not a thunderstorm. I can go weeks without any of these comments and then be laughing with Robin about getting three in a row in 15 minutes at a GP surgery.

My younger sister, Tanya, and her husband, Eli, have two daughters. When one of my nieces was a baby, Eli decided one day to take her for a walk in her buggy. She slept while he walked around a park and listened to an audiobook. A woman walked past in the other direction and said to him, 'What a great dad, well done.' Eli laughed when he told me about this. 'It was the best hour. I was getting some peace, listening to my audiobook and she was asleep. What a great dad I am!'

Friends of ours, Royi and Joanna, have three children and a running joke about him being called a 'superdad' for doing less parenting than she does. 'School drop-off, swimming – I am regularly championed for being a great dad doing these things that Joanna does more often and in addition to the majority of parenting she is responsible for,' Royi said. 'It is absurd that I get credit for this basic stuff. Last week I was called a superdad because I was with my three children and was told that I make it look so easy. I bloody don't.'

Joanna added: 'It drives me mad how often people fawn over Royi for doing dad things. When our oldest was a baby, he took her to get weighed, and he said the health visitors were basically falling at his feet in admiration.'

One of my male friends owns his own business so is able to work flexibly, allowing him to pick up his children from school more often than his wife does. He said the comments he gets are double edged. They seem complimentary at first but can be tinged with resentment. He said:

> It is a constant thing. I go to pick up the kids from school, or take my kids to birthday parties, and the mothers are all in a group. They are not particularly friendly to me – it is like

it is unusual that I am there. I get some comments like 'Oh it's superdad again'. I feel like it's passive aggressive; some of the mothers seem to begrudge that I am available and that I want to be there.

When Solly was a few months old and lockdown restrictions started to ease, I signed us up for a baby class in a music teacher's garden. I was determined not to be self-conscious, assuming I would probably be the only dad. These classes are often marketed at 'mums and babies', although this one had a more neutral name. I very quickly realised that there was one type of person who was not going to be popular. It was not me but a mother who swayed in looking very made up, bragging about how her twins were sleeping through the night at 12 weeks. Another mum then arrived. 'Arghhh, she's pooed and I forgot to bring any nappies,' she said, almost tripping on the play mat. I instantly loved her and handed her one from my bag.

Solly and I went to the class once a week, and I never felt unwelcome or different from anyone else. I offered to step out when the mums wanted to breastfeed, but no one cared. They also did not judge me for shoving a dummy in Solly's mouth at the first sign of a moan. Within a few weeks I was no longer the only father as one of the mums had shared parental leave with her husband and gone back to work. Many dads can feel alienated in these environments, but that was not my experience.

There are plenty of days when the barriers to men being equal parents seem to be falling fast, and others when they creep back up. On a recent Sunday, I had one of those days when ridiculous comments seemed to be flying all around. In the morning, we were at a football class with Solly, and I asked another father a question about local child-friendly activities. 'I don't know really,' he said. 'The only dad thing I do with him is football.'

In the afternoon, I walked into a bookshop with Solly, and he was carrying a packet of biscuits, which I had bought for him to calm him down after he accidentally let go of a helium balloon and it flew away. He had been distraught, crying, 'My bayoon, my bayoon, my bayoon.' A woman walked past us in the shop. 'Oh I bet Mummy will be delighted you're eating those,' she said to Solly, while giggling and giving me a knowing look.

Later, at about 5 p.m., we were out for Solly's dinner at a pizza restaurant. I went to the loo and walked past a family of five at a table, and the mother was letting one of the young children try coffee. She looked up at me and, pointing to the father, said: 'It's not my problem – he's babysitting tonight!'

While society is generally changing, and that is great, we can and should strive for more. As the silly nonsense comments about useless dads gradually die out, national health services should take the opportunity to embrace the changes that are already happening and then push fathers to do more. As the studies already show, it really does not take much. Just a few minutes with a nurse or midwife can give a new dad confidence in holding his tiny baby, changing nappies, bathing and bottle-feeding – skills that add up to lessen the burden on mothers.

No mother should feel like her partner is babysitting their children because he is so rarely involved with their care. It should, surely, be unremarkable for a dad to look after his own son or daughter. Because he should be doing this about 50 per cent of the time at least without a woman having to feel she must help or be nearby. It should be unremarkable for a dad to take his child to a medical appointment or to a baby class. For there to be true equality of the sexes, a dad should be able to take his child anywhere at all without him automatically being asked: 'Where's Mummy?'

CHAPTER EIGHT

BOYS DON'T WEAR PINK

How to Stop Limiting What Our Children Can Be

Solly is a lad. He is such a typical little bloke. Look at him smashing down that tower of bricks; he is so cheeky, a proper boy. These are the types of things people often say about our son, and Robin and I have found ourselves joining in.

Solly is a very physical child and plays fearlessly. He started walking at between 13 and 14 months, not a particularly young age, but he seemed to miss out the bow-legged stage most children go through. Within days of taking his first steps he was running and jumping. At the playground, he would head straight for the highest slide and climb the steps, while one of us climbed behind him, arms out and terrified.

Solly is now just over two years old and loves football. When we leave the back door open, he skips out, heading straight for the balls in the garden, shouting: 'Kick ball goal!' We signed him up for a football class called Little Kickers and he was sent a cute little red kit. When he sees it in the pile of washing, he says: 'My knickers!' He loves the classes and runs around scoring goals and doing goalkeeper-like drop kicks. He can catch balls from a decent distance and has a fierce throw on him. Solly also loves diggers and dinosaurs. Robin and I will watch him, next to girls of his age playing with crayons and puzzles in a much more focused way than he does, and it can be difficult not to come to the seemingly obvious conclusion: boys will be boys.

Solly also loves his rainbow leggings. He only recently started showing preferences for clothes and, given the choice, he always goes for the most bright and colourful option. We bought Solly a pair of leggings covered in rainbow-coloured hearts. If you show him a drawer full of different trousers, shorts and jeans he will point straight at the leggings and say: 'I like this one!' We have to hide them if we want him to wear something else.

Solly is also tender and sweet with babies. He wants to hold them and make them smile. Each time a new child joins his nursery, the teachers will tell us about how Solly has looked out for them. A younger boy joined and was crying during his first day and, we were told, Solly kept fetching him teddies to try to make him happy. A baby girl then joined and Solly insisted on sitting next to her at lunch and helping to feed her.

The nursery has sent us the most adorable pictures of Solly pretending to read to younger children. When Solly plays with his cousin Edie, who is a year older than him, they dress up in pink and purple butterfly wings and then fly around Edie's garden, getting muddy and wet and dragging themselves up a climbing wall. My sister Tanya, Edie's mum, says she loves it when Edie plays with Solly because he brings out the fearless, physical side of her character. As with all children, it is impossible to know how much of their personalities and preferences are due to nature or nurture: their sex or the way gendered expectations have already shaped them.

Before I became a parent, I would have said that society was getting better at not imposing gendered stereotypes. But you have a child, and it is like you are instantly transported to the 1950s (method of transport: hot air balloon, either blue or pink). It is impossible to avoid all of the bizarre ways that we treat baby boys and girls differently, based on the simple fact that they have different body parts under their nappies. We often do it without even thinking. It feels like the biggest cliché to spell it all out. Why do boys equal blue and girls equal pink? Why do the cards and banners say: 'It's a boy!' or 'It's a girl!' as if sex is the key thing that is relevant when welcoming a new human? Why are clothes for boys and girls often so different, from birth? Why does a one-week-old baby girl need a bow on her bald head? Why do we usually grow girls' hair long and keep boys' hair short? Why would men who regularly wear salmon-coloured shirts never dress their baby sons in salmon-coloured Babygros? Why are toys organised in shops by gender? Why do parents dress baby girls in dresses that literally stop them being able to crawl or climb? I write all this, and yet I also would have dressed a daughter in a dress occasionally and I never would have done so with Solly. Why? I would not have painted Solly's room pink. Why? This nonsense is ingrained, and it takes effort to resist it all.

Shopping for Solly continually makes me feel like I am that annoying person who always has to be a contrarian. There is a word in Yiddish for that person: a *dafkanik*. They love to say no, just to be obstinate. They are not much fun to be around at parties. When everyone is counting down to the New Year, they say they refuse to celebrate a meaningless passage of time. They are the one person in a jury of 12 who says 'guilty' when there is no evidence and everyone else is saying 'not guilty', just to feel like they have independent thought. They say 'yeah, *but*' a lot. So many online clothes shops have separate categories for boys and girls. I get bored of the boys' clothes after picking a few with dinosaurs and diggers that Solly will like, and then click onto the girls' section. I ignore the princess slogans but there will also usually be fun colourful jumpers, T-shirts and leggings that I know Solly will love. Why can only girls be colourful? I buy them feeling like a *dafkanik*.

One rainy Saturday, Robin and I were due to take Solly to a farm and realised on the way that we had forgotten his wellies. Solly had fallen asleep in the car, so we stopped at a big supermarket, and I stayed in the car with Solly while Robin went in to buy him a pair. Robin told a sales assistant in the baby-clothes section that he was looking for wellies for his two-year-old. She asked if it was a son or daughter. Robin chose a pair that were navy blue with a few red hearts on them and she said, 'I thought they were for a boy?' She then tried to convince him to swap them for wellies with characters from the TV show *Paw Patrol* on them, saying they were better for boys. Robin declined to swap them and went for the navy boots with hearts.

I love those boots, and so does Solly. They are not in any way 'girly' or pink – not that it would be a problem if they were. And yet just because there are a few hearts on them, literally the symbol of love, there is something inside that tells us they are not for boys. I do not blame the shop assistant for her gut instinct that the heart boots were for girls. This stuff has been embedded deep within us.

It is not just clothes, of course. Dolls and toy buggies are marketed as being for girls and lorries for boys. Play kitchens are for girls, and car tracks are for boys. There have been different building sets specifically targeted at girls, focused on them building a pop star's house, a hair salon and a cupcake café.[1] Even basics like plates and cutlery for toddlers are often gendered: pink and decorated with pretty dolls for girls and blue with cars for boys.

I once had a steaming row about the plate I had picked for Solly's breakfast. We were abroad and I grabbed a plastic plate from a cupboard without looking, put Solly's toast on it and handed it to him at the kitchen table. I then turned around and someone we were staying with was swapping the plate for a blue one with cars. 'The blue one is better for you, Solly, isn't it?' The plate I had given him was a Dora the Explorer one that was, apparently, meant for girls. I could not care less whether Solly eats off a blue or pink plate. Blue is also fine. But the idea that a pink plate had to be replaced for a blue one drove me mad. Solly did not care what plate he was eating off; he just wanted some toast.

Does it really matter if boys and girls are differentiated by colour? Many boys do seem to like rough, physical play and there are plenty of girls who love dolls. Of course, we should not deny any child their preferences. We would never intentionally stop Solly being who he is and playing with whichever toys, or balls, he wants to play with. Surely it is about encouragement rather than limits though. Children should be helped to explore all different kinds of toys, to eat off whichever plates they like and to wear different clothes so they can find their own passions that are genuinely theirs, without having to feel self-conscious.

These influences in childhood may seem harmless, but research suggests the opposite. When children are pushed towards stereotypes – the building toys just for boys and pretty princess games for girls – it restricts their imaginations and shapes how they see themselves when they get older. Experts argue that these kinds of gendered ways of treating children differently contribute to girls growing up with lower self-esteem, body-image issues and eating disorders and boys having worse reading skills and being more likely to be misogynistic when they are older. These stereotyped assumptions in childhood have also been linked to career choices, such as boys being more likely to see themselves becoming engineers and scientists and girls having fewer ambitions to be successful outside the home.[2] The inequality that we still see in the way men and women split parental responsibility is rooted in our children's earliest experiences of what it means to be a boy or a girl.

I will not go through the extensive academic literature in this area – that would require a whole other book, or a series of books – but a couple of the studies have made a particular impression on me, because they suggest just how early children can be affected by adults' gendered stereotypes.

In 2000, psychologists at New York University set up a sloping walkway for babies. The top platform was just over a metre high and led to a soft, carpeted ramp down that could be adjusted at different inclines. The researchers observed 23 mothers with 11-month-old infants and asked them to estimate how steep a slope their babies would try to crawl down, and how steep a slope they would then successfully descend. After that, they all watched as the babies made their attempts. There were volleyball nets secured to all sides of the contraption in case any babies tried to make a leap for it.

The researchers had not initially intended to study gender bias, but the results could not be ignored. Even though there were no reported differences in motor performance according to sex at this age, they found that mothers of girls underestimated their crawling ability and bravery in making attempts, while the mothers of boys overestimated their performance. On average, mothers of boys guessed that they could successfully crawl down slopes five degrees steeper than the inclines estimated by mothers of girls. Mothers of boys thought their babies would have more courage and attempt slopes 13 degrees steeper compared to the estimates made by mothers of girls. In reality, there was no difference in the average crawling ability of the boys and girls. The authors wrote that the averages were not due to a few outliers 'but rather reflected a consistent pattern', adding:

> Mothers of boys expected their infants to be more successful at descending steep slopes than mothers of girls, they expected boys to attempt steeper slopes than girls, and they expected boys to attempt risky slopes and girls to limit their attempts to safe slopes.[3]

How else are we limiting our children, without even realising it, because of these ingrained and unconscious sexist beliefs?

Another team of psychologists at the universities of New York, Illinois and Princeton found that girls are particularly affected by negative gender stereotypes by the age of six. The psychologists initially assessed 96 children of different ages, who were told stories which included a description of someone who was 'really, really smart'. The gender of this particularly clever character was never mentioned. The children were then shown pictures of four people, two men and two women, who were similarly attractive and dressed equally professionally, and asked which of the adults was the person from the story. At age five, the boys and girls typically associated brilliance with their own gender, which was an expected finding as children of this age tend to view their own groups most positively (when I read the study, I had flashbacks of running around my primary school playground, 'Girls are elastic, boys are fantastic'). However, the older children's answers showed a different pattern.

Girls aged six and seven were significantly less likely to pick a woman from the pictures as the person in the story who was described as 'really, really smart'. The researchers then replicated the study with another 144 children. As before, there was no difference according to gender at age five, but the six- and seven-year-old girls were much more likely to see the men in the pictures as cleverer. A third sample of another 64 children also found this difference between girls' and boys' perception of brilliance according to gender at the ages of six and seven. In a particularly depressing finding, the researchers reported that girls who saw men as cleverer were starting to avoid activities that they viewed as being for more intelligent children.[4]

In December 2020, the Fawcett Society, a charity that campaigns for gender equality, released the findings of a commission that it had run into gender stereotypes in early childhood. The work had been started a year and a half earlier and involved a group of leading

academics, politicians, business and public service leaders carrying
out an extensive review of the existing academic research in the area,
hosting events and overseeing their own studies to better understand
the impact of gender stereotypes imposed on young children. One
exercise involved members visiting 141 high street shops to assess
gender stereotypes and conducting online audits of the websites of
33 retailers. They held their own evidence sessions and polled 1,280
parents and 1,027 practitioners working in childhood education.
The report concluded:

> Gender stereotypes are oversimplified generalisations that
> dictate what is acceptable or expected for women and girls,
> and men and boys. The evidence is clear – those limitations
> start early, hold many children back, and cause significant
> problems across society in later life.[5]

The charity's review highlighted how over the past few decades,
research has repeatedly shown how gender stereotypes infiltrate
parents' and teachers' brains and negatively affect how we bring
up our children. The report shared evidence that more than one
in three girls say they are made to feel that their looks are their
most important attribute, contributing to them being unhappy
with their bodies. Expectations on boys to be breadwinners and
not to be emotional reportedly contribute to higher male suicide
rates. The report stated that there is 'significant research' showing
that failing to challenge gendered stereotypes in childhood makes it
more likely that boys go on to be violent towards women and girls.[6]

In their earliest years, boys have been found to be more likely to
have problems reading if they have teachers who have traditional
attitudes to gender. The suggestion is that teachers who were studied
were, effectively, writing off boys as potentially good readers based
on their preconceived ideas about what they thought boys tended to

be like. When boys had teachers with a more egalitarian approach, they were less likely to have problems with reading when they were older.[7]

Other studies have shown that teachers are more likely to dismiss playful boys as 'class clowns' than playful girls;[8] parents tend to praise toddlers in different ways depending on their gender, with more constructive praise for boys;[9] and parents of sons are more likely to save more money for their education.[10]

I met Jemima Olchawski, chief executive of the Fawcett Society, and Andrew Bazeley, then the policy, research and public affairs manager for the charity, at their office in south London to discuss their commission's findings. They described how so many of the things that surround children – their toys, clothes and entertainment – are more gendered than they were 50 years ago. This was a surprise to me. Through my experience of parenthood, I have become aware of how little societal progress has been made in challenging gender stereotyping in childhood. What I did not appreciate was that it has actually been getting worse. 'If you go back 100 years, a picture of a small child in a white dress could just as easily have been a boy or a girl because that is just how we dressed children then,' Bazeley said.

During our discussion, Bazeley pointed me to research from the US indicating that toys are more segregated by gender now than they were in the 1970s. Elizabeth Sweet, a sociologist, analysed advertisements for toys since the early 21st century in catalogues published by Sears, the American department store chain. Between the 1920s and the 1960s, toys in the catalogues were typically divided by gender, with building sets aimed at boys and toys focused on domesticity, such as brooms and mops, marketed as being for girls. However, by the 1970s, at the height of feminism's second wave and with more women working in paid jobs, there had been marked change.

Sweet found that less than two per cent of toys in a Sears catalogue from 1975 were explicitly marketed as either for boys or girls. In fact, many of the pictures advertising the toys challenged gender stereotypes, with boys photographed playing with domestic toys and girls shown building and playing at being doctors and scientists. With increasing commercialisation during the 1980s and 1990s, companies learned that they could sell two of the same toys by clearly marking them out as either for boys or girls. Blue and pink became the default colours they used. In the Sears catalogue from 1995, about half of the toys were gendered, the same rate recorded in the catalogues sold before the Second World War.[11] Bazeley said:

> If you look in general at children's advertising from the 1970s, it was not a gender-equal wonderland; you will still see boys playing with guns and girls playing with kitchens. But what has happened in the 1980s and 1990s, and continues now, is the pink and blue, the colour-coded segregation of girls' and boys' things. The theory is that this happened partly to improve sales. If you sell things separately as blue and pink, you stop families from handing down. You can sell the same bike twice.

The Fawcett Society's commission found that toy shops in Britain have got much better at not explicitly segregating aisles and online categories for boys and girls. However, this still happens in an implicit way. While it is rare to see aisles of toys with banners marking them out as for boys or girls, many toy shops still put domestic toys, which are usually pink, together and then the sporty, blue toys together, so they look to most people like girls' and boys' aisles.

'Society has trained children to like these colours and associate them with their gender, and then the colour coding signals to girls and boys what they should play with,' Bazeley said. 'If your dolls section runs into your home corner section, which runs into your unicorn section and the whole area is pink and bright purple, it is fairly clear what the store is doing even without signs.'

Often toys are bought as gifts by friends and older family members and the safe, easy decision is to buy the gendered toy. Online algorithms push people to more and more gendered choices. 'There is much more manufacturers and stores could do to split things up and make clear that all toys can be for all children,' Bazeley said.

When it comes to children's clothes, there is rarely any subtlety to the segregation. As Robin and I have found repeatedly, clothes stores signal that strong darker colours and hard wearing is for boys, and flimsy, bright and not suitable for active play is for girls. Girls' clothes are often shaped like small versions of women's clothes, even though their bodies will not change in these ways until puberty. The slogans can be ridiculous. Boys' T-shirts are emblazoned with statements about them being naughty monsters, wild animals and adventurers, and the ones for girls are about them being pretty, passive princesses. Olchawski said:

> Children's clothes are the worst. We tell them who they can be on their clothes. It is really uncomfortable the way girls are given this narrow set of things they are allowed to be. Be happy always. Friendship always first. The messages are that you'd better be nice and happy and think of other people first all of the time. But for boys it is about being active and a rebel and a little monster. Look out, here comes trouble! Both are harmful in different ways. Children don't do irony. If their T-shirt says little monster or little princess, that is what they understand.

The clothes that adults select for their children are gendered in much more extreme ways than the clothes they pick for themselves. How often do you see an adult woman in brash, bright pink? Bazeley said:

It sets their framework for understanding gender in their own lives. Children do need to be able to distinguish between men and women. It is an important part of the world and their lives. But when you have an environment which completely separates boys and girls in a lot of ways, it overstates the importance of gender for children, and that is harmful. Boys should see the girls in their class as children just like them, their equals, not as being some sort of other thing that wears pink and has to be kind and gentle whereas he is a monster who wears blue.

Olchawski added that focusing on girls' looks – with them being praised more for being pretty than anything else – sends a strong message that their appearance is uniquely important, which impacts their self-esteem and centres their worth in how others judge them. When I shared that I often felt like I was being annoyingly humourless when I called out these things, Olchawski said: 'Feminists know well the argument that you are being a spoilsport.'

The Fawcett Society's polls found that about half of parents prefer to buy clothes for young children which are advertised by gender, while 28 per cent prefer clothes advertised as being for any child and 22 per cent express no preference. The charity's report argued that while many parents are happy with the status quo on gendered clothing for children, there is also a significant and underserved market for parents who want to have the option to avoid gendered clothing.

'The approach we advocate is not to shift from gender-segregated pink and blue products to a beige, "gender neutral" option, which is how this argument is sometimes caricatured,' the report stated. 'Our aim is for the whole range of experiences and options to be available to all children, and therefore for the whole colour palette to be used without discrimination when it comes to products and media for children.'[12]

There has been some progress in some areas. The campaign group Let Toys Be Toys has successfully pushed many retailers to stop explicitly separating toys by gender.[13] There are many independent businesses online selling all types of clothes for children without specifying that they are for girls or boys. Robin and I love the online store Lindex, which has loads of fun, colourful options modelled by girls and boys.

Many of the most popular children's books now challenge gender stereotyping, and books are not sold by gender in any shops that I have been to. The princess in *Zog*, about a clumsy dragon, refuses to be rescued by a knight and takes charge of her own destiny, becoming a doctor. 'I won't go back to being a princess,' she says. 'And prancing round the palace in a silly frilly dress.'[14] In *Jack and the Flumflum Tree*, it is Rose, rather than the boys, who climbs the tree, 'as nimble as can be', to get the fruit that Granny needs to cure her moozles.[15] Maisie and Ollie play football together in *The Everywhere Bear*.[16]

But something that we have noticed is that while girls are rightly celebrated for being physical, active and daring, there still seems to be a squeamishness about celebrating supposed feminine qualities in boys. It is inevitably a girl who plays in a dreamy, creative way in *The Paper Dolls*, while a boy comes along with a pair of scissors to snip them up.[17] Then the girl grows up, becomes a mother and she passes on this lovely, imaginative game to 'her own little girl'.

Bazeley said this point about perceived femininity in boys had come out strongly in the Fawcett Society's research, with many parents worried about movements away from gendered clothing going too far the other way:

Fundamentally, the fear, the anxiety, is about boys wearing dresses. It is not about girls wearing trousers. We have some really strong societal boundaries about boys transgressing by being like girls, and it is to do with the negativity that we have about femininity. It feels so much more of a transgression of the norm. That is part of a much bigger project to change that perception.

This idea – that girls can be like stereotypical boys, but boys must not be like stereotypical girls – broadly reflects where we are with gender equality in adult life. Society appears to support women having careers as long as they also do most of the caring at home. There can also be a suspicion of men who work in supposedly feminine jobs, so children only usually experience female nursery teachers. It has been reported that at nurseries with male teachers, parents often ask that they do not change their children's nappies. Instead of challenging these attitudes, some nurseries give in to the demands.[18] What message does that send to children about men and women's roles? Olchawski said:

This fear of what is perceived as 'femininity' in men is really fundamental to women's equality because a lot of the inequality women experience in the workplace comes from balancing work and care. If parents were sharing that more, women would have more opportunity to continue to progress their careers after becoming parents. We have spent a lifetime coaching girls in the skills we associate with caring. From giving them dolls, to telling them to be kind, gentle and think about other people. And then lo and behold it feels to people as if girls and women are better at it, or that it might come more naturally to them. We all know that as parents you model what you have seen. So if you are brought up in a household where being a father means one thing and being a mother means something very different, that can be a big part of how we come to understand those roles.

The Fawcett Society's commission has already had significant impact, with it leading to Ofsted, the education regulator, now requiring nurseries and schools to show they are challenging negative gender stereotypes in order to get a 'good' rating. Previously this was only required to get the best 'outstanding' rating. The change will mean 14,000 more schools actively having to challenge gender stereotyping.[19] The charity is also working with a major publisher of British school textbooks and exam papers to improve the content of materials used by thousands of teachers.

Pragya Agarwal is a behaviour and data scientist and Visiting Professor of Social Inequities and Injustice at Loughborough University. She is also a feminist author and the mother of three daughters. In her latest book, *Hysterical*, she explored gender stereotyping and how our brains are affected by gendered messages as we grow up.[20] It is a subject that she has been particularly attuned to while bringing up her children.

In February 2020, she tweeted that one of her daughters, aged three at the time, had taken a children's book about Frida Kahlo, the Mexican painter, to nursery for circle time and was told the boys would not like it. She wrote: 'Not only could she not share her joy of a book she loves but she has also been given a message that girls & boys like diff things. I am livid.'

After studying an array of academic research on gendered preferences, she has come to the conclusion that nurture is much more significant than nature. When we spoke, Agarwal said:

There have been these very hard lines drawn between men and women and about what a father does and what a mother does. It is around children, in the role models they see, and in books and in media. In society it has become embedded that women have this maternal instinct – that all women have it, that they all want children and would be better parents and they are better at nurturing. Men are believed to be the ones who are better working in the public domain but not as good at parenting and nurturing. There is this whole discourse about how much of that is innate and biological and how much of that is socially determined. I firmly believe that these roles are socially determined. A lot of studies try to prove that men are inherently like this and women are inherently like that, but there is actually more in-group variation than between-group variation. We create these myths and we internalise it. I think we have to shatter those myths.

There is a large gap in age between Agarwal's oldest daughter, who was 23 at the time of writing, and her twin daughters, who were six and born through surrogacy following fertility treatment. Like others, her experience is that children's things, from clothes to toys, are more gendered than they used to be:

Particularly with clothes, I did not previously see these slogans that I have seen since my twins were born. I hate that girls are given this message that they are soft and passive and nurturing while boys are supposed to be adventurous and wild. Girls' clothes are made smaller for the same age group. Girls' shoes are very flimsy, and boys' shoes are much stronger and sturdier. We start giving these messages from a very young age.

In writing this book, I have been keen to learn from other parents about how to teach young children, from the earliest years, to be whatever they want to be and not to be limited by the roles societies impose on us based on gender. Agarwal said she tries to create an environment that allows her daughters to make their own choices, as freely as possible. She said her younger girls are 'very active and sporty' but also like to play with dolls and are drawn to 'pink and purple, sparkly, glittery things'.

'I want to celebrate all of them, rather than curbing one aspect just because it feels stereotypically feminine,' she said. 'Giving them autonomy and freedom to choose is the most important thing. It backfires sometimes. My six-year-old tells me, "It is my body, my choice," when I ask her to wear a jacket outside.'

One father who has particular reason to be celebrated for the way he and his wife encouraged their children to defy gendered expectations is Ziauddin Yousafzai. His daughter, Malala, is the world's most famous young activist, who was shot in the head as a schoolgirl because she had fearlessly campaigned for girls' rights to education while living under Taliban oppression in the Swat Valley, Pakistan. Malala began speaking out for women's equality when she was just 11 and has since become the youngest ever recipient of the Nobel Peace Prize, when she was 17. She describes her father, a teacher who ran a school for girls as well as boys in their town, as her 'ally and inspiration'.[21] Given that Malala was brought up to resist the most extreme form of sexist terror, I approached her father, who is also an outspoken activist for equal rights, and asked if he would meet me. I was hoping for a video call, or to meet at a café, but he invited me to their home in Birmingham.

In an outhouse at the back of the garden, Ziauddin Yousafzai served me eight large pakoras, mint sauce, an array of nuts and a cup of tea so creamy that it filmed at the top. We sat on sofas at right angles to each other and he took off his shoes, curling his legs under him while facing me. Every now and again, he would lean forward and use tongs to place more pakoras onto my plate, grinning and urging me to keep eating. 'The more you eat, the happier we will be,' he said. I happily obliged.

I asked him about how he and his wife, Toor Pekai, raised Malala and her two younger brothers to believe in sexual equality despite

living under the Taliban. He answered immediately, without having
to think:

> Children learn from what we do, not what we teach. There is
> no point being a father who talks all the time about equality
> but still sits at the table and waits for his wife to serve him
> and is never there for his children. Children can see hypocrisy.

Yousafzai said that what children see at home, every day, within
their own families, is key:

> Family is the most crucial, basic, important and transformative
> institution that all of us have. It is an informal institution
> which has no written laws, but it creates your values and your
> beliefs. The way we taught equality to our children was just
> through the way my wife was treating me and I was treating
> my wife. The respect and love I had for her and she had for
> me. Our children would see me clean the house, iron their
> clothes and polish their school shoes. They grew up seeing
> there are two adults in this family, a man and a woman, a
> father and mother, and there is no difference in their status
> because of their gender.

This model of a family with parents of genuinely equal status
is, let us be honest, still elusive for many in supposedly progressive
societies. Who serves more? Who does more laundry? Who wakes
more at night while the other parent sleeps?

Where Yousafzai grew up, in a small village in Pakistan, sexual
equality was unheard of. He had a very strict patriarchal upbringing, an extreme example of inequality, with one brother and five
sisters and a father who was an Islamic scholar. When the family
ate, he, his older brother and his father were given the meatiest

parts of the chicken, the thighs and the breast, while his mother and sisters had to make do with what they could scrape from the wings. Only the men and boys had cream with their tea. When he picked up prescriptions for his mother, they would be addressed to 'the mother of Ziauddin'. He and his brother went to school, while his sisters never learned to read or write. Instead, they were prepared to be married from when they were as young as 14. At their local graveyard, headstones for women did not list their names, only those of their male relatives.

Yousafzai said he began to feel the injustices experienced by his sisters because of his own issues as a teenager at school. He had a stutter and was mocked by other boys. The teachers seemed to focus their attention on the lighter-skinned boys and those who were better looking or wealthier. His parents put pressure on him to be influential, ideally a doctor, because of his gender. He was made to trek to the top of a large hill with his mother and an uncle to see a saint, who sucked a large ball of sweets and gave it to his mother, so she could feed little bits of the ball to her son every day until his stutter disappeared. Unsurprisingly, this treatment did not work. He said:

As a boy, I was special, but with a lot of pressure. With more education, I was able to reflect on many things, including this gender inequality around me. I started to feel more empathy, to see that in my society, more boys meant more money, more power, more influence, but more girls was more problems, more honour issues. I wanted to be a champion of women's rights and education for girls. Education empowers and gives you the language, confidence and words to speak for yourself. Education transformed me – it changed my inner being and gave me the values of empathy, equality, justice, love and respect. The earliest years for children are so important because education gives everyone the chance for freedom, whatever the gender.

In 1997, Malala was born. Yousafzai and Toor Pekai named their daughter after Malalai of Maiwand, a legendary Pashtun heroine who was known by her own name and raised her voice to rally warriors and give them strength in battle. The school Yousafzai started in Pakistan three years before Malala's birth had three students when it opened and grew over the next 18 years to the point where there were 1,100 students, 500 of whom were girls. During this period, the Taliban began asserting control over the region and bombed schools, cracking down on girls' education. At home, their daughter was developing an independent and quirky way of thinking and acting. Yousafzai said Malala was unusual compared to many other children because she was talking from 15 months, before she could walk:

> Speaking was always something that was very special about her personality. One morning when she was three or four years, we were having breakfast and she was looking at me. Then she said: 'Do you know what colour you are, what you look like? You look like the colour after you mix milk into tea.' I jumped up and said: 'Well done, Malala, now I know what I look like, thank you.' I was so happy that she was being very creative. My way of parenting was just to watch and appreciate, really.

Yousafzai said he tried to encourage his children's interests, whether or not they were supposedly typical for their gender, but he was also keen to emphasise that they did not force Malala to reject anything typically 'girly' either. They believed in praising their children for their choices, rather than imposing any limits on their imagination. He said:

I never encouraged my two sons that they should have boy things and Malala should have girl things, like bringing her dolls. I treated them as children, and they were free in their choices. Malala had a haircut that was a bit like a boy's cut, and I had no issues with that, I liked that. But she was also very mindful of her headscarf. When someone knocked at the door when she was very small, three, four or five years, she would rush to put a shawl on. I didn't stop her from doing that either. When you don't instruct children and you encourage them to think for themselves then they find their own things and they question things. Malala was very critical, I loved her critical thinking, and I encouraged her to be a free thinker.

As the founder of a school that taught girls in the Swat Valley, Yousafzai became well known in the region for his women's rights activism. A BBC journalist who had interviewed him asked if one of his female teachers would write a blog about their life under the Taliban. They were all too afraid. Another young girl was briefly going to do it but then her father forbade it. Malala, who was 11 by this point, said she wanted to write the blog. She did so under the pseudonym Gul Makai, meaning cornflour in Pashto. Yousafzai and his wife decided that it was not their place to deny their daughter a voice. In the weeks that followed, Malala wrote:

I had a terrible dream yesterday with military helicopters and the Taliban. I have had such dreams since the launch of the military operation in Swat. My mother made me breakfast and I went off to school. I was afraid of going to school because the Taliban had issued an edict banning all girls from attending schools. Only 11 students attended the class out of 27... On my way from school to home I heard a man saying 'I will kill you'. I hastened my pace and after a while

I looked back if the man was still coming behind me. But to my utter relief he was talking on his mobile and must have been threatening someone else over the phone.[22]

Malala also started to write for local news outlets and featured in a *New York Times* documentary, becoming famous in Pakistan in her own right for her activism. In October 2012, when she was 15, a masked gunman boarded her school bus and asked: 'Who is Malala?' before shooting her in the head. The bullet just missed her brain, and she had life-saving surgery in Pakistan before being flown to England for more treatment. Despite significant injuries, she recovered and continued campaigning, and the family remained in England, settling in Birmingham. Malala was awarded the Nobel Peace Prize two years later. She is the youngest ever Nobel laureate.

Yousafzai was about to give a speech at an education rally, and his phone was off, when a friend whispered in his ear that there had been an incident involving his school's bus. There had been a fire or possibly an attack.

As he processed the news, Yousafzai's name was announced as the next speaker and, in shock, he continued with his task and went up to the podium. As he spoke, he felt himself panicking, his forehead sweating, and he cut the speech short, apologising to the crowd. He asked his friend to drive him to hospital and switched his phone on and it rang. It was a principal at another school. He had heard that Malala and two other girls had been shot. 'Honestly, I can't explain what I felt,' Yousafzai told me.

It was like a doomsday for me. I was sucked down by some black hole or something. Even I forgot how to cry. It was like everything in my body had been hacked. I was blank. When I went to the emergency ward, she was there and had this bandage on her left side. I just kissed her and told her you are my beautiful daughter, my brave daughter.

Yousafzai felt instant guilt and went over and over in his head arguments about whether or not he should have prevented his daughter from campaigning with him and allowing her to become a target. 'The Taliban had bombed many schools, but they had never attacked a student or a teacher,' he said. 'I was well known, I spoke against Talibanisation and for girls' education and received threats but, at that time, we didn't think it would ever threaten her life.'

It was incredibly difficult for him to cope with the idea that he had put her at risk, but his wife felt strongly that they had nothing to regret and that Malala would have campaigned loudly, whatever they had said to her:

> Obviously I had these thoughts. And am I responsible for what had happened? My wife and I are best friends and we talked about it. She said: 'Never think like this. You stand for peace and education, and Malala stands for peace and education – we should be proud. The Taliban are responsible, not us. Malala wanted to do this.' When she said this, I was fine.

Yousafzai said that even as a teenager Malala was the driving force behind her own activism:

> You can inspire your children, you can guide them, but you cannot construct them, you cannot engineer them. Already that spark was in her, you can't create that. When Malala was in the hospital and until this day she has never complained or implied what happened to her was someone's mistake. She is forgiving and resilient. Malala is Malala.

The central principle that guides Yousafzai's parenting and school teaching is that adults should not clip children's wings, whatever those wings look like. For him, it is about parents doing less and appreciating more. Watch your child, put your phone down and notice them. When they show preferences, encourage them, whether or not they are ones you share and whether or not they conform to gender stereotypes. He told me about his bewilderment when a man he knows said his daughter was as precious as a 'pearl in an oyster':

> Patriarchal men romanticise it in a way that girls are so precious, so valuable, that they are like a princess or a pearl in an oyster and we have to shield them from top to toe. I am sure he meant it as a compliment but this kind of love deprives a human being of humanity because of her gender. To learn and to be open. It is like they are not human. Why do you romanticise them to keep them invisible and then you romanticise their invisibility? This is not her choice.

Before I left, Yousafzai remembered something he wanted to show me and led me across the outhouse to where his iPad had been charging. It was a video that his younger son, Atal, had uploaded onto social media the previous evening, while revising for his A levels. In it, Atal sits by a computer and performs a rap he wrote called 'A Confession of a Child'. There are references to bullet holes, staying up at night praying his dad would return alive and wishing they had enough money to buy a PlayStation. Yousafzai watched the video with me intensely and while grinning about as widely as humanly possible. 'Honestly I don't understand much of what he says. I have a vague idea,' Yousafzai said, laughing. 'But I feel more happy when my children do things that I don't understand. Then I think they are living in their age. He is such a lovely boy.'

Yousafzai put the iPad away and described how he had recently tried to encourage his son to try to get into Oxford University, where Malala studied, but he realised he was pushing too hard:

Atal told me, you are limiting my choices. Oxford is not the only place, and it is not for every child. Oxford is not for me. It is funny, this idea of being limited by going to Oxford, but I understand him.

Yousafzai said fathers should think about whether they want to be 'future fathers' or 'past fathers':

It is difficult for men in patriarchy to stand against it. When you are in a comfort zone, doing what all other men and fathers do, it is the socially approved behaviour. When you go against that, the first person you come across is yourself, you feel uncomfortable, you question yourself. Will other men criticise me? Will they see me as a weak person, not a real man? Once I defeat that old self of mine, that is it done then. You are free. I believe in future fathers, futuristic fathers, who can see past this comfort zone.

A few days after meeting Yousafzai, I was sitting on the sofa with Solly watching TV. I usually avoid switching on *Peppa Pig* because I find her so annoying and Daddy Pig is such a moron, but I decided to give it another go. The episode was called 'Washing' and it started with Daddy Pig doing the laundry. Promising!

He hung his white football kit on the washing line outside before going to work as he was planning on playing football later. Peppa and her mum talked about 'poor Daddy having to go to work' before they jumped in a muddy puddle and got Daddy's kit all dirty. Maybe not so promising.

The girls and Peppa's brother George then put the football shirt in the washing machine, but Peppa put in her red dress as well and it all came out pink. Mummy Pig was dismayed. 'Pink isn't a very good colour for a football shirt,' she told her children. Daddy Pig came home and when he was shown the kit, he said: 'Hehehe, don't be silly, Peppa, that's one of Mummy's dresses – it's pink.' When he realised that it was, in fact, his kit, he said: 'But I can't wear a pink football shirt.' He ended up playing in his white work shirt and tie instead.

The line about not wearing a pink kit was particularly ridiculous because, as football fans will know, many teams have played in pink kits. Real Madrid, the most successful club in the world, recently had a bright pink away kit. We do not have many rules in our house, but *Peppa Pig* will not be on again any time soon.

In recent years, there has been a notable effort from producers and commissioners to make more progressive children's TV. One programme that gets a lot of praise is *Bluey*, about a family of Australian cartoon dogs. It is funny and playful and features a great dad. The main character, Bluey, is a girl, even though she is blue. Twist! Bluey and her sister, Bingo, play elaborate games with their parents. It captures the magic of imaginative play. The dad character, Bandit, is engrossed in his children's games, silly and has endless patience but is not overbearing. He waits and lets the children figure things out, like riding a bike, by themselves, without panicking if they fall.

One episode is almost entirely Bluey copying everything her dad does and says while he tries to outwit her. He takes the girls to the supermarket, and they pretend Bluey is the parent and he is one of the kids, being scolded for adding vegetables to the trolley. They go to a creek and the children give him a mud facial and manicures. The mum character, Chilli, is also fun and physical. She and her husband launch their girls back and forth on a hammock, pretending it is a pirate ship. Bandit feels like a dad of the moment. He is present, funny and loving, like lots of modern fathers. He is still not quite taking full responsibility though.

He takes Bluey and Bingo swimming and does not bother bringing the bag of essentials that Chilli asks him to take. When she reminds him, he says 'Boring!' and then squirts her with a water gun. They get to the pool and the children's eyes sting because they do not have their goggles. They have to stay in the shade because they do not have sun cream or hats. Mum arrives and saves the day by bringing the boring bag.

We bought a *Bluey* book. In it the mum goes out for one evening and it is such a rare occurrence that the dad should do bedtime by himself that this event gets a name: Daddy putdown. I love watching *Bluey* with Solly, but I feel like a *dafkanik* for being irritated by these details. It is definitely massive progress in comparison to *Peppa Pig* though.

One of Solly's favourite TV shows is *Bing*, on CBeebies. The main character, Bing, is a pre-school-age, black bunny being brought up by Flop, his carer, who is orange and smaller than Bing. They live together but they do not look at all alike and it is never clear whether Flop is Bing's dad or some kind of foster carer. Bing has friends and they all have similar set-ups, with parent figures who do not look like them. Bing is pretty whiny and regularly feels hard done by. Flop, who is voiced by Oscar-winning actor Sir Mark Rylance, is calm, patient and nurturing. Bing will start to have a tantrum and Flop will masterfully guide him away from it, addressing Bing's feelings while gently nudging his thoughts in a way that allows Bing to resolve the problem himself. Some parents hate it because Bing whinges a lot. It is a bit sanctimonious, but it feels exciting to see a male character who is such a great parent. A few times when Solly has started to descend into a tantrum, I have genuinely found myself thinking, what would Flop do in this situation?

Watching a bit of *Peppa Pig* is not going to turn a child into a misogynist pig. That one episode about washing did not have an impact on Solly. But you can see how the messages all around children about what girls and boys should and should not do, say or wear can add up and narrow their ideas about how they should be as an adult, and even who they can be as a parent.

We are trying to follow Yousafzai's advice about being 'future fathers' and showing Solly that it can be natural for men to be parents who are nurturing, loving, creative and affectionate, as well as physical and fun. We are also trying to encourage all of the interests Solly starts to show, whatever they are, however supposedly masculine or feminine, and however similar or different to ours. For the moment, Solly is still a boy who loves playing football in rainbow leggings.

CHAPTER NINE

I HAVE TEN DADDIES!

Embracing Modern Families

In a ball pit at a soft-play café, Solly and an older boy are taking turns trying to hit me on the forehead. I am lying down and kicking hard, so green and blue plastic balls are flying all around us.

'Throw it Daddy Pauly! Throw it Daddy Pauly!' Solly says to the older boy, while lobbing another blue ball towards my face.

Robin has been drinking coffee at a nearby table and arrives to swap with me.

'Daddy Robin here!' Solly says.

The older boy, who Solly has never met before, corrects him, pointing to me and saying, 'No, that's your daddy.'

Solly's reply is instant. 'My two daddies!'

Robin and I look at each other. He has never said this out loud before.

The older boy joins in. 'I have ten daddies!' he shouts, throwing his hands into the air and jumping back into the ball pond.

The older boy's parents, Robin and I tell and retell the story of what happened to each other and laugh over our tepid lattes. It is a glorious moment that sums up how children tend to react when faced with something different. They are themselves. They are accepting and funny. The older boy's response was not to tell Solly that it is weird to have two dads, or that he must have a mum somewhere, or that dads are not good at looking after babies, but to accept it and then become competitive and try to out-daddy him. And then to move on and keep playing. He spent the rest of the soft-play session referring to us both as Solly's daddies. 'Do you want Daddy Pauly? He's over there. Or Daddy Robin?'

As a non-traditional family living in 21st-century Britain, we have almost always been welcomed and accepted with the same joy and warmth as any other family. Society is changing. It is becoming more common to see dads on the school run and less of a rarity to see two-dad or two-mum families, as well as single parents. However, some people refuse to accept the reality of families such as ours, with men as primary parents.

Robin and I both use Twitter. Since we started posting openly about our family, we have both been accused of 'erasing motherhood' and of denying Solly his heritage or treating him like a commodity or a fashion accessory by having him. What would two men want with a baby? Dads through surrogacy are compared to Commanders in Gilead, forcing our handmaids to give us their babies. We have been told that we must have secretly bribed Rachel, Solly's surrogate, to carry him for us.

When I was once at a café with Solly, I was talking to another child's grandmother about how Solly was born through egg donation and surrogacy. I explained how it worked in Britain, with egg donors and surrogates having to act altruistically by law and only being paid to cover their expenses. 'Yeah, but you secretly give them extra cash, don't you?' she asked. When I explained that we definitely did not illegally pay the egg donor or Rachel for us to have Solly, she looked unconvinced. No matter how often Rachel and other British surrogates speak about their personal reasons for wanting altruistically to help other people become parents, they are viewed with suspicion by some and told they cannot possibly know their own minds and that no rational woman could 'give up' a baby. Women who donate eggs for other women with fertility problems are, rightly, praised for their altruism. But when the people they are donating for are men, there are concerns.

Our experience is in no way unique as gay fathers. When the singer Elton John and his husband David Furnish became parents through surrogacy, Germaine Greer, the radical feminist writer, said: 'The concept of motherhood has emptied out. It's gone. It's been deconstructed.'[1] The chief executive of a prominent Christian group in Britain wrote that it was an example of 'the tragic but unsurprising consequences' of our culture drifting 'further and further from God's design'.[2]

In an interview with an Italian magazine, the designer Domenico Dolce, of Dolce & Gabbana, described children born through IVF as 'synthetic', and said they 'oppose gay adoption' and 'chemical offsprings and rented uterus'.[3]

Tom Daley, the British gold-medal-winning Olympic diver, and his husband, Dustin Lance Black, an Oscar-winning film-maker, faced similar comments when they announced they were having a child through surrogacy in 2018.

In the *Daily Mail*, Richard Littlejohn responded to the couple's news with a column headlined: 'Please don't pretend two dads is the new normal'. He described how Daley and Lance Black had posted a picture of their child's pregnancy scan – like many prospective parents do – and wrote: 'Here we have two men drawing attention to the fact that "they" are having a baby. But where's the mum, the possessor of the womb which features in this photograph? She appears to have been written out of the script entirely.' He conceded that homosexual couples could make excellent parents but said people felt discomfort about the 'trend towards treating women as mere breeding machines and babies as commodities'. Perhaps hoping to fend off criticism, he also wrote:

> Before the usual suspects start bouncing up and down, squealing 'homophobia', don't bother. I supported civil partnerships long before it was fashionable and I'd rather children were fostered by loving gay couples than condemned to rot in state-run institutions, where they face a better-than-average chance of being abused.

Well, I guess that's alright then? Of course, Littlejohn also reached for the 'who is the real daddy?' question:

> What I also find slightly disconcerting is that this story was reported virtually everywhere without so much as a raised eyebrow, as if it would be impolite even to ask any questions about the parentage. For instance, is Daley or his husband the father? Was it Bill, or was it Ben? Or neither of them?

After an aside about news of a transgender woman managing successfully to breastfeed her baby after being given hormone therapy to encourage milk production, he concluded: 'I'm looking forward to the photos of Tom Daley breastfeeding his new baby.'[4]

Sifting through this swamp, you find two main arguments: firstly, that gay men having children must be exploiting a mother and, secondly, that this is all selfish and not in the best interests of children, who should be brought up in traditional families.

The problem with the first argument is that critics who claim to care for the welfare of surrogates also appear to be unwilling to listen to the women themselves. When someone tweets this kind of criticism my way, accusing us of exploiting women, I just add as many surrogates on Twitter as I can to the thread so they can speak for themselves. The conversation usually ends there because the critics do not want to believe rational women would choose to be pregnant for other people. Ironically, they feel they should be able to decide what these women do with their own bodies. In my experience, surrogates in the UK – including Rachel, who carried Solly – usually do not see themselves as any kind of mother to the child and do not like to be called surrogate mothers.

I found it interesting that Littlejohn asked, about Daley's child: 'Where's the mum, the possessor of the womb which features in this photograph?' Why is the mother the person who carried the baby, rather than the egg donor? Who is 'the mum' in this family – or in mine? Is there one mum, two mums or none? What is so scary about just speaking in truths? The real-life facts are that Solly does not have one father and one mother. Not all families do. He has one genetic father (Robin) and one non-genetic father (me). He was also born because of an egg donor (who could be called his genetic mother) and a surrogate (Rachel, who could be called his birth mother). When keyboard warriors accuse us of denying Solly a mother, do they mean Rachel or the egg donor? I ask them and they do not know. In the reality of Solly's daily life, he has two parents who are both men. But we believe in celebrating all the different parts of his creation, very much including the extraordinary women who were central to us becoming a family.

The second argument is relevant to many more modern families. Ultimately, is it really in a child's best interests to bring them up in a family that does not look like the norm? This kind of suspicion of non-traditional families is not surprising. Single parents and lesbian mothers have long faced accusations of harming their children just by being themselves and living authentically as parents. Women in heterosexual couples who decide to balance the demands of mother-hood with a career – who split childcare with their partner or agree for a partner to be the primary caregiver – are also among those in non-traditional families who face judgment about their decisions. Children do best with a mother and father in traditional roles is the claim. This is shouted loudly by some but can also niggle quietly at the backs of the brains of more liberal-minded parents. Is it really in our child's best interests for him not to have a mum around all the time? If it is fine that I am at work, why do I feel guilty?

In her book *Mothers and Others*, Sarah Blaffer Hrdy, a biological anthropologist and professor emerita at the University of California, Davis, wrote about the way researchers have typically compared children in traditional families to those raised by single mothers. The research suggests that children in traditional families do better at school, get better jobs and are less likely to have emotional and psychological problems or to get into trouble with authorities.[5] However, Hrdy argues that this comparison is meaningless. She told me it was 'like comparing apples and oranges'.

Society has not traditionally made life particularly easy for single mothers. They are more likely to be in economic hardship, suffering with stress, lacking social support and facing stigma. It is not a huge shock that children who are poorer, and raised by a single caretaker fighting against endless societal hurdles, are less likely to get straight As. This also does not say anything about traditional families compared to other modern family structures not facing hardship.

Hrdy argued that the research has to go further to account for differences caused by historical, economic or social conditions and to differentiate between different types of households, for instance looking at ones in which the single mother had adequate social support. She wondered whether other forms of stable families, with a single parent not suffering economic hardship and sup-ported consistently by other attachment figures, such as involved grandparents or nursery teachers, would do almost as well, just as well or even better than those raised in traditional families. 'We don't know, because we rarely asked,' she wrote.[6]

As I described earlier in this book, Hrdy believes that evolution has relied on children having 'allomothers' – adults other than a genetic mother who provide committed caregiving to a child. In *Mothers and Others*, Hrdy referenced research suggesting how outcomes for children actually appear to be less to do with the structure of the immediate family, and more to do with having a few dedicated people involved in their care, whatever their genetic link to the child, or sex. At its most basic level, a child having more caring figures around, whatever their genetics, can be the difference between life and death.

Hrdy described how in the early 2000s, two British anthropologists, Rebecca Sear and Ruth Mace, re-evaluated a major study by the UK Medical Research Council between 1950 and 1974 of the health of children among Mandinka people in rural Gambia, West Africa. Out of the 2,294 children they studied, 883, almost 40 per cent, died before their fifth birthday. Sear and Mace were looking to see if anyone other than mothers mattered to the survival of the children.[7]

'The results from their reanalysis of the Gambian data were stunning,' Hrdy wrote. 'If the child had older siblings (especially sisters) or if the child's maternal grandmother was living nearby and was herself past reproductive age, the child's possibility of dying before age five fell from 40 per cent to 20 per cent.' She added: 'From the perspective of a Mandinka child, having an older sister on hand to babysit or a maternal grandmother to provide extra food as well as care was, literally, a lifesaver.'[8]

Children still appear to do best with a few close and secure attachment figures, whether or not they are all their parents. In the late 1980s and early 1990s, a team led by Abraham Sagi, an Israeli psychologist, and Marinus van IJzendoorn, a Dutch psychologist specialising in child development and attachment, conducted a series of studies in Israel and Holland comparing children cared for primarily by mothers with those whose mothers shared childcare with other adults. The research included assessing outcomes for children raised in Israel on kibbutzim, communal settlements which typically relied on professional childcare while parents worked.

On the kibbutzim, the childcare tended to be high quality, with good training for the *metapelot* (Hebrew for caregivers), who had chosen this as a career. Children who formed a secure relationship with a childminder were found to be 'more empathic, dominant, purposive, achievement-oriented, and independent' than those who appeared ambivalent towards the carers.[9] Infants who formed these secure attachments to their carers were also judged to be more self-confident and socially sophisticated when they started kindergarten, several years later.

Sagi and van IJzendoorn reported that, overall, 'children appear to profit most from three secure relationships'.[10] They found that a secure attachment to mothers was important and a good predictor of 'later socioemotional development'[11]. But even when this had not happened and mothers had not bonded well with their babies, they benefitted from having other attachment figures. These children were found to have better outcomes when they had close attachments to their fathers and professional caregivers, rather than when this was not compensated for by secure attachments to others.

Hrdy wrote that what the results showed 'is not that having a responsive mother does not matter (of course it does) but that infants nurtured by multiple caretakers grow up not only feeling secure but with better-developed and more enhanced capacities to view the world from multiple perspectives'.[12]

During interviews for this book, I repeatedly asked experts about the conclusions they had come to about the importance of traditional family structures, with a mother primarily responsible for parenting and a father at work. Susan Golombok, professor and former director of the Centre for Family Research at the University of Cambridge and an expert in outcomes for children in non-traditional families, said family structures were much less important than people often assumed:

> Every time a new family type comes along, there is a whole set of concerns that come up. But we see it as our role at the Centre to provide empirical data to address these questions – actually going out and doing psychological assessments of the children. Everybody said the children would suffer from psychological problems and behaviour problems. The research aims to provide objective data on what actually happens. What has become clear to me is that family structure doesn't matter nearly as much for children as everybody thought that it did. What matters much more is the quality of relationships in the family. I am not saying that no child in these families has problems. That wouldn't make sense at all. You get normal variation in new family forms. But what we have found over the years is that this is no different to others – you don't have raised levels of problems compared to the traditional family.

Michael Lamb, emeritus professor of psychology and former head of the Department of Social and Developmental Psychology at the University of Cambridge, said he had been surprised that there was still such rigid thought from many people about gender roles within families:

> The puzzle for me has been that in the 1970s people were asking these questions and there was a feeling at the time – and I certainly believed it – that we were moving towards

less gendered expectations and greater openness. I have since realised I misjudged the direction and pace of change.

In Britain, perhaps the most striking sign of dissent against the reality of modern families were protests in 2019 held at the gates of a state primary school that chose to teach pupils about families with same-sex parents. There were months of vitriolic demonstrations outside Anderton Park Primary School in Birmingham. Some parents objected to a programme of lessons called 'No Outsiders', which encouraged children to accept different types of families and to be tolerant of other religions and races. This was not sex education – it was about people and families. One of the books they read was about two male penguins raising a chick together.[13] The school had been rated outstanding by inspectors, and the No Outsiders programme was devised by Andrew Moffat, an assistant headteacher who was shortlisted for a prestigious Global Teacher prize.

Protesters used a megaphone to chant threats, upsetting and confusing the children inside. They accused the headteacher, Sarah Hewitt-Clarkson, of promoting homosexuality. They said the school had a 'paedophile agenda'. Concerns, more generally, about women's roles in society were also raised. In an interview with a Sky TV news reporter, one of the demonstrators shouted: 'God created man and then he created woman for man's pleasure and for his companionship. He did not create man for man.'[14] After weeks of confrontations, the protesters were forced to leave because the local council went to the High Court and obtained an injunction.[15]

These protests were hateful. But they were also futile. Modern families exist and the numbers are growing. Between 1991 and 2019 there were about 390,000 babies born as a result of IVF and donor insemination cycles, according to the UK's Human Fertilisation & Embryology Authority (HFEA).[16] In the US, there were more than 75,000 babies born following assisted reproduction in

2020 alone.[17] Many of the parents in these families are same sex or single women. Wonderfully, it is becoming increasingly difficult to pretend to children that families only exist in one traditional form. Every child at Solly's nursery knows about two-dad families because they know Solly. They also know about two-mum families because there are twins at the nursery with two mums. They know about single-parent families, because their classmates, friends and family members exist in these families. They are also aware of children whose fathers are as present in their lives as mothers.

On a sunny afternoon in June, I got a train to a coastal town in the south east of England to meet Freddy McConnell, a transgender single father with two children. We sat and talked at a café while his gorgeous five-month-old baby played in a buggy next to him, occasionally contributing to the discussion by making high-pitched noises, like a chirpy little dinosaur. We walked together on a promenade overlooking a pebbled beach and then up and down a pier. We got ice cream. We stopped on a bench for a bottle feed. In theory, McConnell is a remarkable modern parent, defying stereotypes about what a family looks like by just being himself. But the truth is, our meeting was not remarkable at all really. We were two relatively new parents going for a walk with one of our babies. We spent a lot of the time chatting about routines, baby clothes, dummies, potty training, toddler sleeping and parenting podcasts that we liked. We got on well. That is the truth about modern, supposedly radical families. Whether it is a man or woman pushing the buggy and doing the feeds, and whatever the number of parents at home, we are all pretty much doing the same stuff. Like all parents, getting through the day and trying to do our best.

As we walked along the coast, McConnell calmly juggled caring for his baby while answering my questions and, a couple of times, waving and saying 'hey' to friends passing in the other direction.

Like most dads involved in day-to-day childcare, the only vaguely negative reactions he has faced in his local community have been the occasional patronising ones from people who assume a man with a baby will not know what they are doing. McConnell asked me not to use his children's names. When he posts on social media he uses 'LB' for his baby and 'SJ' for his older son, who was four at the time of writing. McConnell said:

> Yesterday in Sainsbury's one of the staff was gently, but annoyingly, trying to tell me that I shouldn't have socks on my baby. She was saying to LB: 'You need to tell daddy that you're too hot, don't you? You need to tell daddy that you don't need socks on.' LB was not too hot.

He laughed and said these comments were very infrequent, maybe once every six months, and they did not seem to be any worse than the comments mothers can get, just different:

> My sister who has kids always used to get judgy comments about being able to cope, whereas I just sometimes get treated like a bit of a doofus. Older blokes will say, 'You on duty today?' I just say yes, because technically I am on duty, like I am every day.

Sometimes when Robin and I are having a hard couple of days, we will wonder how single parents manage on their own. We rely on each other continually. I could only be with McConnell for the afternoon as I had taken the day off work, and Robin was doing the nursery run. I assumed single parents would feel that they had it harder, by doing double, and just, incredibly, coped. I asked McConnell how he managed as a single parent and his response changed my perspective:

Maybe I am a bit of an anomaly or an outlier, but I genuinely look at couples who parent together and think, how do you do it? With friends, you often hear about the arguments and the struggles, and you don't necessarily hear about the day-in, day-out times that one parent was cooking dinner while the other was changing a nappy, which is obviously going to help things run more smoothly. But the idea of me having to negotiate a living space with another adult as well as my children, potentially disagreeing about which school to send them to or which name to give them, I would find that really hard. It doesn't feel like it is about being in control, it is just there is so much going on and there is a simplicity to being a single parent.

McConnell said he had been relatively lucky with sleep as a parent and LB was already sleeping through the night when we met. He added:

> I have been exhausted at times. But mums I know would sometimes describe the frustration of just listening to their partner snore while they were up breastfeeding at night. I wouldn't be able to deal with the injustice of that. I'd rather be by myself, in my own little bubble, doing it my own way.

During our few hours together, we bumped into McConnell's younger brother. His parents also still live nearby and help out with the kids. While parenting in a little bubble, he is not on his own. 'I have family very nearby and close friends who I just happened to be pregnant at the same time as in my small hometown, and I lean on them and they lean on me,' he said. 'It is such a cliché, and it doesn't necessarily take a village, but I do have a village, and I am extremely grateful for it.' In particular, he described the importance to his family of reliable, good-quality childcare:

I love nursery. I have such respect for early years workers. SJ loves them. They do things with him that I couldn't do, or wouldn't do. I am not the type of parent who is like 'let's do crafts, or let's play make believe for an hour'. LB also goes to nursery for four hours one day a week so SJ and I can go swimming or do a shop together. I don't feel any guilt about them going to nursery.

LB and SJ are unusual in one very specific way: they do not currently have birth certificates. McConnell has been taking legal action to try to be officially registered as their father, or parent, rather than as their mother. While McConnell is legally male, the law in Britain remains that the person who gives birth to a child is automatically their mother on their birth certificate, even if they have a Gender Recognition Certificate. McConnell said that a key argument made for him to be listed as the mother on his children's birth certificates was that his children should know the truth about their birth. But this is also exactly what he wants. He wants his children's birth certificates to reflect the reality – that they were born to a trans man. He would be delighted for his children's birth certificates to refer to him as their parent, or specifically as their transgender father, because this is what he is, by law. For the time being, while the case is being decided, his children do not have birth certificates, although his eldest was granted a passport. McConnell lost his case in the UK at the Court of Appeal and was denied a hearing by the Supreme Court but is now taking it to the European Court of Human Rights.[18]

Whatever the legal solution to this question, it seems clear that the status quo is not right. The law, as it stands, appears to be contradictory. How can you legally be a man and a mother at the same time? McConnell explained how the UK court judgment found that he was female for parenthood but male for all other purposes, and that the word 'mother' is now, essentially, a gender-neutral term because trans men can be mothers. He said this was 'illogical'. Currently, in the UK, if you are a transgender man and your partner gives birth, you can in practice be listed as the child's father on their birth certificate. But if you give birth you have to be the mother.

McConnell knows a couple who are both trans men and have two children, one carried by each of them. This means that they are both listed as a mother on one of the birth certificates and as a father on the other one. How is that an accurate record? How can you, at once, be a mother to one of your children and a father to the other one? McConnell also knows another trans man who gave birth to a child and is listed as the mother on the birth certificate but, in the box for occupation, wrote: 'Full-time father'.

A similar issue with birth certificates applies to children born through surrogacy. Solly's original birth certificate states that his mother was Rachel, his surrogate, and his father was James, who is Rachel's husband. The parental order that we got at court replaced this, but the original birth certificate still exists. A researcher in 200 years' time could look at the paperwork and assume this means that Rachel and James got pregnant with their own child and then decided to give him to us. A much better, and accurate, way to record how Solly was born would be for me and Robin to be listed as his parents and then for this to be linked to a surrogacy and donor conception register, so he and others born through surrogacy and donor conception could have access to all of the genuine details.

In McConnell's case, if he ends up having to be on his children's birth certificates as their mother, the historical records would not reflect the reality. Children should know how they were born. Some cite concerns about the erasure of motherhood and these changes skewing figures on the numbers of women giving birth. But surely more information is better.

McConnell said little is known currently about the numbers of trans dads giving birth. Why could we not improve records and, therefore, have reliable statistics on the total numbers of births each year, including how many of these were through surrogacy and to transgender men? What if a child is born to a transgender dad who later detransitions? Should the child not be able to know, when they are older, the truth about their birth? McConnell said: 'Everyone should know the origins of their birth and that has to include taking into account surrogacy, donor conception and trans parents. No one should be allowed to lie to their kids about how they were born.'

McConnell is a calm parent. When LB stirred in the buggy, he did not rush to respond. He kept talking and walking, but I could see him also waiting and watching to see if LB would settle back to sleep. I felt calmer being around him, strolling against the wind, by the sea.

Throughout my adult life I have dealt with periods of feeling intense anxiety. It usually happens when I slow down. I can be at work on a deadline, dealing with a serious legal issue minutes before publishing a big news investigation, and I am fine. I have reported from a live terror attack in Kenya, hiding behind the wheels of cars while gunfire went off metres away, and I felt weirdly calm. I regularly work undercover, and I do not find it overwhelmingly stressful. My mind is busy and occupied. But then it will be the first day of a holiday abroad in a gorgeous, quiet resort and over dinner I will feel a panic attack starting, sweeping over my head and gripping my chest. For many years I have taken an elective serotonin reuptake inhibitor (SSRI) anti-anxiety medication, which works for me. The periods of anxiety happen in the months after I get convinced by a GP to try coming off them. However, I have not had a period of anxiety like this since becoming a father. There is something about the busyness that suits me. I was particularly calm when Solly was a newborn. My mind stopped racing as I had a baby to care for and focus on completely. The adrenaline had somewhere to go.

I told McConnell about my experience of mental health as a father and he instantly agreed, turning towards me:

That's so funny, that is exactly what I find. I am an anxious person so I thought I am going to be an anxious parent, but I'm not. There are practical things all the time to do. They are either tired, hungry or uncomfortable in their nappy. So if you are tuned into that and go through what you have to do, you are like, I am needed, I know exactly what my task is. I have told that to friends who are anxious and think that means they would be an anxious parent. It is not necessarily true. I am a problem solver and parenthood feels like constant problem solving. And feeling needed, which is lovely. I really love hanging out with my kids.

Before I left, we stopped to pick up takeaway pizza as a treat for SJ after he finished nursery. While we waited, McConnell went to the toilet and handed LB to me. After a bit of cooing, I turned LB around into a position that Solly loved as a baby, cradled arm to belly and facing out. LB was not such a fan and puked a little pool of milk on the floor. McConnell came back and handed me a muslin. 'I think you've got a bit on your arm,' he said. We walked to the nursery and then I said goodbye and headed to the station.

The next day, I did Solly's nursery run and counted four dads and two mums picking up their children during the period I was there. One mum and dad had walked together. She had a dog on the lead, and he was wearing a baby sling. When I rang the nursery doorbell, the one male teacher who works there answered. That weekend we went to a barbeque at a male friend's house while his wife was working, as she often does on a Sunday. The friend very calmly multi-tasked grilling steaks and chicken while frying vegetables, comforting his toddler, setting out food for the kids and then bottle-feeding his nine-month-old baby. Robin and I watched him in awe, not because he was a man doing childcare but just because he was a great parent, managing all this on his own while we often find it challenging looking after one kid together.

For every bigot shouting at the school gates about women being created for men's pleasure, there are also lots of modern families, and people, all around, just getting on with their lives. Children are learning about different families and less narrow roles for men and women just by being among them. Change could be faster, but it is already happening.

EPILOGUE

WHEN ARE YOU HAVING ANOTHER ONE?

Now that Solly is two years old, we are starting to get the questions. When are you having another one? Do you want another one? How does it work with you? Who will be the dad this time?

The truth is, we do not really know. In theory, we would love to have another child, if possible, one day. Having a baby is not straightforward for many people, whether or not fertility treatment is needed, and that certainly includes gay male couples. These days there are not as many opportunities to try the old-fashioned way, but our attempts have, once again, been unsuccessful. We feel relaxed about it. We are already an atypical family. If we end up just having Solly, that will have been more than enough. If we have another and the gap ends up being quite big, that is fine too.

There are some things I am absolutely sure about though. I love Solly more than I could ever have imagined loving anyone. If I had another child, I would love them just as much. The genetic make-up of any child we had would have no bearing at all on how much I would love them. The same goes for Robin. While we have had some tough days, Robin and I can actually do it. We are fully involved primary parents and Solly is a smiley, sociable, funny kid who is doing brilliantly. We are not in any way exceptional. Men can, and should, do this.

If Robin and I did have another child, would we notice any changes in how fathers with babies are generally treated, compared to a few years ago? The pandemic has meant more fathers being at home, working flexibly and seeing more of their children. If we had another child, would there be more men at baby classes? Would nurses be less surprised to see one of us at appointments? Would we still be getting calls from health visitors shocked that a dad had answered? Would we be less anxious about taking parental leave? What would we do differently?

As with when we had Solly, I would hope we could both be with a new baby from birth, and then throughout the days and weeks afterwards. Every parent should have this time at the beginning of their children's lives, as long as the mother, or whoever has given birth, consents. I would not want to go home from hospital early to get some rest. I would want to have skin-to-skin contact, if possible. I would really hope Robin would get pooed on again.

I would also be much more relaxed about sleeping easily while Robin did his share of the night waking and feeds, whichever one of us went back to work first. If there is one clear thing I have learned over the past two and a half years, through trying to parent equally and in writing this book, it is that the key is trying to share the mental load. This means being fully on when you are on, but also that you can relax when you are not, because you know the other parent will be fine. They can settle the baby on their own, even if their technique seems incomprehensible to you.

If you do not trust your partner enough to believe, deep down, that they can cope on their own for a period of parental leave, it seems unlikely that you will share the responsibility fully in the long run. If, on a rare night out, you are checking your phone every half an hour to make sure your partner has successfully got the children to sleep, you are probably still carrying around most of the mental load. If you are calling your partner when they are at the office because you do not know how to pack the kids' school bags on your own, you are probably not sharing the stresses of parenting equally. Of course, this is all down to what people really want. You have to be committed to parenting equally to truly let go in these moments.

Roles within families are changing, and the institutions that we rely on as parents have not been keeping up. Governments that claim to care about gender equality are being disingenuous if, simultaneously, they are neglecting to fund parental leave policies fairly and ensuring that fathers take this time off, as well as mothers. Ministers cannot be believed when claiming to want to close the gender pay gap, while failing to subsidise childcare properly so that parents, and mostly mothers, can go back to work when they want to. These changes are needed ethically – because anything other than gender equality is a disgrace – but they are also investments in our children's futures that will benefit us all.

Will these issues still be debated when Solly's generation become mothers and fathers? There is only so long that governments can keep neglecting to support children properly in the first thousand days. There is increasing noise from the media about the need to better fund childcare, and politicians seem to be, gradually, waking up to the idea that childcare reform would be a vote winner. It also seems likely that shared parental leave will keep evolving, so that more men take it. By the time Solly is an adult, surely there will be many more MummyDaddies in many different countries wheeling their babies around parks and malls.

In writing this book, I have seen many examples of how parenting roles are evolving and how institutional changes can boost gender equality. The way hospital design is transforming birth experiences in Denmark. How use-it-or-lose-it paternity leave in Iceland and Sweden has allowed a new generation of babies to have months of direct care from their fathers. The school systems in Estonia and

Finland, showing the extraordinary benefits of properly funding early years education. The new $10-a-day childcare policy in Canada, because equal parenting is also good economics.

I have been encouraged by the work of academics from the world's top universities, whose research over the past five decades has started to show how dads are, contrary to assumptions, primed to be parents with equal responsibility.

More than anything, I have also been inspired by meeting families who are proving that, despite societal pressures, parents can do things differently. Freddy McConnell doing the nursery run by the seashore. Duncan Hames taking control of weaning and voting in parliament while carrying his baby in a sling. Lucy Greenwood working as a judge while her phone incessantly buzzes with calls from her daughter's school. Molly in the supermarket with her son. Carly Newman battling through every societal hurdle to balance work with childcare, asking her son's nursery if she can pay just a few days late. Ziauddin Yousafzai feeding me pakoras and sharing the wisdom that 'children learn from what we do, not what we teach'. Catherine Cho's husband passing her their baby to breastfeed during the nights, before taking the baby away, burping her, changing her and putting her to sleep, so his wife can have a little less on her mind.

Solly has still got a while until he has to worry about this stuff. Last night, he laughed in his sleep. It was about 11 p.m., after a particularly hot day. Temperatures had reached 40°C, the hottest heatwave ever in the UK, and Solly's nursery was one of many that shut early.

With Robin and I both working, we split the time looking after him in shifts. Robin picked Solly up from nursery at 1 p.m. and took him to a soft-play centre with air conditioning and iced coffees. I then took over when they got back, feeding Solly fish fingers and ice lollies and splashing in a paddling pool in our garden while Robin went back to work. I did bath time, and Robin did bedtime while I made a call to my boss, who had been trying to get hold of me for a few hours.

Later, as Robin and I got ready for bed, there was a loud cough from the audio monitor that links to one in Solly's room. Then he cackled – a full-on belly laugh – for a couple of seconds, before going quiet again. What was he thinking about? Robin and I lay in bed and speculated. A paddling pool full of blueberries? A giant fish finger riding a digger? One of his nursery teachers falling into a puddle? Who knows. It was joyous.

A LETTER FROM PAUL

There are so many books, and it can be a struggle to get the time to read, by yourself, without a manic toddler, or boss, demanding your attention, so I am incredibly grateful that you have spent some of your time with mine. My publishers at Thread are all about thought-provoking, inspiring and smart-thinking ideas that start conversations. If you are keen to read more of this sort of thing, you can sign up at the following link. Your email address will never be shared, and you can unsubscribe at any time.

thread-books.com/sign-up

While writing *The Equal Parent,* my intention has never been to tell anyone how they should live their lives or how to be a good parent. Frankly, I am just about managing most of the time. I decided to try to write a book about dads being equal parents while lying in bed one evening, thinking about how no one ever calls women 'hands-on' mothers. I rolled over to my husband's side and spent the next half an hour keeping him awake with ideas. He had lots of ideas too but said he would rather carry on talking about it in the morning. We have not stopped discussing the subject since. Living in a two-father family has forced us to try things differently, without expectations about parenting roles or guilt for defying them. You may have nodded along, agreeing that men can be equal parents, or you may have found the way we share things utterly bizarre. Both are fine! I don't want everyone to agree with me, but it would be great if reading this book sparked discussions.

With that in mind, I would love to hear what you think. If you loved it, please consider writing a review. They really help, particularly first-time authors. You can also get in touch with me directly on Twitter, Instagram, or at my website: paulmorganbentley.com.

Thank you so much for reading *The Equal Parent*.

Paul

ACKNOWLEDGMENTS

I have had so much help in writing this book and am very grateful to everyone who contributed. Firstly, Claire Bord at Thread. I have had many editors and sub-editors during my career as a journalist. Claire has been the dream editor. Frustratingly, it has been impossible to argue with her suggestions as every one of them has made *The Equal Parent* much better. Thank you also to the wider team at Thread who have backed this book with such enthusiasm and, specifically, to Myrto Kalavrezou, Alex Holmes, Maureen Cox and Richard King, a kindred spirit who also believes passionately that dads can be equal parents.

Julia Silk, my agent, is one of those people who introduces herself to you and, before you know it, an hour has passed and you feel like you have a new best friend. I am so thankful to Julia for responding to my blind email book submission with such warmth and excitement and for all of the long and funny phone calls we have had since. She found the perfect home for *The Equal Parent* at Thread, and I am very grateful.

Thank you also to all the very brilliant scientists, academics, politicians, campaigners, activists, community workers, authors and other parents who gave me their time for free to be interviewed for this book. In particular, thank you to Evalotte Mörelius, Nils Bergman, Jenna Wall, Leah Hazard, Esben Bala Skouboe, Sarah Blaffer Hrdy, Catherine Cho, Mary Ann Sieghart, Jim Waterson,

Danny Harmer, Jo Swinson, Duncan Hames, Lucinda Platt, Andrew Bazeley, Jemima Olchawski, Carly Newman, Joeli Brearley, Lucy Greenwood, Susan Golombok, Molly, Anna Machin, Michael Lamb, Jeremy Davies, Elliott Rae, Owen Thomas, Kieran Anders, Pragya Agarwal, Ziauddin Yousafzai and Freddy McConnell.

I also relied on discussions with close family and friends including my sisters Tanya and Debbie, my brother Josh, my brothers-in-law Eli, David and Sam and sisters-in-law Carly and Alexandra, as well as Deborah, Paul, Charlotte, Mark, Aaron, Michelle, Alex, Andrew, Royi, Joanna, Natan, Josh, Daniel, Aryeh, Robert, Lydia, Noam, Gabriella and Caroline. And to Rachel, James, Charlie and Jack (and Reggie) – you have made our family possible, and we will never be able to express fully how much we love you.

I am also very grateful to all of the unnamed people quoted in the book – and in some of the chapter headings – for providing useful material. I will forever have a soft spot for the chemist in Willesden Green who called me MummyDaddy and slipped freebies into Solly's buggy when he was a few months old.

Balancing work, writing a book and looking after Solly has been a challenge. I am a firm believer in the importance of alloparents – the few regular carers around us that we rely on to help us look after our children – in part because I have seen how each of these relationships has helped Solly to become the fun, sociable and empathetic person that he already is. We are so lucky to have found a nursery where Solly feels so safe that he runs to cuddle the teachers in the morning. To Robin's parents, Karen and Martin – thank you so much for looking after Solly so often and coming up with such fun and inventive trips and activities. Wednesdays with you are the highlight of Solly's week, and we would struggle without you.

And to my parents, Esther and Simon. I am so lucky to have parents who are also my best friends. Our weekend days together are pure joy. I will always strive to have a home that is as loving, fun, chaotic and full of delicious, fattening food as ours was when I was growing up, and yours still is. Thank you for providing so much material for this book and for therapy sessions. I love you.

Finally, my boys. Robin, my husband, writing partner, first reader and editor. Thank you for allowing me to write about our life in such detail. Of course, this book could never have existed without you. We do everything as a team, and this is as much your story as it is mine. But, also, I never would have had the courage to have tried to write this without having been inspired by your own writing career. There are very few people who could get up one day, without any advice or direction, and just think – you know what, I am going to try to write a book. You did it, and you made me believe I could too. Thank you. Solly, I really hope that you don't hate me when you're older because I shared so much about you in this book. You can get me back if you want and write your own version of events. I feel incredibly grateful to have you, and your other dad, in my life.

NOTES

Introduction: You Know What You're Letting Yourself In For, Don't You?

1 County Durham and Darlington NHS Foundation Trust, 'For dads and partners', cddft.nhs.uk/our-services/division-of-women,-children-and-sexual-health/maternity/pregnancy,-labour,-birth-your-baby/labour-and-birth/for-dads-and-partners.aspx

2 *Chambers Concise Dictionary* (Chambers Harrap Publishers, 2004).

3 Abraham E., Hendler T., Shapira-Lichter I., Kanat-Maymon Y., Zagoory-Sharon O., Feldman R., 'Father's brain is sensitive to childcare experiences', *Proceedings of the National Academy of Sciences* (2014).

Chapter One: Go Home and Get Some Rest: Panic and Bonding in the Days after Birth

1 World Health Organization and the United Nations Children's Fund, *Baby-friendly Hospital Initiative Training Course for Maternity Staff: Participant's Manual* (5 August 2020).

2 United Nations Children's Fund, 'Skin-to-skin contact', unicef.org.uk/babyfriendly/baby-friendly-resources/implementing-standards-resources/skin-to-skin-contact

3 Erlandsson K., Dsilna A., Fagerberg I., Christensson K., 'Skin-to-skin care with the father after cesarean birth and its effect on newborn crying and prefeeding behavior', *Birth* (2007).

4   Huang X., Chen L., Zhang L., 'Effects of paternal skin-to-skin contact in newborns and fathers after cesarean delivery', *Journal of Perinatal & Neonatal Nursing* (2019).

5   Ayala A., Christensson K., Christensson E., Cavada G., Erlandsson K., Velandia M., 'Newborn infants who received skin-to-skin contact with fathers after caesarean sections showed stable physiological patterns', *Acta Paediatrica* (2021).

6   Shorey S., He H.G., Mörelius E., 'Skin-to-skin contact by fathers and the impact on infant and paternal outcomes: an integrative review', *Midwifery* (2016).

7   Betran A.P., Ye J., Moller A-B., Souza J.P., Zhang J., 'Trends and projections of caesarean section rates: global and regional estimates', *BMJ Global Health* (2021).

8   NHS, 'Overview: Caesarean section', nhs.uk/conditions/caesarean-section

9   In 2020 the proportion of all deliveries in the United States that were by caesarean section was 31.8 per cent. Centres for Disease Control and Prevention, 'Births – Method of Delivery', cdc.gov/nchs/fastats/delivery.htm

10 Mörelius E., Örtenstrand A., Theodorsson E., Frostell A., 'A randomised trial of continuous skin-to-skin contact after preterm birth and the effects on salivary cortisol, parental stress, depression, and breastfeeding', *Early Human Development* (2015).

11 Dzeaye N.G., 'Prolactin and testosterone levels in first-time fathers during skin-to-skin contact with their infants soon after birth by caesarean section', University of Cape Town, open.uct.ac.za/bitstream/handle/11427/5939/thesis_hsf_2014_dzeaye_nv.pdf?sequence=1&isAllowed=y (2014).

12 Dewar C., 'Edinburgh midwives say men using postnatal ward "like a hotel" are "compromising patient care"', *Edinburgh Evening News* (14 January 2020).

13 NHS, 'NHS maternity statistics, England – 2020–21', digital. nhs.uk/data-and-information/publications/statistical/nhs-maternity-statistics/2020-21

14 Data from Freedom of Information requests sent by the author to 123 trusts that manage NHS hospitals. Out of 74 trusts that responded, 19 said they usually allowed partners to stay with the mother or birthing parent throughout the time after the child was born. In some cases, partners are only allowed to stay for a maximum of one hour per day. Birthing units run by midwives are often able to be more accommodating of partners staying for longer with mothers and babies.

15 In a response to a Freedom of Information request from the author, Northumbria Healthcare NHS Foundation Trust stated: 'All birthing partners are encouraged to come prepared to enable them to stay from the point of admission until discharge home', adding that there was '24-hour access to the antenatal/postnatal ward for birthing partners, with a second visitor welcome to attend a scheduled appointment' (29 December 2021).

16 NHS, 'Northumbria Specialist Emergency Care Hospital', nhs.uk/Services/hospitals/Overview/DefaultView. aspx?id=101968

17 Hazard L., *Hard Pushed: A Midwife's Story* (Hutchinson, 2019).

18 Hildingsson I., Thomas J., Olofsson R.E., Nystedt A., 'Still behind the glass wall? Swedish fathers' satisfaction with postnatal care', *Journal of Obstetric, Gynocologic and Neonatal Nursing* (2009).

19 Roberts M., 'NHS vs private maternity care: what are your options?' *Which?* (12 July 2022).

20 The Leeds Teaching Hospitals NHS Trust, 'Planned new maternity centre will be largest in the UK', leedsth.nhs.uk/

about-us/btlw/future-hospitals/latest-news/2022/06/01/
planned-new-maternity-centre-will-be-largest-in-the-uk
21 Frizzell N., *The Panic Years* (Penguin, 2022), pp.283–284.

Chapter Two: Who Does the Nights?
The Mother and Father Instinct

1 Galbally M., Lewis A.J., van IJzendoorn M., Permezel M.,
   'The role of oxytocin in mother-infant relations: a systematic
   review of human studies', *Harvard Review of Psychiatry* (2011).
2 Feldman R., Weller A., Zagoory-Sharon O., Levine A.,
   'Evidence for a neuroendocrinological foundation of human
   affiliation: plasma oxytocin levels across pregnancy and
   the postpartum period predict mother-infant bonding',
   Psychological Science (2007).
3 Gordon I., Zagoory-Sharon O., Leckman J.F., Feldman R.,
   'Oxytocin and the development of parenting in humans',
   Biological Psychiatry (2010).
4 Feldman R., 'Oxytocin and social affiliation in humans',
   Hormones and Behaviour (2012).
5 Atzil S., Hendler T., Zagoory-Sharon O., Winetraub Y.,
   Feldman R., 'Synchrony and specificity in the maternal and
   the paternal brain: relations to oxytocin and vasopressin',
   *Journal of the American Academy of Child and Adolescent
   Psychiatry* (2012).
6 Abraham E., Hendler T., Shapira-Lichter I., Kanat-Maymon
   Y., Zagoory-Sharon O., Feldman R., 'Father's brain is sensitive
   to childcare experiences', *Proceedings of the National Academy
   of Sciences* (2014).
7 Hrdy S.B., *Mothers and Others: The Evolutionary Origins
   of Mutual Understanding* (The Belknap Press of Harvard
   University Press, 2011).

8 Hrdy S.B., *Mother Nature: Natural Selection & The Female of the Species* (Pantheon Books, 1999), p.535.

9 Hrdy S.B., 'Born Human: How the Utterly Dependent Survive', a speech given for the Center for Academic Research & Training in Anthropogeny at the University of California San Diego. Available online at: uctv.tv/shows/CARTA-Birth-to-Grandmotherhood-Childrearing-in-Human-Evolution-Sarah-Blaffer-Hrdy-Born-Human-How-the-Utterly-Dependent-Survive-28217 (6 August 2014).

10 Sear R., Mace R., McGregor I.A., 'Maternal grandmothers improve the nutritional status and survival of children in rural Gambia', *Proceedings of the Royal Society Series B: Biological Sciences* (2000).

11 van IJzendoorn M.H., Sagi A., Lambermon M.W.E., 'The multiple caretaker paradox: Data from Holland and Israel', *New Directions for Child Development* (1992).

12 The Lullaby Trust, 'Dummies and SIDS', lullabytrust.org.uk/safer-sleep-advice/dummies-and-sids

13 NHS, 'Overview: Postnatal depression', nhs.uk/mental-health/conditions/post-natal-depression

14 Oster E., *Cribsheet: A Data-Driven Guide to Better, More Relaxed Parenting, from Birth to Preschool* (Souvenir Press, 2019).

15 Hiscock H., Bayer J., Gold L., Hampton A., Ukoumunne O.C., Wake M., 'Improving infant sleep and maternal mental health: a cluster randomised trial', *Archives of Disease in Childhood* (2006).

16 Oster E., *Cribsheet: A Data-Driven Guide to Better, More Relaxed Parenting from Birth to Preschool* (Souvenir Press, 2019), p.177.

17 Cho C., *Inferno: A Memoir of Motherhood and Madness* (Bloomsbury Circus, 2020), p.7.

18 NHS, 'Postpartum psychosis', nhs.uk/mental-health/
    conditions/post-partum-psychosis
19 Walker M., *Why We Sleep* (Penguin Books, 2018), p.7.
20 Ibid., p.3.

Chapter Three: You'll Still Go to the Office a Bit, Right?
Reimagining Parental Leave

1 Whipple T., 'Are you man enough to take five months'
   paternity leave?', *The Times* (9 August 2014).
2 HM Government, 'New shared parental leave arrangements',
   gov.uk/government/news/new-shared-parental-leave-
   arrangements gov.uk/shared-parental-leave-and-pay (17
   January 2011).
3 In December 2021 the Institute for Fiscal Studies, an economic
   think tank, reported figures from the UK's HM Revenue &
   Customs suggesting that in the 2018/19 financial year 'just
   10,700 couples took up paid shared parental leave, which is less
   than 2% of the 654,000 women who took up maternity leave
   in that year'. Institute for Fiscal Studies, 'Women and men at
   work' (6 December 2021).
4 HM Government, 'Shared Parental Leave and Pay', gov.uk/
   shared-parental-leave-and-pay
5 For the first six weeks after having a child, UK statutory
   parental leave pay covers 90 per cent of the parent's average
   weekly earnings before tax. After this point, it then falls to a
   maximum of just over £155 per week for the next 33 weeks.
   (In the 2022/23 financial year, the flat rate was £156.66. You
   either get the flat rate or 90 per cent of your average weekly
   earnings, whichever is lower.) The final 13 weeks of the year
   are then unpaid. To put this £156.66 per week into context,
   the national minimum living wage for workers in the UK
   aged 23 and over became £9.50 per hour from April 2022, so

statutory weekly parental leave pay is the equivalent of what someone on minimum wage earns in less than 17 hours, or less than half the lowest amount an employer can legally get away with paying a worker per week. A further problem with the policy as it stands is that it is not available to all fathers, including ones who are self-employed or on zero-hours contracts.

6 Sevilla A., Smith S., 'Baby steps: the gender division of childcare during the COVID-19 pandemic', *Oxford Review of Economic Policy* (2020).

7 Miliband E., *Go Big: How to Fix Our World* (The Bodley Head, 2021), pp.60–61.

8 Institute for Fiscal Studies, 'Women and men at work', (6 December 2021), p.2.

9 Workers in the US only have a basic federal legal right to up to 12 weeks of unpaid leave around the birth of a child, and only about one in five has access to any form of paid family leave through their employer. There are some slightly better local entitlements. In 2004, California was the first state to implement a comprehensive paid family leave law. Workers with paid family leave insurance can receive wage replacement benefits for up to eight weeks, partially paid at 60 to 70 per cent of earnings, depending on income and up to a cap of $1,357 per week in 2021. See Petts R.J., Engeman C., Kaufman G., Gatenio Gabel S., 'United States country note' in Koslowski A., Blum S., Dobrotić I., Kaufman G., Moss P. (eds), *17th International Review of Leave Policies and Related Research 2021*. Available at: leavenetwork.org/annual-review-reports (2021).

10 Eydal G.B., Gíslason I.V., 'Iceland country note', in Koslowski A., Blum S., Dobrotić I., Kaufman G., Moss P. (eds), *17th International Review of Leave Policies and Related Research*

2021. Available at: leavenetwork.org/annual-review-reports (2021).

11 Cederström C., 'State of Nordic Fathers', *Nordic Council of Ministers* (2019).

12 Haataja A., The Social Insurance Institution of Finland (Kela), 'Fathers' use of paternity and parental leave in the Nordic countries' (2009).

13 Chronholm A., 'Fathers' experience of shared parental leave in Sweden', *Recherches Sociologiques et Anthropologiques* (2007).

14 Individual parents in Sweden can take 240 days of leave, with 195 days paid at 77.6 per cent of earnings, up to a maximum of SEK486,000 (about £38,000) and then at a flat rate. There is some ability to transfer the allocation between parents but 90 of the days each cannot be traded. Parental leave can be taken at any time until the child turns 12 years old, although only 96 days can be used after the child turns four. See Duvander A.-Z., Löfgren N., 'Sweden country note' in Koslowski A., Blum S., Dobrotić I., Kaufman G., Moss P. (eds), *17th International Review of Leave Policies and Related Research 2021*. Available at: leavenetwork.org/annual-review-reports (2021).

15 Sieghart M.A., *The Authority Gap: Why Women Are Still Taken Less Seriously Than Men, and What We Can Do About It* (Doubleday, 2021),

16 Sieghart's book, *The Authority Gap: Why Women Are Still Taken Less Seriously Than Men, and What We Can Do About It*, cites studies exploring outcomes in more gender equal relationships, including: Carlson D.L., Hanson S., Ftzroy A., 'The division of child care, sexual intimacy, and relationship quality in couples', *Gender & Society* (2016); Holter O.G., '"What's in it for men?": old question, new data', *Men and Masculinities* (2014); Croft A., Schmader T., Block K., Baron A.S., 'The second shift reflected in the second generation: do parents' gender roles at home predict children's aspirations?',

Psychological Science (2014); and Miller E., Jones K.A., McCauley H.L., Chugani C.D., Coulter R.W.S., Abebe K.Z., 'Cluster randomized trial of a college health center sexual violence intervention', *American Journal of Preventative Medicine* (2020).

17 Brammar J., twitter.com/jessbrammar/status/1387694989266853888 (29 April 2021).

18 Topping A., twitter.com/LexyTopping/status/1387733454465421315 (29 April 2021).

19 Aviva, 'Takeup of equal parental leave at Aviva remains high after four years', aviva.com/newsroom/news-releases/2022/06/takeup-of-equal-parental-leave-at-aviva-remains-high-after-four-years (13 June 2022).

20 Netflix, 'Starting now at Netflix: unlimited maternity and paternity leave', web.archive.org/web/20160328051636/https://media.netflix.com/en/company-blog/starting-now-at-netflix-unlimited-maternity-and-paternity-leave (4 August 2015).

21 Gross E.L., 'Goldman Sachs has upped the ante for paid parental leave on Wall Street', *Forbes* (5 November 2019).

22 Accenture UK, 'Rebalancing work and family', accenture.com/gb-en/blogs/blogs-rebalancing-work-and-family (6 March 2019).

23 Institute for Fiscal Studies, 'Women and men at work' (6 December 2021), p.27.

24 Swinson J., *Equal Power: And How You Can Make It Happen* (Atlantic Books, 2018), p.157.

25 Ibid., p.157.

26 Ibid., p.151.

27 Cooke L.P., 'The case for paid fatherhood leave', University of Bath Institute for Policy Research blog, blogs.bath.ac.uk/iprblog/2021/12/06/the-case-for-paid-fatherhood-leave (6 December 2021).

Chapter Four: Which One of You Is Quitting?
Returning to Work in the Nursery Years

1 HM Government, 'School admissions: School starting age', gov.uk/schools-admissions/school-starting-age.

2 Calver T., 'Held back: the mothers who can't afford to return to work', *Sunday Times* (5 June 2022).

3 Save the Children, '870,000 mums in England can't get the childcare they need', savethechildren.org.uk/news/media-centre/press-releases/870-000-stay-at-home-mums-in-england-want-to-work-but-cant-get-the-childcare-they-need (16 March 2018).

4 The figures are from country comparisons by the Organisation for Economic Cooperation and Development (OECD), showing childcare costs, net of any government subsidies and tax breaks, as a percentage of household income. The calculations assume both parents earn 67 per cent of the average wage and are raising two children, aged two and three. OECD, 'Net childcare costs', doi.org/10.1787/e328a9ee-en (2022).

5 Rastrigina O., Pacifico D., Damwerth R., 'Net childcare costs in EU countries', *OECD* (2020).

6 Lovegrove S., twitter.com/SharLovegrove/status/1518570492063535139 (25 April 2022).

7 Sylvester R., 'Want your child to have the best education in Europe? Move to Estonia', *The Times* (6 November 2021).

8 Figures based on gross median weekly earnings for full-time and part-time employees in the UK in 2021. Office for National Statistics, 'Employee earnings in the UK: 2021', ons.gov.uk/employmentandlabourmarket/peopleinwork/earningsandworkinghours/bulletins/annualsurveyofhoursandearnings/2021#employee-earnings-and-hours-worked (26 October 2021).

9 Pregnant Then Screwed, 'Press release – 1 in 4 parents
have had to cut down on heat, food & clothing
to pay for childcare', pregnantthenscrewed.com/
one-in-four-parents-say-that-they-have-had-to-cut-down-on-
heat-food-clothing-to-pay-for-childcare (25 March 2022).

10 OECD, 'Net childcare costs', doi.org/10.1787/e328a9ee-en
(2022).

11 Social Mobility Commission, 'The stability of the early
years workforce in England', assets.publishing.service.gov.
uk/government/uploads/system/uploads/attachment_data/
file/906906/The_stability_of_the_early_years_workforce_in_
England.pdf, p.28 (5 August 2020).

12 Hansard House of Commons Debate. Volume 700, Childcare,
column 221WH, 13 September 2021. [Online]. Available
from: hansard.parliament.uk/Commons/2021-09-13/debates/
d6d0fe4d-196f-4d78-bc82-7afbd1f10efa/WestminsterHall.

13 Department for Education, 'Statutory framework for the
early years foundation stage', assets.publishing.service.gov.
uk/government/uploads/system/uploads/attachment_data/
file/974907/EYFS_framework_-_March_2021.pdf (31 March
2021).

14 HM Government, '15 hours free childcare for 3- and
4-year-olds', gov.uk/help-with-childcare-costs/free-childcare-
and-education-for-2-to-4-year-olds.

15 HM Government, 'Free education and childcare for
2-year-olds', gov.uk/help-with-childcare-costs/free-childcare-2-
year-olds.

16 HM Government, 'Universal Credit and childcare', gov.uk/
help-with-childcare-costs/universal-credit.

17 HM Government, '15 hours free childcare for 3 and
4-year-olds', gov.uk/help-with-childcare-costs/free-childcare-
and-education-for-2-to-4-year-olds.

18 HM Government, 'Tax-Free Childcare', gov.uk/tax-free-childcare.

19 Tew I., 'Families let £3 billion in tax-free childcare benefits go unclaimed', *The Times* (28 May 2022).

20 National Day Nurseries Association, 'Stop Underfunding – Start Building Futures', ndna.org.uk/wp-content/uploads/2021/09/1258_NDNA_A4_Report_PDF_England_AW-1.pdf (9 September 2021).

21 Sylvester R., 'How to teach a toddler, the Scandi way', *The Times* (4 March 2022).

22 Hunt M., 'MPs call for end to £10k penalty on new fathers', *The Daily Telegraph* (22 February 2020).

23 Pregnant Then Screwed, 'Press release – nearly a fifth of parents have had to leave their jobs because of the cost of childcare', pregnantthenscrewed.com/press-release-nearly-a-fifth-of-parents-have-had-to-leave-their-jobs-because-of-the-cost-of-childcare (28 October 2019).

24 Peck S., 'Fathers' "raw deal" on flexible working', *The Daily Telegraph* (27 January 2014).

25 Brands R., twitter.com/RainaBrands/status/1499017094024806403 (2 March 2022).

26 Greenwood L., twitter.com/Intarblawyer/status/1501117965491703809 (8 March 2022).

27 Institute for Fiscal Studies, 'Women and men at work' (6 December 2021).

28 OECD, 'Programme for International Student Assessment 2018 results: Combined executive summaries', oecd.org/pisa/Combined_Executive_Summaries_PISA_2018.pdf (2018).

29 Sylvester R., 'Want the best schools in Europe? Try Estonia', *The Times* (5 November 2021) and Times Education Commission, 'Bringing out the best: How to transform education and unleash the potential of every child', nuk-tnl-editorial-prod-

staticassets.s3.amazonaws.com/2022/education-commission/
Times%20Education%20Commission%20final%20report.pdf
(2022).

30 Education Policy Institute, 'Divergent Pathways: the
disadvantage gap, accountability and the pupil premium',
epi.org.uk/publications-and-research/divergent-pathways-
disadvantage-gap-accountability-pupil-premium (2016).

31 Sylvester R., 'How to teach a toddler, the Scandi way', *The
Times* (4 March 2022).

32 OECD, 'Programme for International Student Assessment
2018 results: Combined executive summaries', oecd.org/pisa/
Combined_Executive_Summaries_PISA_2018.pdf (2018).

33 Government of Canada, 'Toward $10-a-Day: Early
Learning and Child Care', canada.ca/en/employment-social-
development/campaigns/child-care.html (modified 2022)
and Shakil I., Gordon J., 'Canada's Trudeau secures national
childcare legacy with Ontario deal', *Reuters* (28 March 2022).

34 Fortin P., Godbout L., St-Cerny S., 'The impact of Quebec's
low-cost child care on women's participation rates, domestic
income and government budgets', *Revue Interventions
Économiques/Papers in Political Economy* (2013).

35 OECD, 'Programme for International Student Assessment
2018 results: Combined executive summaries', oecd.org/pisa/
Combined_Executive_Summaries_PISA_2018.pdf (2018).

Chapter Five: Who Is the *Real* Dad?
Why Parenting Is Active, Not a Genetic Condition

1 Golombok S., *We Are Family: What Really Matters for Parents
and Children* (Scribe Publications, 2020).

2 Golombok S., Spencer A., Rutter M., 'Children in lesbian
and single-parent households: psychosexual and psychiatric
appraisal', *Journal of Child Psychology and Psychiatry* (1983).

3 Kirkpatrick M., Smith C., Roy R., 'Lesbian mothers and their children: a comparative study', *American Journal of Orthopsychiatry* 1981) and Green R., Mandel J.B., Hotvedt M.E., Gray J., Smith L., 'Lesbian mothers and their children: a comparison with solo parent heterosexual mothers and their children', *Archives of Sexual Behaviour* (1986).

4 Golombok S., *We Are Family: What Really Matters for Parents and Children* (Scribe Publications, 2020), p.23.

5 Tasker F., Golombok S., 'Adults raised as children in lesbian families', *American Journal of Orthopsychiatry* (1995).

6 Golombok S., Perry B., Burston A., Murray C., Mooney-Somers J., Stevens M., Golding J., 'Children with lesbian parents: a community study', *Developmental Psychology* (2003).

7 Wainright J.L., Russell S.T., Patterson C.J., 'Psychological adjustment, school outcomes and romantic relationships of adolescents with same-sex parents', *Child Development* (2004).

8 Golombok S., Blake L., Slutsky J., Raffanello E., Roman G., Ehrhardt A., 'Parenting and the adjustment of children born to gay fathers through surrogacy', *Child Development* (2017).

9 UK government statistics show that, in 2011, 117 parental orders were granted in family courts in England and Wales following surrogacy births. In 2021, the figure was 435. Ministry of Justice, 'Family Court Statistics Quarterly: Family Court Tables: January to March 2022: Table 4', gov.uk/government/statistics/family-court-statistics-quarterly-january-to-march-2022 (30 June 2022).

10 Law Commission, 'Building families through surrogacy: a new law. A joint consultation paper', s3-eu-west-2.amazonaws.com/lawcom-prod-storage-11jsxou24uy7q/uploads/2019/06/Surrogacy-consultation-paper.pdf (6 June 2019)

11 Golombok S., Blake L., Slutsky J., Raffanello E., Roman G., Ehrhardt A., 'Parenting and the adjustment of children born to gay fathers through surrogacy', *Child Development* (2017).

12 Golombok S., *We Are Family: What Really Matters for Parents and Children* (Scribe Publications, 2020), p.159.

13 Ibid.

14 Golombok S., Mellish L., Jennings S., Casey P., Tasker F., Lamb M., 'Adoptive gay father families: parent-child relationships and children's psychological adjustment', *Child Development* (2014).

15 Golombok, S., Blake, L., Casey, P., Roman, G., & Jadva, V., 'Children born through reproductive donation: A longitudinal study of child adjustment', *Journal of Child Psychology and Psychiatry*, (2013).

16 Ibid.

17 Golombok S., Ilioi E., Blake L., Roman G., Jadva V., 'A longitudinal study of families formed through reproductive donation: parent-adolescent relationships and adolescent adjustment at age 14', *Developmental Psychology* (2017), and Golombok S., *We Are Family: What Really Matters for Parents and Children* (Scribe Publications, 2020).

18 Golombok S., Readings J., Blake L., Casey P., Mellish L., Marks A., Jadva V., 'Children conceived by gamete donation: the impact of openness about donor conception on psychological adjustment and parent-child relationships at age 7', *Journal of Family Psychology* (2011), and Ilioi E., Blake L., Jadva V., Roman G., Golombok S., 'The role of age of disclosure of biological origins in the psychological wellbeing of adolescents conceived by reproductive donation: a longitudinal study from age 1 to age 14', *Journal of Child Psychology and Psychiatry* (2017).

Chapter Six: Daddy-Led Weaning!
How New Fathers Can Share the Domestic Load

1 NHS, 'Infant Feeding Survey', digital.nhs.uk/data-and-information/publications/statistical/infant-feeding-survey/infant-feeding-survey-uk-2010 (20 November 2012).

2 Centres for Disease Control and Prevention, 'Breastfeeding Report Card: United States, 2020', cdc.gov/breastfeeding/pdf/2020-Breastfeeding-Report-Card-H.pdf (2020).

3 Burrows G., *Men Can Do It! The Real Reason Dads Don't Do Childcare and What Men and Women Should Do About It* (ngo.media, 2013), p.74.

4 Wicks J. *Wean in 15* (Bluebird, 2020) became a number 1 Sunday Times bestseller in May 2020. The Sunday Times Bestsellers, 'Manuals', *The Sunday Times* (24 May 2020).

5 Swinson J., *Equal Power: And How You Can Make It Happen* (Atlantic Books, 2018), p.161.

6 Ibid., pp.169–170.

7 Syrda J., 'Gendered housework: spousal relative income, parenthood and traditional gender identity norms', *Work, Employment and Society* (2022), and Roddam T., 'Married mothers who earn more than their husbands take on an even greater share of housework', *University of Bath*, bath.ac.uk/announcements/married-mothers-who-earn-more-than-their-husbands-take-on-an-even-greater-share-of-housework (31 March 2022).

8 Fawcett Society, 'Parenting and Covid-19 – Research evidence', fawcettsociety.org.uk/Handlers/Download.ashx?IDMF=f1d5b1c3-d5e0-4497-8078-1bad6ca4eb5a (2020).

9 Andrew A., Cattan S., Dias M.C., Farquharson C., Kraftman L., Krutikova S., Phimister A., Sevilla A., 'How are mothers

and fathers balancing work and family under lockdown?', *Institute for Fiscal Studies* (2020).

10 Sevilla A., Smith S., 'Baby steps: the gender division of childcare during the COVID-19 pandemic', *Oxford Review of Economic Policy* (2020).

11 Machin A., *The Life of Dad: The Making of a Modern Father* (Simon & Schuster, 2018).

12 Bowlby J., *Child Care and the Growth of Love* (Penguin, 1953), and Bowlby J., *Attachment and Loss: Vol 1. Attachment* (Basic Books, 1969). Also Lamb M.E., 'The changing faces of fatherhood and father-child relationships: from fatherhood as status to father as dad', in Fine M.A., Fincham F.D. (eds), *Handbook of Family Theories: A Content-Based Approach* (2013).

13 Lamb M.E., 'Fathers: forgotten contributors to child development', *Human Development* (1975), p.245.

14 Lamb M.E., 'Mothers, fathers, families, and circumstances: factors affecting children's adjustment', *Applied Developmental Science* (2012), p.101.

15 Ibid., p.101.

16 Ibid., p.105.

17 Ellis-Davies K., van Rijn-van Gelderen L., Winstanley A., Helmerhorst K.O.W., Rubio B., Vecho O., Lamb M.E., Bos H.M.W, 'Parental sensitivity and intrusiveness in gay-, lesbian-, and heterosexual-parent families with infants conceived using artificial reproductive techniques: do parents' gender and caregiver role matter?', *Early Childhood Research Quarterly* (2022), p.177.

18 Ibrahim M.H., Somers J.A., Luecken L.J., Fabricius W.V., Cookston J.T., 'Father–adolescent engagement in shared activities: effects on cortisol stress response in young adulthood', *Journal of Family Psychology* (2017).

19 Lamb M.E., 'Interactions between eight-month-old children and their fathers and mothers', in Lamb M.E., *The Role of the Father in Child Development* (Wiley, 1976), and Lamb M.E., 'The development of mother-infant and father-infant attachments in the second year of life', *Developmental Psychology* (1977).

Chapter Seven: Sorry, It's Just for Mums: Why Dads Need to Be Seen at Baby Appointments

1   Cho C., *Inferno: A Memoir of Motherhood and Madness* (Bloomsbury Circus, 2020).

2   Draper S., 'Equal parenting and shared parental leave: the challenges and benefits of being a stay-at-home dad', *Dad: Untold Stories of Fatherhood, Love, Mental Health and Masculinity* (MusicFootballFatherhood, 2021), p.51.

3   Burgess A., Goldman R., *Bringing Baby Home: UK Fathers in the First Year after the Birth*, Contemporary Fathers in the UK series (Fatherhood Institute, 2022).

4   Nuffield Foundation, 'Babies let down by post-natal services that ignore fathers', nuffieldfoundation.org/news/babies-let-down-by-post-natal-services (13 June 2022).

5   Ibid.

6   Burgess A., Goldman R., *Bringing Baby Home: UK Fathers in the First Year after the Birth*, Contemporary Fathers in the UK series (Fatherhood Institute, 2022), p.38.

7   Nuffield Foundation, 'Babies let down by post-natal services that ignore fathers', nuffieldfoundation.org/news/babies-let-down-by-post-natal-services (13 June 2022).

8   Panter-Brick C., Burgess A., Eggerman M., McAllister F., Pruett K., Leckman J.F., 'Practitioner review: engaging fathers – Recommendations for a game change in parenting interventions based on a systematic review of the global

evidence', *The Journal of Child Psychology and Psychiatry* (2014).

9 Wells M.B., 'Literature review shows that fathers are still not receiving the support they want and need from Swedish child health professionals', *Acta Paediatrica* (2016).

10 Høgmo B.K., Bondas T., Alstveit M., 'Going blindly into the women's world: a reflective lifeworld research study of fathers' expectations of and experiences with municipal postnatal healthcare services', *International Journal of Qualitative Studies on Health and Well-being* (2021).

11 HM Government, 'Pregnant employees' rights', gov.uk/working-when-pregnant-your-rights

12 Burgess A., Goldman R., *Who's the Bloke in the Room? Fathers During Pregnancy and at the Birth in the UK*, Contemporary Fathers in the UK series (Fatherhood Institute, 2018).

13 Earls M.F., Yogman M.W., Mattson G., Rafferty J., 'Incorporating recognition and management of perinatal depression into pediatric practice', *Pediatrics* (2019).

14 Panter-Brick C., Burgess A., Eggerman M., McAllister F., Pruett K., Leckman J.F., 'Practitioner review: engaging fathers – Recommendations for a game change in parenting interventions based on a systematic review of the global evidence', *The Journal of Child Psychology and Psychiatry* (2014).

15 Feinberg M., Jones D., Kan M., Goslin M., 'Effects of family foundations on parents and children: 3.5 years after baseline', *Journal of Family Psychology* (2010).

16 Family Foundations, 'About Us', famfound.net/about-us

17 NHS, 'Domestic abuse in pregnancy', nhs.uk/pregnancy/support/domestic-abuse-in-pregnancy

18 Burgess A., Goldman R., *Bringing Baby Home: UK Fathers in the First Year after the Birth* (Fatherhood Institute, 2022).

19 Fatherhood Institute, 'Guide to developing a father-inclusive workforce', fatherhoodinstitute.org/uploads/publications/460. pdf (2010).

20 Burrows G., *Men Can Do It! The Real Reason Dads Don't Do Childcare and What Men and Women Should Do About It* (ngo. media, 2013), p.1.

Chapter Eight: Boys Don't Wear Pink:
How to Stop Limiting What Our Children Can Be

1 LaFrance A., 'How to play like a girl', *The Atlantic* (25 May 2016).

2 The Fawcett Society, 'Unlimited potential: Report of the Commission on gender stereotypes in early childhood', fawcettsociety.org.uk/Handlers/Download. ashx?IDMF=17fb0c11-f904-469c-a62e-173583d441c8 (2020).

3 Mondschein E.R., Adolph K.E., Tamis-LeMonda C.S., 'Gender bias in mothers' expectations about infant crawling', *Journal of Experimental Child Psychology* (2000), pp.311–312.

4 Bian L., Leslie S-J., Cimpian A., 'Gender stereotypes about intellectual ability emerge early and influence children's interests', *Science* (2017).

5 The Fawcett Society, 'Unlimited potential: Report of the Commission on gender stereotypes in early childhood', fawcettsociety.org.uk/Handlers/Download. ashx?IDMF=17fb0c11-f904-469c-a62e-173583d441c8 (2020).

6 Ibid.

7 Wolter I., Braun E., Hannover B., 'Reading is for girls!? The negative impact of preschool teachers' traditional gender role attitudes on boys' reading related motivation and skills', *Frontiers in Psychology* (2015).

8 Barnett L.A., 'The education of playful boys: class clowns in the classroom', *Frontiers in Psychology* (2018).

9 Gunderson E.A., Gripshover S.J., Romero C., Dweck C.S., Goldin-Meadow S., Levine S.C., 'Parent praise to 1- to 3-year-olds predicts children's motivational frameworks 5 years later', *Child Development* (2013).

10 Freese J., Powell B., 'Sociobiology, status, and parental investment in sons and daughters: testing the Trivers-Willard hypothesis', *The American Journal of Sociology* (1999).

11 Sweet E.V., 'Toys are more divided by gender now than they were 50 years ago', *The Atlantic* (9 December 2014), and Sweet E.V., 'Boy builders and pink princesses: gender, toys, and inequality over the twentieth century', University of California, Davis (2013).

12 The Fawcett Society, 'Unlimited potential: Report of the Commission on gender stereotypes in early childhood', fawcettsociety.org.uk/Handlers/Download. ashx?IDMF=17fb0c11-f904-469c-a62e-173583d441c8 (2020).

13 Ibid.

14 Donaldson J., Scheffler A., *Zog* (Alison Green Books, 2010).

15 Donaldson J., Roberts D., *Jack and the Flumflum Tree* (Macmillan Children's Books, 2019).

16 Donaldson J., Cobb R., *The Everywhere Bear* (Macmillan Children's Books, 2017).

17 Donaldson J., Cobb R., *The Paper Dolls* (Macmillan Children's Books, 2012).

18 Morton K., 'Parents uncomfortable with male practitioners changing their child's nappy', *Nursery World* (12 September 2019).

19 Fawcett Society, 'Small but mighty steps to tackle gender stereotypes', fawcettsociety.org.uk/blog/small-but-mighty-steps-to-tackle-gender-stereotypes (16 December 2021).

20 Agarwal P., *Hysterical: Exploding the Myth of Gendered Emotions* (Canongate, 2022).

21 Malala Fund, 'Malala's Story', malala.org/malalas-story

22 Yousafzai M., 'Diary of a Pakistani schoolgirl', *BBC News*, news.bbc.co.uk/1/hi/world/south_asia/7834402.stm (19 January 2009).

Chapter Nine: I Have Ten Daddies!
Embracing Modern Families

1 Buckley J., 'Greer attacks Elton for listing husband as "mother"', *Daily Mail* (25 May 2015).

2 Christian Concern, 'Germaine Greer: Motherhood has been deconstructed', archive.christianconcern.com/our-concerns/ bioethics/germaine-greer-motherhood-has-been-deconstructed (30 May 2015).

3 Ward V., 'Dolce & Gabbana's attack on gay adoptions leaves Sir Elton raging', *The Daily Telegraph* (16 March 2015).

4 Littlejohn R., 'Please don't pretend two dads is the new normal', *Daily Mail* (16 February 2018).

5 Hrdy cites books that argue for the importance of the traditional family structure, including: Popenoe D., *Life Without Father: Compelling New Evidence that Fatherhood and Marriage are Indispensable for the Good of Children and Society* (The Free Press, 1996) and Blankenhorn D., *Fatherless in America: Confronting Our Most Urgent Social Problem* (Basic Books, 1995).

6 Hrdy S.B., *Mothers and Others* (The Belknap Press of Harvard University Press, 2011), p.145.

7 Sear R., Steele F., McGregor I.A., Mace R., 'The effects of kin on child mortality in rural Gambia', *Demography* (2002).

8 Hrdy S.B., *Mothers and Others* (The Belknap Press of Harvard University Press, 2011), p.108.

9 Van IJzendoorn M.H., Sagi A., Lambermon M.W.E., 'The multiple caretaker paradox: data from Holland and Israel', *New Directions for Child Development* (1992), p.15.

10 Ibid., p.22.

11 Ibid., p.22.

12 Hrdy S.B., *Mothers and Others* (The Belknap Press of Harvard University Press, 2011), p.132.

13 Griffiths S., 'Children get caught in the LGBT crossfire', *The Sunday Times* (14 April 2019).

14 Johnson B., 'Angry protests continue over Birmingham school's "okay to be gay" lessons', *Sky News* (17 May 2019).

15 Woolcock N., 'Judge bans protests over LGBT lessons', *The Times* (27 November 2019).

16 Human Fertilisation & Embryology Authority, 'Fertility treatment 2019: trends and figures', hfea.gov.uk/about-us/publications/research-and-data/fertility-treatment-2019-trends-and-figures (2021).

17 Centres for Disease Control and Prevention, 'ART success rates', cdc.gov/art/artdata/index.html

18 Booth R., 'Trans man loses UK legal battle to register as his child's father', *Guardian* (16 November 2020).